The French Effect

Books By Patricia Sands

The Bridge Club

The Promise of Provence

Promises to Keep

I Promise You This

Drawing Lessons

The First Noël at the Villa des Violettes

A Season of Surprises at the Villa des Violettes

Lavender, Loss & Love at the Villa des Violettes

Deck the Halls at the Villa des Violettes

The Secrets We Hide

Lost At Sea

A New Leash on Life

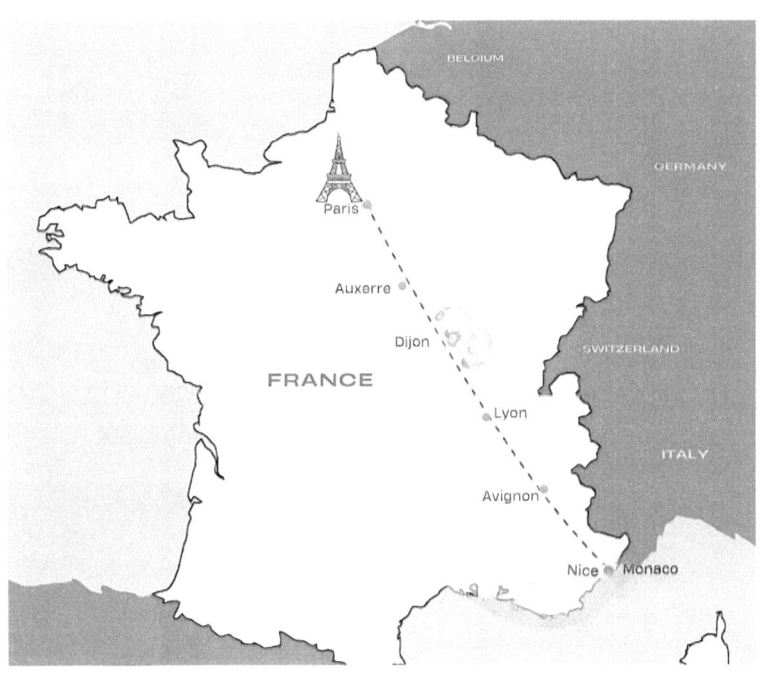

The French Effect

PATRICIA SANDS

Copyright © *2025* by Patricia Sands
All rights reserved.

This is a work of fiction. The characters, incidents, events, and dialogues in this book are of the author's imagination and are not to be construed as real. Any resemblance to actual events or persons, living or dead, is completely coincidental.

No part of this book may be reproduced or transmitted in any form or by any means, electronic or mechanical, including photocopying, recording, or by any information storage and retrieval system, without permission in writing from the authors.

Paperback ISBN: 978-1-0691281-2-6

Cover Design: Lauren Faulkenberry
www.faulkenberryarts..com

To all those seeking a pause from the real world—may this story be your quiet escape and carry you far away.

Chapter One

Nora Bennett was having a moment.

Wrapped in the silence of her thoughts in her cozy home office, she doodled intricate patterns on a paper on the desk in front of her.

She was supposed to be writing her latest novel, but the words were not coming ... and hadn't been for a few days. Nora did not want to admit she had a bad case of writer's block, but it was the truth.

She doodled some more.

Through the window, she watched snowflakes twirling and floating around, as if in no hurry to land. When they finally settled gracefully on the ground, bushes, and tree branches, everything looked pristine and untouched. The ultimate winter wonderland.

She had never figured it out but was certain there must've been a psychological explanation for the peace that flowed through her on snowy days. For as long as she could remember, it had been that way.

Probably one of the biggest reasons was the fact that Jeremy, her beloved late husband, had proposed to her in a memorable snowstorm like this one, at the top of their favorite ski run on

Blue Mountain. Down on one knee, as friends of theirs got off the chairlift and gathered around, he had spoken the sweetest words to her. Then he dropped the ring box in the deep, powdery snow, which had turned Nora's tears of joy into tears of laughter as he dug it out. The tears of joy returned as he tenderly placed the ring on her finger and whispered promises they believed would come true.

Nora had grown up in northern Ontario, where white winters were the norm, and happy childhood memories always surged back with fresh falling snow. She especially loved a winter storm with big fluffy flakes, and this was the first one this year. Early too. Since it was only mid-November, it would all probably melt in a few days. But she hoped it was a sign of what was to come.

Chickadees and cardinals were taking turns at the snow-topped bird feeder, while a noisy blue jay squawked its displeasure at the visitors from the apple tree in the corner of the yard. Nora was glad she had filled the feeder earlier in the week. The cardinal was Jeremy's favorite bird, as well as hers, and she went to the pine sideboard, steps away in the hall, to pick up his binoculars to enjoy the show at the feeder even more.

Just then, her phone beeped with a text from her daughter Chloe, an artist living in Paris.

> Chloe: Are you home? I've got the most exciting proposition for you and we have to talk about it now! I'm in a meeting but will FaceTime within half an hour. Can you be somewhere to take the call?
>
> Nora: I will be here and can't wait to talk to you. xo

She wondered what the exciting issue might be. Nora never knew what to expect from her exuberant daughter. Chloe had blossomed from a teen who had her share of struggles into a thoughtful, grounded young woman filled with resilience, kindness, and fire. She expressed such passion in her art, and Nora was deeply grateful she had found her path.

She went back to the window with the binoculars.

This was her happy place: her garden in the small yard of her grandmother's 1850s cottage home she had inherited at twenty. Small-town life suited her, and she never regretted returning sixteen years ago with her thirteen-year-old daughter after being widowed the previous year.

The loss of Jeremy, a true soulmate and best father ever, to a sudden brain aneurysm had been devastating. But he had ensured she and her daughter were taken care of by taking out a generous insurance policy early in their marriage. Nora and Chloe had slowly found healing here in the comfort of the cottage and the closeness to nature. Hiking and skiing became their seasonal obsessions.

Both agreed they did not miss city life.

The red-brick, story-and-a-half house had been a weekend escape even before Chloe was born and already provided a comfortable ambiance in those early years. After Jeremy's passing, mother and daughter shuffled existing furniture around and moved in their favorite early-Canadian pine pieces that Nora and Jeremy had collected at auctions in their first years together.

Art from their city house filled each room including the van Gogh, a Pissarro, and several Monet prints, bought on her splurge-worthy Paris honeymoon. Chloe's treasured posters of van Gogh's sunflowers brightened her bedroom. She had begged for them on her first visit to the Art Gallery of Ontario when she was six.

Without question, the Christmas trunk had been the first item loaded into the moving van that had brought their possessions from the city. A battered pine blanket box filled with cherished decorations going back to Nora and Jeremy's childhoods, its unpacking was a tradition every December 1^{st,} after a ceiling-high blue spruce was brought home the weekend before. Its sweet piney aroma always filled the house with a cozy festive vibe.

Chloe had grown up hearing her mom teasingly referred to by Jeremy as Mrs. Claus. Nora's devotion to their family traditions made each Christmas special. Year after year, her magic filled the house once the trunk was opened and the tree securely fixed in the living room. The ritual of admiring each of the decorations and placing them on the tree and around the house was almost a religious undertaking. The tissue paper surrounding each one was carefully unwrapped and inevitably Nora told the story of the ornament's provenance, even though the three of them knew it by heart.

That seasonal magic was contagious and eagerly embraced. Friends and family gathered for shortbread baking, carol singing and hearty meals year after year.

Mother and daughter shed tears when they closed the door of the house in the city for the last time. But before long, it felt like the cottage had always been home. Friends and family pitched in to make the transition as seamless as possible. The memories of Jeremy moved in with Nora and Chloe, helping bring comfort as the two became settled.

Nora and Chloe grieved together, at times weeping in each other's arms and other times curled up alone in a quiet corner of the house. They talked openly about the pain brought into their lives by the loss of Jeremy. As years passed, there were still tears, but both women knew those tears were firmly rooted deep in their hearts. Expressions of eternal love.

Nora dedicated herself to being strong and positive for her daughter's sake. Jeremy's passing had left such a hole in their lives. More than anything, she'd wanted Chloe to grow up knowing her father was watching over them. His spirit was with them.

Jeremy continued to be Nora's loving partner and soulmate in her heart, and she still talked to him about everything. He had been the best reader of the first drafts of her novels and she trusted his comments and critiques. This she missed. She had a supportive writing group she had belonged to for years, but it wasn't the same as sitting by the fire or out in the garden or snuggled in bed sharing her writing with him. That loss had been another adjustment.

She wore his favorite silk nightgowns to bed every night. Those intimate memories had not faded. On some nights, she closed her eyes and could sense his hands caressing her, making her feel cherished and loved as he always had. She was convinced it was all she needed.

They had committed to a date night every two weeks after Chloe was born, and Nora had never stopped that ritual. She chose whichever weekend night she did not have any plans, poured herself a glass of wine, and got cozy with a good book, always trusting Jeremy was with her. Some of those nights didn't go so well. After repeatedly playing "If the World Was Ending" she would be in a puddle of tears with an empty wine bottle, angry at herself for being unrealistic.

When Chloe left for art school in Toronto, Nora missed her, but Toronto was less than two hours away and she came home most weekends. Nora felt no regrets about continuing life alone in the town where she had made trusted friends.

The Girls, as Nora and her friends collectively referred to themselves, were fully invested in all the area had to offer. They appreciated the easygoing small-town atmosphere, with the north-south streets all named after trees and the east-west streets in the oldest part of the village using the numbers one through ten.

The lively main street, with its nineteenth-century architecture from the busy, long-gone shipbuilding days, offered abundant varieties of bars, cafés, and shopping. The outdoor lifestyle options of skiing, hiking, boating, golf, biking, tennis and the recent addition of even more pickleball courts, meant life was active year-round. Throughout the region there was a vibrant cultural scene of theatre and music, including concerts and a movie festival. Vineyards and craft breweries flourished amidst the farms and apple orchards in the rolling agricultural countryside.

Life passed by without many glitches until Chloe moved to

France. Then Nora began to drink way too much white wine and consumed more chocolate than anyone should. Even though she hiked, played tennis twice a week, and skied in the winter, the pounds piled on. And her self-esteem tanked.

Her friends gently offered advice and assistance, which Nora carefully ignored. Chloe chided her on video calls and expressed concern. Nora made unkept promises.

She knew Jeremy would be disappointed but would also be her best champion in her heart when she did start making good decisions. Even that was not enough to get her on the right track at first.

After a year or so of total lack of self-care, a proliferation of ads about losing weight through online dance programs kept popping up during her scrolling. She knew they were a direct message from Jeremy. Dancing had been their thing. She began with one class a day, and quickly added another because it was so much fun. She was amazed at how the pounds slipped away. Replacing the white wine with smoothies helped too. It had been a struggle to ditch the chocolate. Truth to tell, she still cheated occasionally.

Keeping fit, reading, and writing became the driving forces in her life, and she finally turned things around. Volunteering at the library, she took on the task of helping with a memoir class and found it a satisfying endeavour. A few of the group had serious stories to tell and appreciated her assistance as she guided them through the writing process. She was pleased to use her experience to help them.

And it might have been due to Jeremy that her few attempts at online dating had failed too. No one measured up to him. She knew he would have wanted her to be happy and move on with her life. She had tried ... sort of. But it wasn't long before she gave up on romance with anyone new.

As Chloe matured and subsequently fell in love in Paris, she had conversations with Nora about finding someone to share her life with again. Nora listened and at times considered it ... possibly

... might not be a bad idea. But in the end, she always circled back to the same quiet certainty – it simply wasn't a path she felt called to follow.

"My girlfriends are the best," she argued. "We keep each other busy and happy. What more do I need at this stage in my life?"

The Girls had grown close over the last fifteen or so years. Some had married, some not. Together they skied, played tennis, hiked, volunteered, wined and dined, laughed, talked, and sometimes cried. Life moved smoothly through the years, and one thing Nora gratefully never felt was alone.

Chapter Two

Her phone rang, startling her from her fixation on the bird feeder. As expected, it was Chloe. Nora was always happy when she received a call from her daughter rather than a text.

"Hey, Mom! What are you doing?" Chloe paused for a moment and chuckled as she said, "Um ... hello? Just a reminder I called you on FaceTime and your video is on!"

Nora snorted. "Oops! Didn't notice that."

"Obviously," Chloe said. "I was staring into your ear!"

Laughing, Nora held the phone in front of herself and grinned at her daughter. She quickly ran her fingers through her ash-blonde highlighted hair, cropped just below her ears.

"Gah! Sorry about that! Sorry about my messy hair too. I may not have combed it today. No makeup either," she said.

"You look just fine, Mom. You always do ... even with bedhead." Chloe paused for a moment and scrunched her eyes before she said, "Were you writing with music blaring? You kind of have that look."

"Well, yes ... and no, to answer your question. I have been attempting to write. But it's not working. I did decide to play some music, but I turned it off when a magical snowstorm began. You know how I feel about the first snowstorm ... especially when it's perfect."

Chloe nodded and gave a thumbs-up. "Obvs, you're still not over your writer's block! That's a bummer. And I know how you adore first snowstorms. I can hear you sighing across the Atlantic."

"Got that right," Nora replied. "It's an absolutely beautiful soft snowfall—so quiet and serene. I've been jumping for joy at the window. Literally."

"I get the picture," Chloe said.

"I'm already fantasizing about getting on the slopes and hope it's as good a winter as last year. It's all relative, as we know. I had twenty great ski days last season, so no complaints."

"And since you are strictly a fair-weather skier now, those must have been picture-perfect days. But as a change of scene, how about Christmas in Paris with a side trip to the vineyards of Provence? That's what I'm calling about."

Nora grinned. "Ha! Any time in Paris sounds good to me. But are you serious? I was just there in June and, um, as we know, you do enjoy your independence and your busy life. Isn't it a bit soon for me to be there, lurking?"

"Mom! You don't lurk! You know Olivier and I love having you visit us. We can hardly keep up with you."

Chloe had gone to Paris to study art after graduating from OCAD University at the Art Gallery of Ontario. Her plan to stay for one year turned into two, and then three, before she married her charmingly serious Frenchman, Olivier, and that was that. Nora believed Chloe had made good decisions, as she had never seen her often-temperamental daughter so decidedly happy and content.

It had been three years since Chloe married Oli. Nora made at least one visit each year and always rented a studio apartment near them, so they all had their privacy.

"Okay, I just like you to tell me that, so I don't worry about being an overbearing mother."

They stared at each other intensely before bursting into wide smiles. They had always shared the same sense of humor, and Chloe knew how to make Nora laugh without saying a word. Nora looked at her daughter for a moment. Twenty-nine with flawless skin, her long dark hair pulled back in a casual ponytail, flashing a brilliant smile thanks to two years of agonizing braces.

"Well, moving on," Chloe said, "here's why I called! I'm so excited about this! My dear neighbor, Madame Tremblay—Giselle—whom you have met briefly before, is going to Mexico in ten days and staying there for six weeks. I believe it was a sudden decision after she banished her most recent gigolo, although she did not say that to me. It's me being nosy and gossipy. Her regular dog-sitter just became ill and is hospitalized, so she is frantically looking for someone reliable. She was thrilled when I suggested you might do it. You would stay at her apartment with Atticus, her Doberman pinscher—"

Nora interrupted with a shriek. "That humongous muscular behemoth who looks like he's smarter than a person and totally intimidates me?"

Chloe's laugh ended in a loud snort. "Okay, I know he has a rather menacing appearance, but he really is a softie. Truly a sweetie pie who loves to snuggle. I've spent enough time with him to know. You simply haven't been around him enough."

"But like, right this minute? This week? It means I have to leave ... like ... in seven days. You know I can't do that!"

"Well, yes, that's what it means. I know you can do it."

Chloe was well aware that hasty adventures were definitely not Nora's thing. She worried about the cost, the weather, and anything else she could dredge up in her imagination. And yet she loved to travel. Whether it was a road trip to cottage country or something which involved an airport departure, once she overcame her concerns, she settled right into the experience.

Nora asked, "Why don't you have the dog stay with you while Madame Tremblay is away?"

"Because, as you might recall, Jezebel cannot tolerate him and creates such a hissy fit whenever he's at our place. It's pure jealousy. It simply would not work. And I don't want him to stay in his apartment all day and have someone drop by only to feed and walk him. He loves company."

Now it was Nora's turn to laugh. Chloe and Oli's cat was a real piece of work and as spoiled a feline as Nora had ever seen. But still very lovable, at least when Atticus was not in their presence, as Nora had witnessed several times in the past. Jezebel loved to cuddle on Nora's lap when she visited their apartment.

There was quiet on the line.

"And yes, you can do it," Chloe said, breaking the silence. "Just throw some winter clothes in a bag and get over here. Besides, you've been talking about getting another dog. This might help your decision. It's been five years since Maggie crossed the rainbow bridge."

She's right. I have been considering a rescue dog.

"Well—" Nora began but was interrupted.

Chloe turned her phone around to pan the camera over the fabulous view of the Paris skyline through her living room window. Sunshine bathed the magnificent panorama.

"Doesn't this tempt you? Just think, Mom. Christmas in the City of Light. How divine would that be? I know you've been a Christmas curmudgeon since I left home ... but trust me, this will change you back to who you were!"

Nora's heart wrenched. She had to admit the Christmas trunk had not been opened since Chloe married. It had been a conscious and painful decision. Christmas without Jeremy had been difficult enough, but she had maintained her festive persona for Chloe's sake. Together, and with their friends, they had continued the rituals and kept the season meaningful.

With Chloe absent, though, she'd packed it all away in the trunk. She had encouraged Chloe to stay in France for the festive season each year and celebrate all the wonderful traditions she had heard about with her new family in Provence. It had felt like the right thing to do. She'd wanted her daughter to create her own Christmas magic in her new life.

And if she was honest with herself, she had thought it would be too difficult to be in the midst of a family Christmas without Jeremy. It was easier to celebrate with her friends, so she could make excuses for being absent when she felt like it.

"The Christmas lights in Paris are not to be believed." Chloe babbled on at warp speed. "We haven't had Christmas together since I married Olivier. Do you realize that? He and I have so many new traditions to share with you, and I know you will love them. And you can work on your projects here... Or better yet, take time off. Give yourself a break."

Nora laughed before replying. "Whoa... Take a breath, sweetheart. You do have a point. Christmas in the City of Light would be more than divine, and I may be ready for this now. What fun to see the city lit up ... oh, that tree in Galeries Lafayette ... and hit all the holiday markets. But you know I will have to write while I'm there. That's what I do ... when I'm not blocked."

"I know, I know. I get it. But you can ease up a bit, I'm sure. Besides, a change of scene might be just the spark you need to beat the block."

"Of course. On another topic, however, I'm not sure I can handle Atticus. The few times I saw him he seemed strong and intimidating."

"Mom, you are grasping! He's just a dog ... and actually very well behaved, as I keep telling you."

Nora held the phone away and excused herself after she sneezed. "Ah sorry, dear. I didn't feel that coming."

Chloe didn't miss a beat. "Giselle actually loves the idea of you doing it. She said she would be nervous to have a stranger stay in her apartment, as all sorts of weird things are happening these days: people having parties or stealing things or leaving the place a mess. At least she told me she had read about these problems. But she would be thrilled to have you stay and thought we would all be happy living so close to each other. What do you say?"

Nora was silent for a moment. "Well, uh ... I still don't speak French very well."

Chloe snorted. "Atticus will help you learn. I believe he's fluent ... he-he ... Seriously, I think dogs understand pretty much any language. C'mon, Mom, that's a pretty feeble excuse."

"Yeah, you are right." Nora realized it was a stretch.

"Oh! There's more! She wants to pay your airfare!"

"Not necessary," Nora said.

"That's what I said too. But Giselle said she would have to pay someone way more than your airfare would cost. So, you shouldn't feel badly about it. She would be insulted if you refused her offer. Her words. The French are like that. Come on! Say you will!"

"Let me think about it. Madame Tremblay may be a spur-of-the-moment person, but you know I'm not."

"Tell me about it," Chloe muttered. "But as you know, everything always works out. Come! It'll be fun!"

Nora had to smile listening to her über-optimistic daughter. She always wondered what she had done right to raise a young woman who always looked on the bright side.

"Well," Nora said hesitantly, "if I decide to do it, I will come a few days early so Madame Tremblay—er, Giselle—can introduce me to Atticus and be with us while we hopefully get comfortable with each other."

"We have a futon here you can sleep on for a night or two before she leaves. Wait until you see how well-behaved he is. He's been diligently trained. And you can always hire a dog-walker if you feel unsafe outside with him. Which you won't. But at least you know you can do it if you have any concerns."

"Oh, my dear, dear girl." Nora looked at Chloe with such love. "How did you become the calm, clear thinker of the two of us?"

Chloe crossed her eyes and made a silly face. "Sure, sure. But hey! This is excellent. I'll ask Giselle to email you to organize dates. I'm so excited, and Olivier will be too."

The snow had stopped. Nora sat stunned by all that had transpired in her conversation with Chloe. She popped in her earbuds and clicked on her Charles Aznavour playlist. *This might be just what I need to get in the mood for Paris.*

Chapter Three

Two days later, Nora took out her suitcase and tentatively began to organize her clothes.

Madame Tremblay's call had her slowly turning the corner on her decision.

"Please call me Giselle," Chloe's neighbor had said when she'd phoned earlier in the morning. They chatted for fifteen minutes, during which time Giselle tried to convince Nora that she would fall in love with Atticus. "But take your time to think about it and send me an email tonight with your decision. No rush."

No rush! Just a few hours to respond to that charming French accent and delightful personality which made her feel welcome and so needed.

Then Chloe had texted, and Nora sensed her excitement.

> Chloe: Giselle just called and said she thought she had persuaded you! I can't tell you how happy I am.

Nora's mind was not fully made up, but she had to admit she was more drawn to the idea than she expected. Chloe was right, she had recently considered getting a rescue to replace her dear Wheaten terrier, Maggie, who they'd had for eleven years. Living with a dog again for a while might help her reach a decision. Even if this dog wasn't fluffy and cuddly.

As her suitcase filled, she pictured herself wearing the clothes in Paris and her concerns diminished. French women always looked elegant no matter how casual they dressed, but she could hold her own too.

A few cashmere sweaters, two silk blouses, some camisoles, two pashminas, one suede mid-calf skirt, one little black dress, three pairs of leggings, and two pairs of jeans plus her favorite red dress, casual but swishy, for the holidays. Undies, three silk nightgowns—she did always treat herself when it came to those items, just as Jeremy liked. Shoes, boots, waterproof down jacket.

"I'll wear my gorgeous, long leather coat on the plane, so I'll have it if I need to get dressed up," she told Chloe.

She could do this. She would. Maybe. She needed to think about it some more. But still she added things to her suitcase.

In the past when she'd visited Chloe in Paris, she had easily rented her house for the month. She didn't have time to advertise it this time on such short notice, but her friends would help spread the word about the vacancy.

She reminded herself that Paris never failed to be the best experience. It had started when Jeremy suggested the City of Light for their honeymoon. They saved everything they could for a year to make it happen. Ever since that visit she'd been hooked, even though it took Chloe studying there to bring her back.

She thought about her visits each year since Chloe had first been there as a student. It hadn't taken long to rediscover how wonderful the city was for walking, with every street and corner offering something special. It might be a shop or a gallery or something as simple as a small detail on a building or a cat sleeping in a window or a curious bit of graffiti. The aromas from cafés, restaurants, and boulangeries were another satisfying story. Exploring on foot allowed Nora to be surrounded by layers of history and architecture, and there were always narrow cobblestone streets to turn down and be transported to another era.

On every trip, she regretted not having paid enough attention to high school French. Even more so when she listened to Chloe speak so fluently.

She'd always experienced a little twinge of guilt that she lived in a country with two official languages and only spoke one. Maybe it was time to change that, and she could use her time in France to practice. She downloaded a "Daily French Lessons" app and vowed to use it.

As she packed, she felt those sights, sounds, and smells she'd been thinking about, as if they were wrapped around her. More than once, she sat on the edge of her bed and slipped into her thoughts.

She might not have had good luck falling in love with a man after Jeremy, but she was definitely infatuated with Paris. Walking was her jam, and whenever she was in France, she settled immediately into spending most of her days doing just that. Best of all, she felt perfectly safe and happy on her own there.

"Mom, you are the perfect flâneuse," Chloe had said during her mother's first visit. "The French have this wonderful verb, flâner. It means to wander around, stroll, or browse. A woman is a flâneuse and a man a flâneur."

Closing her eyes, Nora could almost smell the intoxicating aromas of freshly baked baguettes, croissants, and pastries wafting through the streets in the earliest morning hours until they were replaced later in the day with the seductive smells of French cuisine: butter, garlic, simmering sauces, and always cheese—strong and pungent or creamy and sweet.

The air was often rich with the essence of fresh coffee, inviting her to stop at a sidewalk café and sit while French life passed by. Nora smiled at the thought now. She loved to sit sipping a café au lait, feeling like a Parisienne.

This trip might be just what she needed. She always tried to sound happy and upbeat when she spoke with Chloe, but if she was honest, this year had been a struggle.

Her freelance copyediting and memoir ghostwriting business

was covering costs. That wasn't the problem. The reality was, lately she'd found it a challenge to tell other people's stories. She always loved encouraging others to record their histories and appreciated the importance of it. But recently the joy was fading, and she recognized it was due to a general malaise within her.

Worst of all, she was suffering from a bad case of writer's block with her latest romance manuscript under her pen name, Belle de Beauvoir. Her own words were somewhat a problem. She struggled to find them recently.

She hated to admit she felt invisible and irrelevant, like some of her friends expressed and other aging women she often read about. But she did. Thank goodness menopause had finally passed. It seemed after turning fifty there were so many other issues, like knee and hip replacements, other illnesses, and the challenges of dealing with troubled zillennials moving back home or caring for aging parents. She was glad none of those things were in her life at the moment, but it was a toss-up amongst her friends as to whose lives might start to fall apart.

Loss had become a quiet companion; her parents and several other dear ones were gone. Some mornings it was the first thing to greet her and, in time, it taught her how to love what remained more fiercely.

Three of her best friends were dealing with challenging health issues. Cancer was the worst, and Nora had spent many hours sitting with her friend, Laura, as she had undergone debilitating chemo treatments. Gloria's double knee replacement had not gone well; she still struggled to walk without a walker or cane and was in terrible pain. Margie had suddenly developed some kind of neurological problem affecting her balance and was dealing with ongoing tests, scans, and other regular doctor appointments. All three of them were depressed.

Not to mention the toll the divorces and strained marriages around her exacted on her own sense of happiness.

And now Nora was feeling low but had refrained from mentioning it to her friends. She went again to see the grief counselor she'd visited in her early years when she'd dealt with Jeremy's loss. She wondered if that was the problem: on her own, she was doing more grieving than healing.

The advice she received from the counselor was simple: It might be time to move on from feeling Jeremy's presence so intensely.

"It's been seventeen years, Nora. He will always be in your heart but not beside you every day. You need to look beyond yourself now and recognize being in your fifties presents an exciting new chapter far more positive than you are describing. Jeremy won't be on this journey. This one is up to you. You need to accept it. All I'm hearing right now are negatives. You've told me how Jeremy would have wanted you to be happy. Keep holding on to those words."

She'd left the counselor's office feeling even worse. In the ladies' washroom, she wiped tearstains from her cheeks. The face looking back at her in the mirror seemed crumpled with anxiety. How could she stop relying on Jeremy's spirit to keep her happy?

She tried to follow the counselor's advice. She read books, listened to podcasts, went out with her friends, and watched *Under the Tuscan Sun* and *A Good Year* repeatedly. Nothing worked.

At the other end of the spectrum from her close friends with problems, her friend Cynthia had sold absolutely everything and moved to a small coastal village in Italy. Her regular emails and photos made Nora question why she herself wasn't planning an adventure like that. Really, there was nothing holding her back from making a move like Cynthia had. Nothing.

If only she was impulsive.

She let out a long sigh as she took a break from packing and went into the kitchen to boil water for tea. Sipping from her favorite china cup and saucer set that once belonged to her mother, she thought some more about her inability to be decisive. Then she called Cynthia.

"Pronto!" Cynthia answered in a cheery voice.

After a few minutes of Cynthia entertaining her about her new life and Nora catching Cynthia up on gossip in the Girls' lives, Nora blurted out her indecision about dog-sitting in Paris.

"Nor, stop being a worrywart! Biting the bullet and moving here was the best thing I could have done. I was in such a slump after my divorce, as you know. I've met interesting people here. Lovely, friendly locals, and a bunch of expats. I wake up happy every day. Of course, I miss the gang, but I bet you will all come to visit. Just do it, my friend! You're going for six weeks, not forever!"

Chapter Four

Five days later, on November 27, Nora was on her way to Paris. Using some of her Aeroplan points, she'd upgraded to Premium Economy. At the airport, she purchased a neck pillow and hoped for a good sleep on the way over.

Things had already worked out better than expected. Gloria's sister, who lived in Toronto, had jumped at the chance to rent Nora's house for the six weeks. She was thrilled to be there to help Gloria and spend the holidays out of the city.

Three days earlier, Chloe had called with an urgent request for Nora to put her ice skates and wool socks in a box and ship them to her. "We're going to a skating party on New Year's Eve. No arguing. Just do it."

So she had.

The Girls had taken her out for a bon voyage dinner earlier in the week and been so excited for her. She tried to hold onto those vibes as she sat waiting to board the plane.

"We want at least one full report a week and daily postings on Instagram."

"You are the queen of taking photos, so it shouldn't be a problem."

"Yeah! Pictures of your apartment! And Paris, Chloe and Oli, and the dog."

"And hot French guys!"

"Yes! Lots of hot French guys!"

There had been a lot of laughs that night, and her friends teased her mercilessly about never being impulsive. She had gone to bed feeling so grateful for each one of those women.

A few hours into the flight, the attendants served dinner. After a glass of wine with a surprisingly delicious airplane meal of boeuf bourguignon, she settled into her seat, wrapped her shawl around herself, and snuggled into the cozy neck pillow. Here she was, taking a chance for the first time in a long time.

She hoped she wouldn't come to second-guess her decision. She had promised Cynthia and the rest of the gang she wouldn't. And Chloe. And herself. So that was that. Now she needed to relax and enjoy whatever lay ahead. At least she would try.

Her chat with Cynthia had clinched it. She had been so convincing. "At this stage in our lives, some of us are at a turning point, Nor. Happiness. Satisfaction. New goals. It's all ahead of us. Who knows how we will move forward? Some of us might be very happy where we are. Change is up to us. Besides, you get to spend six weeks with Chloe!"

Chloe jumped up and down, waving madly as Nora entered the arrivals area. When Nora reached her, Chloe threw her arms around her mother and they hugged, rocking back and forth with pure joy.

"Maman! Tu es ici!"

Nora grinned as she replied, "Oui, ma fille! Me voilà!"

"Ooh là là," Chloe said. "Getting right into the Frenchy vibe! Woohoo!"

They laughed, hugged again, and shared a few more words in French. During their weekly video chats, Chloe often encouraged Nora to learn more words and expressions, and tested her on the things she was learning on her French app too. Nora happily showed off, especially now that her daughter was fully bilingual.

"I took the Metro here, but we'll grab a taxi home. C'est plus facile de parler! Easier to talk!" said Chloe.

Waiting in the taxi line, Nora took a good look at her daughter. How could she be twenty-nine already? Tall and willowy, with hair the color of rich, golden chestnut, halfway down her back, she'd gotten it all from her dad. But she had the same bright blue eyes as Nora.

Video calls were great, but it was the best thing to be together in the flesh. Nora reached out again and hugged her daughter. Chloe's hug back sent a joyful frisson right down to her toes.

The drive was familiar to Nora now. Once they left the airport chaos behind, she soon felt the rhythm of the layered city streets. Before they got to the good part, they had to pass through some unattractive neighborhoods with graffiti-covered buildings and dingy strips of industrial service centers. Then they joined the fast-paced traffic on wider boulevards before turning into the quieter areas that led to Montmartre.

She squeezed Chloe's hand, and they grinned at each other as the view changed to the more charming, historical, timeworn buildings that gave the neighborhood its charm.

"I knew you'd be glad you came," Chloe said. "We're going to have such a good time."

As the car began the steep climb to Montmartre, curving and twisting, Nora caught a glimpse of the white domes of the Sacré Coeur. They turned onto a cobbled street and passed several cozy cafés and galleries before stopping in front of an unremarkable white limestone, five-story building with a set of slightly battered blue doors.

Nora's heart did a little jump at the sight of the residence, which had been built in the early 1880s. Chloe and Olivier had moved into a small flat on the fourth floor. On that same floor,

Vincent van Gogh had lived with his brother, Theo, from 1886 to 1887. Her imagination raced whenever she thought about it.

Nora always rented a small studio nearby when she'd visited Chloe in the past, so to stay in the same building as Chloe—and Vincent—was a thrill.

Her son-in-law Olivier bounded out the double blue doors and greeted Nora with the classic bise, a gentle air kiss on each cheek. "Bienvenue! C'est un grand plaisir de te revoir!"

Nora caught herself just in time before almost giving him a hug. She always found it unusual not to automatically hug anyone she loved, but she had pretty much adjusted to the fact it was not done in France. However, Olivier reached around to give her a light, almost awkward, hug and they laughed as Nora said Chloe had taught him well.

"I'm so happy to see you again too. Such a surprise on such short notice, right?" Nora noted Olivier seemed more handsome each time she visited. She had observed during previous visits that Frenchmen aged very well.

Olivier chuckled. "Chloe is most impressed with you taking this chance."

"So am I," Nora said, rolling her eyes.

Chloe led the way up the wide marble staircase to the building's third floor, which was the fourth floor everywhere else in the world.

As she always did, Nora admired the elegant wooden apartment doors, each fitted with ornate brass escutcheons surrounding enormous keyholes which were no longer used but never failed to captivate her. They looked like they hid intriguing stories with secrets worth hearing. All the doors now had small modern locks installed elsewhere on the wood. They had no character but provided the necessary security.

"Just walking down your hallway brings me right back into

the romance of France. How I love these doors and keyholes," Nora exclaimed.

Once inside the tiny but bright apartment, Olivier put Nora's suitcase next to the futon with a wry grin. "Your palatial space for three days."

"And look, Mom! We found this great privacy screen at a vide-grenier last weekend."

"It's perfect," Nora said. "I want to go to some of those flea markets while I'm here."

"Oh, we will, no doubt about that! And look…" Chloe added. "Jezebel is already settled on your futon to welcome you."

They laughed as Nora curtsied to the fluffy feline and sat down beside her, giving her a scratch on the head. Jezebel immediately climbed on her lap and began to purr.

"Of course, she believes you have come specifically to see her," said Chloe.

Nora settled back into some overstuffed cushions. She looked around with a satisfied smile at the rustic exposed wooden beams and stone walls. "You did a fabulous job stripping those beams. I love the effect. I'm quite happy to snuggle with Jez for a while if you two have work to do."

"We're good for now, and if you aren't tired, Mom," Chloe said, "we thought we would dash over to Le Moulin for your first lunch. After all, it's kind of a tradition when you arrive. N'est-ce pas?"

Olivier chimed in his support for the suggestion. "On y va!"

"Oh, you two are adorable. Of course, it's a tradition. I slept most of the way over, so I'm in good shape and I am hungry. Breakfast on the plane was not edible. Can you believe they had no croissants? On Air France? Allez zou!"

Chapter Five

Le Moulin de la Galette was a short walk down the street. The weather was mild and the sun shone brightly on the busy sidewalk. It was the kind of day that brought people out for the simple pleasure of enjoying the outdoors.

"This would be a spring day at home. It's hard to believe Christmas will soon be here," Nora commented as they strolled along.

"It's turned into a perfect day to welcome you, Mom," Chloe said. "But don't get your hopes up. We had very cold temperatures last week and they're predicting more to come. Maybe you'll get snow here too … to give you a sense of home."

Nora laughed. "I would love to see snow in Paris. But there's no way anything would ever make me feel totally at home here. I always want to be excited about Paris vibes in every way."

"A true Paris romantic," Olivier said. "Pourquoi pas?"

The entrance to the bistro was topped by one of the two remaining original windmills in Montmartre. Nora insisted on taking a few photos of them in front of the landmark. "Get used to it!" she warned, her eyes dancing..

Chloe nodded with a shrug. "C'est la vie avec Maman." She had grown up the subject of endless photos.

Built in the early 1700s and one time a mill which ground flour, the iconic structure had also been a guinguette or tavern for drinking and dancing, a music-hall, and open-air café. For the last few decades, it had been a popular bistro with two terraces where celebrity watching was part of the fun.

"Mmmm, they've not lost their touch in the kitchen," Nora exclaimed as she swirled a plump escargot in garlic butter before popping it in her mouth. The baguette that came with her meal soaked up the butter in a way that made it...

"Orgasmic," Chloe murmured. They all nodded and conversation paused for a moment, except for satisfying sighs and hums as they enjoyed the food. Nora followed that course with traditional coq au vin and, when she finished, sat back with a satisfied smile while they all shared a selection of cheeses.

"Ah, I am back in France. I can't tell you how good this feels."

The café's cosy atmosphere was festive as some of the staff hung garlands of evergreen boughs over the bar and others brought out boxes of decorations. Chloe told Nora they were beginning a competition that very day with some of the other bistros and bars.

Nora laughed. "You know what it's like at home. Christmas decorations have been up since Halloween in all the shops."

"They wait until December first to get started in France. Much more civilized," said Chloe.

"La Fête de Noël is serious in Paris!" Olivier said as they all raised their glasses. "We can't wait until you see how the city lights up for the season."

Conversation was lively as the two young artists spoke about their latest work. For the past months, they had been collaborating on pieces about Paris life for an exhibit in the gallery in Nice owned by Olivier's father, Pierre.

Chloe described the work like this. "We feel the collection reflects a contrast of energy and vision—bold color palettes, impulsive textures as we captured cityscapes, and the energy of different arrondisements."

Olivier added, "For this exhibit, we tried to straddle abstraction and emotional realism. In other words, we hope we balance abstract with real, honest emotions."

Nora hoped she would understand the meaning of their work once she saw it. It sounded complex.

But when they showed her photos of a few paintings, she was overwhelmed. Their work looked real and honest. She felt pulled in by the light and texture seen even in the photos. Her heart filled with pride for both of them.

Nora was also pleased to see how well Chloe and Olivier complemented each other as they related stories of their daily lives with relish and affection. Each time she visited in the three years since the wedding, Nora felt such motherly satisfaction to be in their company and see their relationship continue to flourish.

Several glasses of wine fueled the conversation and laughter. It was midafternoon when they left the bistro and Nora had begun to experience the fog of jet lag.

"I knew that was lunch and dinner I was eating, and I am stuffed. I'll have nothing more to eat today, thank you very much. But I can't go to sleep yet. I'm going to walk around and stop in a few galleries to keep myself awake."

"Bonne idée," Chloe said, and Olivier agreed. "We will be at our studio for a few hours. Keep us posted on your whereabouts."

Nora laughed. "Pas souci! No problem! I'll be fine and then I'll crash after a long soak in your glorious tub."

"Sounds like a good plan, Mom. Oh, by the way, your skates arrived. I kept forgetting to tell you. You might even want to use them before New Year's, as there are lots of skating rinks at the Christmas markets."

Nora was surprised to learn that. "You never know," she said. "Let's see how I settle in."

"For sure," Chloe said, giving her a hug. "We'll see you in the morning."

"Thank you for that magnificent déjeuner, and don't worry, I know my way around. I'm going to stop at the next terrace I come to and have an espresso for an extra shot of energy. I've been practicing getting used to it so I can really feel French."

The next café terrace was only a short walk away. Café des Deux Moulins was featured in the movie *Amélie*, and Nora ordered an espresso now. Sitting in the shade of the building, she wrapped the blanket hanging over the back of her chair around her legs. She wasn't cold but liked the cozy feeling.

The espresso was hot and strong. The jolt of caffeine hit Nora in minutes and she was soon ready to continue exploring. She left some money on the small plastic dish the waiter had placed on the table when he brought her coffee. Paying the bill like this in France was something she thought was brilliant. Just leave your cash and go.

Walking up a narrow cobblestone street, the white domes of the Sacré Coeur came into view. As she arrived in the busy atmosphere of Place du Tertre, she spotted several inviting cafés and promised she would check them out on her future strolls. Even in the cold weather, artists were painting at their easels and encouraging people to stop and sit for a portrait.

She continued to the steps of the Sacré Coeur, and at the top she stopped to drink in the expansive view over the city. Taking several photos, she chuckled, thinking how many she already had from previous trips. The view was one of those shots she took year after year ... just because.

She wasn't certain exactly what it was that made the slate rooftops of Paris such an iconic visual. Through the years she had heard artists describe how the cool blueish-grey tone of the slate and matte texture scattered light differently during the day. She liked how Olivier had once told her the angled mansards, crooked chimneys, and weathered tiles created a visual signature of the city. Seeing this from above was almost an emotional experience to her. She understood how so many painters were inspired by the expansive vista, particularly in the late 1800s, when van Gogh lived here. She closed her eyes and pictured them: Toulouse-Lautrec, Modigliani, Monet, Degas, van Gogh, Gaugin, Cezanne, Pissarro.

The thought that she now lived near the same space as Vincent van Gogh and his brother, Theo, was becoming an obsession. But why not? The fact was simply too special to ignore.

The brothers' apartment was one over from Chloe and Olivier's, on the other side of Giselle Tremblay. They told Nora it was privately owned and had been empty for some time. No one seemed to know why it wasn't occupied.

"Not even Giselle knows!" Chloe had said. "And she knows everything!"

When she found a spot to rest, Nora allowed herself a few fantasies about Vincent living in the neighborhood. She pictured him painting feverishly in the golden light of late afternoon, like it was now. She wondered if he always wore a hat in Montmartre, as he was so often pictured, or was that more in Provence? And did he always smoke as he painted? She remembered reading about him saying he sometimes spent his last money on tobacco rather than food.

The warm sun washed over her as she sat on the stairs watching and enjoying the stories that played out among the colorful characters, excited tourists, and blasé locals wandering about. No doubt there were a few pickpockets in the mix, but she hadn't spotted any today.

She walked down the stairs and over to 62 Boulevard de Clichy. There, all that remained of the famous Café du Tambourin was a plaque on the wall by the entrance. It stated how artists including Vincent had frequented the bar in the 1800s.

Nora stood there, recalling how she and Jeremy had rushed to find the café on their honeymoon and how sad they felt to learn it had closed and gone bankrupt in 1887. They had laughed at not doing better research before their trip and wandered down the street to another bar for a glass of wine.

She felt stalled in a bittersweet moment of emotional limbo, a state not unknown to her. Thinking of Jeremy often brought it on. She pushed herself to get going and took the stairs back up the hill.

As she slowly climbed, she contemplated how she might be influenced by the fact she was staying next door to where Vincent had lived. Before she'd left for Paris, she had fantasized about writing a story based on Vincent's affair with a bar waitress and considered it might be the answer to her writer's block.

Recording some ideas on her phone, as she often did when it came to her writing, she promised herself to do some serious thinking about it once she was settled with Atticus.

After she returned to Chloe and Oli's apartment, Nora checked about their arrival time. She assured Chloe there was no need to rush home to her, since she was heading to bed after her bath and most definitely was not interested in anything to eat.

When the bathtub was filled almost to the top, Nora added a drop of lavender essential oil, at Chloe's earlier insistence. "It'll help you sleep, Mom. Trust me," her daughter had said.

Nora sank into the water up to her neck with a deep sigh. Having a long soak had been her best way to relax for her entire life. Feeling calmed by the warmth and fragrance of the water, she was filled with gratitude to be back in Paris and that Chloe had made it happen.

She told Jeremy all about her thoughts and emotions since she had arrived. Memories of their honeymoon filtered into her head, and she promised to visit all their favorite places during her stay. As she had done each previous visit.

But this time she would have company. She hoped she and Atticus would get along. She hadn't admitted to Chloe that she was still a bit nervous about living with a Doberman. She had googled a lot of information about the breed and everything indicated that even though they were sleek and muscular, they were also gentle and sensitive. She was hopeful.

The next morning at nine o'clock, she and Chloe had a rendezvous scheduled with Giselle and her dog. Nora banished the thought for now, her concerns about Atticus still simmering. Instead, she let herself linger in the moments of her first day, quietly grateful, and aware that a long-dormant happiness was beginning to stir.

Chapter Six

THE LOUD PURRING IN NORA'S EAR CONFUSED HER FOR a split second. Jezebel lay draped across the top of her head, apparently very content. Nora gave the cat's ears a rub and reached to pull the cord that lifted the blind on the window next to the futon. Turning her head, she was just in time to see a burst of vibrant color as the sun began to rise over the rooftops.

"What better way to start my day here?" she murmured to Jezebel as she pulled the fluffball into her arms for a snuggle. "Did you know I love Paris?" Jezebel softly placed a paw on Nora's lips as if to shush her, which made her laugh. Jezebel stretched, gave Nora a haughty look, and leapt to the floor.

Nora lay back, chuckling. *That cat does have attitude*, she mused.

She saw she was alone and a note lay on the kitchen counter with instructions for the espresso machine. Beside that was a plate with two fresh pains aux raisins.

Nora's face lit with a wistful smile. Ever since her honeymoon, this was her first morning taste of France—a buttery, spiral pastry filled with silky custard and plump, golden raisins. Each bite was a satisfying indulgence, warm with nostalgia and sweetness.

Of course, Chloe remembered it was her mother's favorite

breakfast pastry and had already been to the boulangerie before she left for the studio. The plate was covered with a reusable beeswax wrap. It was one of the many items Nora had noticed in the kitchen which showed how eco-friendly the young couple was trying to be.

Nora's eyes teared up when she saw one of the best-loved items from her Christmas trunk on the counter next to the pastries. The music box with the dancing Santa doing a jig to "Jingle Bells" had been a gift from Jeremy to Chloe when she was five. It was usually one of the first things out of the trunk, and Nora had sent it to Chloe for her first Christmas in Paris. It filled Nora's heart to see it again.

She opened the small drawer along the bottom of the box where they always stored chocolate kisses. *Even in France*, she thought, and smiled as she tasted one of the obviously handcrafted treats in there now. When the drawer was opened, the music began and Santa leapt into action. It was impossible not to shimmy and hum along.

Once her coffee was ready, she wrapped a silky pashmina over her nightgown and sat at the table. The view out the window looked down Rue Lepic and across the neighborhood.

In the dim light of dawn, she imagined the streets coming alive with bohemian vibes in Vincent's day. Before she came to France, she had looked up everything she could about that period. The very thought fired her imagination.

Women in long dresses would make their way to the markets along the narrow winding streets. A donkey cart might trundle along filled with firewood. Scruffy dogs would poke around, visiting their favorite haunts for a scrap.

Nora pictured herself walking in the artist's footsteps.

It was time. Nora felt like she was going on a blind date ... apprehensive and suspicious. Atticus was waiting to meet her.

Chloe tapped on Giselle's door and Nora expected a heart-stopping bark from inside. But there only came Giselle's cheery "J'arrive!" before she opened the door and greeted Chloe and Nora each with a dramatic bise. "It's lovely to see you again, Madame Bennett."

Nora had met Giselle briefly on two of her previous visits and found her unforgettable. Her blazing copper hair was piled in a messy knot on top of her head. Her sparkling green eyes glistened with curiosity and enthusiasm.

"And you, Madame Tremblay," Nora replied. She was well aware how important it was to be courteous in France and use *Madam* and *Monsieur* until told otherwise. "But please call me Nora."

"Mais oui, if likewise you will call me Giselle."

Out of the corner of her eye, Nora saw Atticus seated on the floor behind Giselle, as still as a statue. His dark eyes stared at her. His taut, muscular body made no move, but appeared ready to spring on command.

Nora gulped. Giselle grinned and took her hand. "Atticus has been waiting to greet you. See what a good boy he is?" Nora gulped again and forced a weak smile. Giselle slipped Nora a small dog treat and said, "After you say hello, ask him to sit and then offer this in your open palm. It will be the beginning of his love affair with you. I promise."

With a simple hand gesture from Giselle, Atticus stood and approached them. Giselle spoke to him in a gentle voice, in French, "Mon coeur, c'est notre amie Nora."

Nora gingerly reached out her hand to pet his head and he pushed into her palm. It was a friendly gesture, but she felt his strength. She asked him to sit and offered the treat, which to her surprise, he delicately accepted. And that was that. The dog bounced around to each of them for some attention, his hind end happily wiggling, before sitting quietly by Giselle.

"See? Un chou à la créme! A cream puff! And nothing to fear. He will be your best friend. The treat I gave you for him was his favorite, which he only receives on very special occasions. He won't forget your kindness."

Nora laughed nervously but beckoned Atticus to her. He sat by her and eagerly accepted her attention as she stroked his sleek body and admired his black-and-rust coat. Then he moved back to Giselle and stared at Nora with his dark, expressive eyes.

"Oh my gosh, he is gorgeous. His coat is like velvet. Not scary at all when you get past the first impression. And he doesn't have pointy ears!" said Nora.

"That's one of the things I love about him," Giselle said, with obvious affection. "But even with his soft, floppy ears, he makes me feel safe. I did not want him to have them cropped. No one can guess what a sweetie he is at first glance. He commands respect, non?"

Suggesting they sit down, Giselle placed a tray on the coffee table with three tiny cups of espresso and a plate of mini croissants accompanied by a small bowl of strawberry confiture.

Giselle was a woman of an indeterminate age who commanded attention. Her smile was infectious, her energy palpable. Nora had never met anyone quite like her.

The three women chatted for a while before Chloe left to get ready to go to the studio with Olivier. "We've got a Zoom call before we go, Mom, so we will be home a while longer."

Giselle showed Nora around the apartment, assuring her there was little to feel responsible about except a few houseplants and Atticus.

"Please make this your home," Giselle said. "You are doing me such a favor and allowing me to jet away with no guilt. Mille mercis!"

She opened the door to a light-filled room with floor-to-ceiling windows that showcased the same breathtaking view over the city as Chloe's living room had. Sunshine cast warm light over the worn wooden floor. "My studio, my sanctuary," Giselle murmured.

"Chloe told me you were an artist she admired and that she had learned much from you."

Giselle looked at the floor modestly. "Your daughter is so talented, as is Olivier. We learn from each other. It's exciting to watch them progress and I love their youthful company."

The room was filled with organized chaos. A tall easel held a work in progress at least five feet tall. Paint-spattered oilcloths were strewn on the floor. Tubes of paint lay scattered on a battered wooden table along with jars of brushes of all sizes, graphite pencils, charcoal sticks, and a selection of palettes both used and new.

Nora took the scene in and noted the peace reflected in Giselle's eyes as the woman ran her fingers over a stack of open sketchbooks piled on a stool.

"My bibles," she whispered.

Unfinished canvases, multicolored splashes of paint, and pinned-up sketches adorned the walls. A faint smell of oil paint and turpentine hung in the air.

"Chloe told me you are a writer. But if you ever have the urge to dabble, feel free to be part of the energy. It sustains me. Mon dieu, it might be the perfect place for you to be inspired and write."

Giselle quickly cleared one end of the table. "Voilà! Consider this your spot! The room has its own vibe. You know the van Gogh brothers once lived next door, and I have always sensed something special exists that has lasted since then. When you decide to work in here, close your eyes and try to breathe it in."

Nora nodded, speechless at first. Giselle was inspiring. Then as she looked around at the art on the walls, she said, "I hope you will show me more of your work before you leave."

Giselle flashed a smile. "With pleasure, although we don't have a lot of time. I'll have to be concise and not blather on … which is my style. Come by tonight and we will open champagne."

They walked back out to the kitchen area. Giselle picked up a small bag and handed it to Nora.

"These are the special treats like the one I gave you. If you always have one or two in your pocket, Atticus will be the most obedient boy always."

Giselle showed Nora the cupboard with his food and more treats and toys, explaining his daily schedule. Atticus shuffled with excitement and picked up a well-worn stuffed octopus chew toy with cloth legs that popped and crinkled as he whipped it around.

Giselle and Nora laughed, and Giselle played tug with Atticus for a few moments. "As you can see, he enjoys this and will play it any time."

Nora told her about Maggie, her Wheaten, and how much she'd loved having a dog. "Atticus is already bringing back memories. Don't worry, we'll have fun together."

"We have been out for our early morning walk, but I thought we would take a stroll around the neighborhood before lunch." Giselle paused as if a thought had just occurred to her. "Would you like to come with us?"

Without hesitation, Nora said, "Perfect! Just knock on the door when you're ready. I will be catching up on some work and happy to take a break anytime." She felt ready for an adventure, just from talking to Giselle.

Atticus had calmly accompanied them on their apartment tour and seemed perfectly comfortable with Nora's presence. He sat on command and presented his paw for her to shake before she left.

Chloe and Olivier were about to leave for their studio when Nora returned to their place. With their coats already on, they were finishing up two last cups of espresso.

"Whoa! I remembered Giselle as being vivacious, but I'd forgotten what a ball of fire that woman is. And her studio! Wow!

She radiates passion and joie de vivre!" Nora joined Chloe at the kitchen table.

Chloe and Olivier laughed. "Having her as a neighbor is quite the experience. Never a dull moment and, well, just so much laughter."

"And so many bottles of champagne in that studio," added Nora.

"As you saw," Chloe said, "she's a talented artist and actually has quite the following in France and beyond. But she is immensely modest, never brags. She loves to talk about the artist's life ... the creativity and inspiration ... and I have learned things from her that I've seen or heard nowhere else. She's an original."

Olivier said, "She's also incredibly sweet and thoughtful. And what a life! She was a model for Gucci for years and can tell you wild stories that are hard to believe, but are true. She probably didn't tell you that her family has lived in this building since it was built. Her great-great-great grandparents were friends with Theo van Gogh and knew Vincent when he was here."

Nora's mouth gaped. "She did mention the brothers but not her family's friendship with them! What a history."

"Yes," said Olivier. "That is something you often find in France. Families have been connected for centuries and often live in the same place generation after generation."

Chloe added, "It's something that fascinates me about living in this country. I've heard such wild family histories going back through the Revolution and Napoleonic Wars, and of course, the Occupation. We just don't have the same kind of historic connections in Canada, for the most part. I love hearing the French stories."

"You're right. Those history-filled stories are not something we often find at home. It fascinates me too!" said Nora.

Chloe gave her a sly grin. "Hmm, imagine the stories you might be inspired to write here."

Nora nodded and changed the subject. "And I believe Atticus and I are already friends."

"Oh, Mom! Now you know why I wasn't concerned about you getting along with him. Isn't he the sweetest? Who knows, you might decide to get a dog again when you go back home."

"Ha! Don't get carried away! But our meeting went very well. I feel so happy! I was worried for nothing."

Chloe rolled her eyes at Oli. "What else is new?"

"Respect your maman," Olivier chided her.

They said their goodbyes and the two artists left for work.

Nora sat at the tiny dining table with her computer. She organized her work so she could go out with Giselle first and get to everything else later in the afternoon. She figured she would need about two hours to catch up with email and work on a copy edit due to a client by the end of the week. She would worry about the inevitable social media demands later. Her calendar held nothing urgent.

But she was eager to get excited about a new story. If she could just smash through her writer's block.

Chapter Seven

"I have an idea," Giselle said when she and Atticus collected Nora just before noon. "If you have good walking shoes." Her hair, wild and tousled earlier, was now pulled neatly into a sophisticated knot at the nape of her neck.

"Dites-moi," Nora said. "Oops. I shouldn't have said that. I'm not quite ready to dive into a deep conversation in French yet. And I do have good walking shoes on."

"Chloe told me you were looking forward to seeing all the Christmas decorations around the city. It will take you many days and you will love them! For a start, we could walk from here to the large department stores on Boulevard Haussmann in about an hour. The windows are done up in the most amazing scenes and animations."

"Fabulous idea!" said Nora. They left the building and started down the street.

Jittery about Atticus again as they set off, Nora began to relax as the dog displayed perfect manners and seemed to be enjoying the walk as much as she was.

As they strolled, Giselle entertained Nora with a running commentary on the history of the cobblestone streets and narrow laneways they passed. Conversation was light and easy, and more than once Nora gave an inward shake of her head, still adjusting to the shift from her snowy little ski town to the world of Paris.

Nora found Giselle intriguing and admired her passion not just for the city but for life as well—its art, its beauty, its history. And love. Everything the woman spoke about seemed to have an element of love to it. It filled the air around her.

"Each little street here has a story tucked into it, just waiting to be told," Giselle said, sweeping her hand in front of her. "The cobblestones echo with the footsteps of generations past. Artists have never stopped coming here to passionately create. Throughout my life, each day quietly reaffirms my love for Montmartre. It's like a dream from which I never wake up and I can't imagine living anywhere else. I adore everything about this city and this neighborhood in particular."

"I can't help but agree. Each time I visit, I'm aware of such gifts to the senses. There is so much beauty, for one thing … and right now all the aromas from the boulangeries and cafés. I keep taking it all in, breath after breath! Maybe you noticed… I can't help myself."

They both laughed.

"Paris is definitely a love affair for the senses." Giselle's voice dropped to a low, soft tone as she said, "We look for pleasure in everything—art, literature, language, food, drink, fragrances… La séduction is life in France. Be open to it, ma belle."

Her words hit a quiet nerve and Nora recognized a long-buried ache for something like that kind of passion. Giselle spoke of it with such ease. Nora wondered how it would be to experience everything with such lightness. As easygoing as she appeared, Nora held back on many things that might make her happier. She had become an expert at shoving desire into an interior compartment and tossing away the key.

She walked along quietly for a moment, considering that the word 'seduction' was not part of her life. Certainly not without Jeremy.

Atticus kept pace easily with them, and Nora noticed how

Giselle stopped to give him a chance to sniff around from time to time. On one such occasion, Giselle said, "This is like reading the news for dogs. They need to discover what's been going on, just like we do."

He showed no concern when Giselle answered a phone call and passed the leash to Nora. Nora felt his strong pull, but he stayed at her heel. She felt in control, and that was the important thing.

The slender sidewalks bustled with activity. Cafés were beginning to fill, and the two women found themselves dodging pedestrian traffic until they reached the bottom of the steep streets of Montmartre.

The tree-lined and broad Boulevard de Clichy, long a haven for artists still oozed with bohemian life. Strolling became much easier on the wider sidewalks.

Giselle pointed out where the original cabaret in Paris, Le Chat Noir, once operated. "Those exciting bohemian times have disappeared here, and now the place is a bar and hotel." She sighed. "I wish I could time travel back to the days when Degas and Toulouse-Lautrec lived here, and Emile Goudeau gathered his avant-garde group of poets and intellectuals who shaped the artistic and anarchic spirit of Montmartre. Just imagine, Nora, how that life must have been."

Nora grinned at Giselle's enthusiasm as she brought those years to life. They shared a few chuckles as Giselle mused how the numerous sex shops that now dotted the street transitioned the atmosphere from artistic rebellion to commercialized taboo.

"I'm not a prude," Nora said, "but I've been kind of shocked on my last visits to see how many of these stores have opened."

"Alors, there's even one with a book section," Giselle said, laughing. "Literature for everyone!"

They passed the iconic Moulin Rouge, and Giselle entertained with hilarious and racy stories about long ago experiences at the nightclub. "When you live here as long as I do, nothing surprises any more. Although I must admit, I have not darkened the door of this place for decades. It really exists for the tourists now but still gives them a taste of how things once were."

The vibe changed to sophistication on the wide Boulevard Haussmann, with its cream-colored stone structures and wrought-iron balconies. The street was lined with commercial buildings and boutique shops offering clothing and home accessories. Car traffic became heavy.

"This is the magic of Paris. Every part of the city has its own distinctive look and character," Giselle said. "Polished and chic here. You will find hidden charms down many historic covered passageways, remnants of the nineteenth century."

"Chloe has taken me to some of those. I can spend hours browsing all the fascinating shops one finds. Some sell the most obscure items, like vintage fountain pens and tin soldiers," said Nora.

They reached the elegant building that housed the high-end department store Galeries Lafayette, with its breathtaking stained-glass dome ceiling. Giselle suggested they go to the rooftop terrace to enjoy the panoramic view and have some lunch.

"Let's have a bit of a rest and look at the windows later. I've worked up a small appetite. How about you?" she asked. "Or would you like to do some retail therapy first?"

Nora laughed. "I've done a fair bit of damage here on past trips. I'm fine to have a light lunch now."

They walked through Galeries Lafayette and admired the impossible-to-ignore ceiling. In the center of the store, they stopped to gasp at the eighty-two-foot Christmas tree that was decorated dramatically each year. Around the world, people waited to see what the new theme would be and photos were posted internationally. This year, the tree featured thousands of LED lights programmed to create a mesmerizing display of patterns and colors.

Giselle led them to the elevator that went to the restaurant and they were fortunate to get a window table. Nora commented the panoramic view, all the way across rooftops to the Eiffel Tower, was as delicious as their meal.

Afterward, they spent some time on the street taking in the always dazzling and imaginative festive windows celebrating the store's 130th holiday season. Each of the eleven windows showcased a whimsical winter scene with a futuristic twist.

"Simply overwhelming!" Nora gushed. "It's going to take a few return trips to take in all those details!"

"Merde!" Giselle exclaimed as her phone rang again on their way home. "Sorry, I have to take this call."

She handed the leash to Nora, who took charge of Atticus but this time with a twinge of nerves. She wondered if he was just being nice the first time she had taken charge.

Now he stopped and turned to look at her. Their eyes met as if he was contemplating the situation, and then he calmly carried on. Nora felt she had received his approval.

When they reached the foot of Montmartre, they hopped on the funicular to avoid the climb. Atticus showed no hesitation.

"Obviously a seasoned pro," Nora commented and Giselle nodded.

"I'm sure you will take this alternate route many times during your stay," Giselle teased. "Those stairs can be killers."

"Agreed. But I plan to get used to them," Nora said. "If nothing else, Atticus will get me out every day. There are so many arrondissements I haven't explored."

"The more you walk the streets of Paris, the more you feel its rhythm ... its heartbeat. To me the city is a never-ending love affair. I can see you are already beginning to fall under its charm, especially since you've been here before and have had a taste of the love potion it offers."

Giselle's voice caressed the air. Nora thought, *She makes Paris sound like a seductress.*

After wandering over to Rue Lepic, Giselle said she was going to meet a friend for a coffee. Nora declined the invitation to join them.

"Thanks so much for today. I enjoyed the walk, the chat, the lunch, the windows ... everything! And I'm so happy that Atticus is relaxed with me." She reached down and gave his head a rub before handing the leash back to Giselle.

Atticus' little stub of a tail wagged as mightily as Nora thought it could and that made her smile.

"Well, not to take up all your time... But because I won't see you after tomorrow, I would love it if you and Olivier and Chloe could join me tonight at Au Lapin Agile for a glass or two of champagne. It is one of my favorite hangouts, and I have someone I would love for you to meet."

"I'll let the young people decide. I might still be a bit jet-lagged. In fact, I think I'll have a quick nap now and get myself on track."

Chapter Eight

Later in the afternoon, after a two-hour nap, Nora made a pot of tea and Jezebel joined her to snuggle on a grouping of down-filled Moroccan floor pillows. She watched the sky transform into a rich tapestry of amber, pink, and lavender through the massive window in the salon. The last rays of the sun cast a golden hue over the rooftops of the city below.

As the city lights began to flicker on, the landscape looked like a vast fairyland. "Magique," Nora whispered to the cat. "Impeccable." Jez purred loudly and butted her head into Nora's hand whenever Nora stopped stroking her.

Nora pulled up a Joe Dassin playlist on her phone. His soothing voice and French lyrics were the right accompaniment to the scene.

As darkness slowly settled, Nora's eyes rested on the lights of the Eiffel Tower in the distance across the rooftops. A beacon in the night sky. Suddenly it burst into a spectacular dancing show of lights that twinkled like stars. She smiled; she'd forgotten the surprise since her last visit and the pleasure it brought. When the lights returned to their steady graceful flow, she wondered who had come up with an idea so simple that created such a burst of happiness.

"Brilliant," she murmured to Jezebel, planting a kiss on her.

She finished her tea and felt herself relaxing after the busy two days. There was no stress, no worry about what might occur next. A moment of wonder filled her as she thought of how she was already opening herself to change. *I did that. I'm making it happen. Maybe it is the start of something new. And I don't think I'm worrying. Well, maybe just a bit... Hopefully Atticus will love me.*

Then she dozed off.

When Chloe and Olivier arrived home from the studio, Nora woke and gushed about the lights on the Eiffel Tower sparkling on the hour after dusk.

"It began on January 1, 2000, as a temporary celebration for the millennium," Olivier explained. "But everyone loved it so much that the council decided to make it permanent."

Chloe added, "It's amazing how people react to it. A small thing that makes everyone smile."

"That's exactly what it did to me," Nora said.

After Chloe had texted they were on the way home, Nora prepared a small charcuterie board, raiding the fridge.

They stood at the kitchen island grazing and sipping a Vincent Delaporte 2013 Sancerre *Silex Cuvee Maxime.* They had all become Sancerre wine devotees when they'd spent several days exploring the Loire Valley on Nora's visit two years prior.

Chloe put her glass on the marble counter and wrapped her arm around Nora. "Giselle texted us about going out to one of her favorite haunts later. We can nibble a bit here and then have some fabulous food at Au Lapin Agile. Are you up for it, Maman? Did you have a good rest after your long walk?"

"I had an excellent two-hour nap after my lunch excursion with Giselle and Atticus. I'm up for anything now."

Olivier smiled as he and Chloe exchanged looks. "Be ready for some fun. Giselle is in party mode. Her final words in her text were 'On se déchaîne!'"

"Let's get wild," Chloe translated with a laugh. "Au Lapin

Agile is the place to do it, Mom. We've never taken you there, but I know you'll love it. It's a true French cabaret... Edith Piaf all the way! Prepare to sing, and possibly dance! You never know."

"And the dress code for this event that sounds a little dangerous?"

"Anything goes. But maybe smart casual tonight with Giselle. You're great at that, Mom."

Chloe was right, Giselle was in party mode. Nora spotted her waving to them as soon as they entered the small, crowded space. The room was filled with benches and odd wooden tables and chairs. A most eclectic collection of art covered every bit of wall space.

Chloe whispered to Nora, "Imagine how at one time art here was by van Gogh, Picasso, Degas, and other masters! I would love to time travel in here!"

Looking around at the cabaret's interior, Nora felt like she had stepped back in time. The décor was vintage, and the ceiling featured exposed beams.

Giselle's fiery red hair tumbled to her shoulders in cascading waves, contrasting against the full-length conservative black turtleneck wool dress she wore that emphasized her curvaceous body. With a long cigarette holder in her hand, she blended in with the bohemian vibe of the room, even though her cigarette was unlit.

The room buzzed with energy: bustling waiters, spirited conversation, and laughter even as in one corner a woman sang accompanied by a trio. There was no stage; the patrons and entertainers were cheek by jowl. Chloe had explained the music was like folk music and popular French songs going back to the 1800s.

"People often sing along," she said. "Imagine Edith Piaf belting it out here."

Once they reached the table, a middle-aged couple named Mark and Marie greeted Chloe and Olivier like old friends, and a handsome man, introduced as Luc duValois, kissed Nora's hand. He appeared to be in his thirties, tall with dark-brown curly hair slicked back but not quite in control. He exuded undeniable natural charm, had a smooth, sensual French accent, and appeared totally smitten with Giselle, who returned his affections. Nora couldn't take her eyes off them but attempted to be subtle.

As Giselle made introductions all around, the waiter brought two unopened bottles of champagne for their table and left.

"That will get us started," Giselle commented as Luc ceremoniously popped a cork and everyone cheered.

"We like to do that ourselves," he said to Nora. "It's more festive."

Champagne flowed and they enjoyed one musical performance after another. Everyone at the table was thoughtful about including Nora in the conversation. She implored them to speak French, and Chloe said she would translate when needed. Nora told them she was determined to become better at speaking and understanding French.

"Diving in is often the best way," Luc said to her. "Sois courageuse. Be fearless ... and maintain a sense of humor."

"Nous essaierons de parler lentement," Giselle added.

Everyone agreed, with sympathetic laughter. They would do their best to speak slowly.

Nora knew exactly what they meant. The French did speak quickly and slowing down would help. And be appreciated.

The owner, introduced by Giselle as Frédé, joined them when he took breaks from being a guitarist. "You will stay after hours, non?" he asked the group as it got closer to closing time. Nora raised her eyebrows at Chloe and Olivier. They both looked at her and grinned as the others uttered enthusiastic assurances.

"Absolument."

"Totalement."

"Bien sûr!"

Satisfied with the results, Frédé left the table to check on other guests.

"The owners are descendants of the original Frédéric Gérard, who bought the club in 1900. He was known as Frédé too," Luc told Nora. "They have remained true to the bohemian atmosphere he established, and we love it. Not too many tourists are aware of this place, so the crowd is mainly locals, and we love it that way."

The others nodded.

At one o'clock in the morning the club was closing, and Nora looked around at her friends for signs they would be leaving soon. Giselle patted her hand. "Not us, chérie. This is our special time."

More champagne appeared and Nora was amazed that everyone seemed so light-hearted and animated but still quite sober. She felt more than a little inebriated but decided they were more experienced at drinking champagne. And besides, one only sipped champagne. It seemed to heighten everyone's charisma rather than cloud it.

I'll just have to get better at this, she told herself.

Melancholic accordion music played now, which puzzled Nora as it was a distinctly different sound compared to anything she'd heard earlier that evening. Luc helped Frédé clear a large area near the stage by pushing tables and chairs out of the way.

"Nora, I see the look on your face." Giselle sat beside her. "I am guessing you did not know that tango is extremely popular in France ... and has been since the early 1900s. Before World War One, Paris was overcome by tangomania! The dance became fashionable here but also spread to small villages throughout the country, and it has remained part of our culture ever since. Dancers came from Argentina in the early days to perform and give classes. Watch Mark and Marie, they are professionals, and we all learn from them. But tonight, they are just here for fun and pleasure."

The idea of trying to keep up with professional dancers after a night of champagne didn't sound very appealing. "Oh dear, I have no idea how to tango, although it sounds fascinating. Maybe tonight I'll just watch."

Giselle gave her a warm, knowing smile. "Attends ... just wait. You will be surprised."

Everyone but Nora got up and moved to the cleared space. Frédé extended his hand to her. In the most exotic French accent Nora swore she had ever heard, he said, "Giselle tells me you are visiting, and you do not know how to tango?"

Nora froze, feeling a twinge of panic. She didn't want to make a fool of herself. "Yes, I'm visiting, and no, I do not know how to tango. I'm sorry."

"Ah, non, non. Do not worry. I will show you. It's really very simple. Here is a good quote about this dance I always share with those just learning: 'Tango teaches us that joy isn't always loud—sometimes, it's found in balance, trust, and the beauty of surrender.' Just remember those three words and you will do it. The French love it because it is all about plaisir."

With that he swept her into his arms. "This is called the abrazo ... the embrace. It's where it all begins."

Nora hoped she didn't feel like a stiff board to him. She certainly felt like one to her.

"Nora, look at me."

Frédé's captivating dark eyes drew her in with a soft but magnetic energy. His voice exuded a quiet confidence, inviting her into his world. "Just melt in my embrace and trust me. It's as simple as that. We can start with something smooth and uncomplicated."

Nora swallowed a gulp. This was intoxicating. He was intoxicating. The music played—a slow tune, rich and melancholic. They began to dance.

Frédé guided her every move. His hand rested in the middle of her back with a comforting amount of pressure, and after a few moments of awkwardness, she felt as though she was floating.

"Oui, c'est ça," he murmured. "Relax into the music and my movement. It's all about communication. And trust."

The music went on far longer than any song she had ever danced to, and she began to hope it wouldn't end. When they did go to sit down, Frédé grazed her hand with his lips. "Magnifique! Let's have a rest and then, if you like, we can dance to another piece."

"I would like that. But please be honest... Did I really do it?"

His laughter was warm and genuine. "You really did it, Nora. Mais oui!"

He brought her another glass of champagne, and they watched the others move around the floor. Mark and Marie danced with effortless grace—a blur of intricate footwork and practiced elegance. From time to time, Chloe and Olivier would pause them to ask for a tip—an impromptu lesson or a secret to make it look so smooth and flowing.

"How long must one practice to get that good?" Nora asked Frédé.

"Not as long as you might think. Once the partners know what is expected, a bit of practise can bring it all together. But as you may have realized, a tango can be as simple as the steps we were doing. There is no rush to get complicated. Did it please you?"

"It did, even though I was terrified of making a mistake and tromping all over your feet."

"But you did not do that, even though you were terrified, because you let me guide you. That is the secret in the beginning. When you are more experienced, partners can take turns doing the guiding and the dance can become passionate, emotional, and dramatic."

As they sipped more champagne, he explained the recorded music they danced to. "What sounds like an accordion is something called a bandoneon. It truly is the soul of tango music. Then there is a violin, piano, guitar, and double bass. This is a tango orchestra. The sound they create pulls at the heart and can be beautiful or heartbreaking. Yet it is always emotional and seductive."

"Even though I was mainly focused on not messing up, I felt that emotion. I love sitting here watching how the dancers are so passionate. Their movements shape a story in notes and even the pauses become dramatic. It's an entirely new education for me."

Frédé touched his champagne flute to Nora's. "Magnifique, my new friend. You are catching on. Are you ready to go again?"

Surprised at her own eagerness, she nodded. Frédé stood and held out his arms. Then she was once again in the embrace. The abrazo.

As the evening went on and more bottles were opened, the dancing continued. From time to time, they all changed partners. To Nora's relief, everyone she danced with kept the movements simple, and each dance gave her more confidence.

At one point, Giselle swept her into her arms. "Viens, ma belle. Dance with me. You are doing just fine. How do you like it? Do you feel the plaisir?"

Nora laughed. She already knew this was classic Giselle.

Chloe grinned at them as she and Luc swept by. Olivier was dancing with Marie.

The hours passed. The bubbles flowed. Nora fell in love with tango.

Chapter Nine

Nora's phone rang at half past nine the following morning. It was Chloe. "Mom, did I wake you? I just ducked out of a meeting but thought you might need a wakeup call this morning."

"Well, I did hear the church bells earlier but immediately fell back to sleep. I totally forgot to set my alarm when I fell into bed last night. Thanks for calling. I'll get up and jump in the shower. Giselle will be here soon. She has someone she wants me to meet."

It had been years since she'd slept in so late, but today she'd finally broken her streak. Thanks to a raucous night of champagne, music, and merriment, she'd collapsed into bed sometime around three. But it had all been so very worth it.

Especially the tango.

She laughed out loud as the memories danced into her thoughts. She would never forget last night. She had learned to dance tango. Very basically, but she'd done it and loved it. The entire experience had seemed almost surreal and yet it wasn't.

When they'd chatted during breaks, the others regaled her with stories of how the French love this dance. They shared stories of growing up with people doing it in their small villages. Giselle told hilarious anecdotes about tango spots along the Seine.

"Particularly, le Quai de la Tournelle is perfection when the weather turns warm," she'd said. "I can't begin to tell you the number of characters one meets there. Nora, you must come back in the summer, and we will go together. All of us!"

Dancing tango by the Seine under the stars was magical, they all agreed.

A quick shower left her feeling refreshed and her head somewhat cleared. She would have to ask Chloe about champagne hangovers and how to avoid them while still enjoying the bubbles.

She organized her things and laid the clothes she had already unpacked on the futon. Her plan was to simply throw them over her arm to take them next door.

Giselle expected her to move in around nine thirty and had promised to come over and help in spite of Nora's protestations that she had very little to take with her.

With a flight booked at three in the afternoon, Giselle insisted she was all set to go and had plenty of time to help. When they had stumbled out of Au Lapin Agile well after two, she bade goodnight to Nora with a message that in the light of day made little sense.

"Just think about it. I'm taking you to meet someone who may have an unforgettable story to tell."

Nora tried to unscramble her rather blurred memories and recall the rest of the conversation. If she remembered correctly, Giselle had explained there was an elderly reclusive relative she wanted Nora to meet. Something about the Resistance, something about a memoir. It didn't make a lot of sense.

She made an espresso and sipped it at the kitchen island. It was a rainy day and the view out the windows had been transformed. The rooftops glistened under low-hanging clouds, creating a more somber ambiance than a sunny day. Faint trails of gray smoke spiraled from chimneys, and Nora chuckled as a brief Mary Poppins image popped into her head. Wrong country though.

Giselle texted her and was at the door with Atticus minutes later.

"Good grief!" Nora exclaimed. "How can you look so bright-eyed and full of energy after our late night?"

"Years of practice, ma chérie, many years of intense practice." She raised an eyebrow, giving Nora a look filled with wisdom. "It's part of living in Paris. Trust me."

"I must thank you for an amazing experience last night, in so many ways. Your friends, the music—"

"Ah, the tango," Giselle interrupted, flashing her bright smile. "I'm so happy you loved it. It will change your life, and I'm not being dramatic. Everyone should experience that dance. And I'm glad you enjoyed my friends, who are now your friends. Another of the joys of life."

Nora wanted to hug Giselle but of course did not. She was overwhelmed by the positive energy this woman brought to her. She reached out and took Giselle's hand, and they grinned at each other. No words were necessary.

In no time they had transferred all of Nora's belongings. Giselle had insisted on helping in spite of Nora's protests.

Atticus had walked back and forth with them, supervising with curiosity.

"Eh bien. Allez zou! Let's go. Ma tante Marie-Louise is waiting for us," Giselle said as they put on their coats. "She lives a few minutes away."

Two streets from their apartment building, Giselle led Nora onto a narrow cobblestone alley that could easily have been missed if one hadn't known it was there. They were on a secluded cul-de-sac lined with some of the tiniest houses Nora had ever seen, nestled quietly between larger two-story townhouses. They stopped in front of a worn stone façade covered in ivy, the leaves brown and dry in the winter cold. A wrought-iron gate, its black paint lightly flecked with rust and softened by time and weather, guarded the entrance to a flagstone path. A wreath of cedar boughs tied with bright-red ribbon graced the wooden front door.

"These houses rarely change hands. Generations of my blessed late mother's family lived here for almost 150 years. My aunt has been here since the 1950s. I mentioned it last night—you do remember, right?" She looked in Nora's eyes and chuckled.

"I have to admit my memory is rather blurred. That was quite an evening! But I do recall you speaking to me about your aunt. If my memory serves me right, she has a remarkable story to tell."

"Très bien! And yes, I'm hoping you will feel inclined to encourage her to open up and share her journey. So far, I have not had any luck, but it strikes me that you are someone who may have the right touch with her. At any rate, I'm sure you will enjoy her company."

Nora's thoughts began to clear and her conversation with Giselle from earlier in the morning was filtering back into her head. "Right! You told me an amazing tale about her past. And you mentioned even though she has a full-time caregiver, you visit with her a couple of times a week."

"Formidable! You do remember." Giselle grinned.

"As you know, my French isn't great. I hope we can converse."

"Your French is better than you give yourself credit for. But you will be pleasantly surprised," Giselle said, giving her a cryptic look.

She tapped the brass door knocker shaped like a hand and opened the door into a small foyer.

A bell tinkled lightly as they entered. A young girl with a pixie cut and the brightest green eyes Nora had ever seen immediately appeared and bised with Giselle before she greeted Atticus with a scratch on his head. He sat perfectly still, but his tail wagged nonstop.

"Yvette, bonjour ma belle. This is my friend from Canada, Nora, who is going to stay with Atticus while I'm gone."

Nora offered her hand with a smile.

"Enchantée," Yvette said, shaking Nora's hand. "Please come

in. Tante Marie-Louise is reading in the garden. The sun is lovely and warm this morning, and she is snuggled in her couverture chauffante."

As they walked through the house, Nora commented on how Atticus was so quiet and calm. Giselle said, "He and my aunt have a special love affair going. He seems to understand she is elderly and must be treated with respect."

They walked through a narrow kitchen, immaculate and organized, and out to a postage-stamp-size patio surrounded by vine-covered stone walls. A tall infrared heater stood in one corner radiating warmth.

A petite, fragile-looking, white-haired woman with bright-red nails and matching lipstick was wrapped in a soft pink blanket on a high-backed wicker chair. Giselle undid the leash and let Atticus greet her first.

Her blue eyes sparkled as she reached a hand to pet him and whisper some words before he sat for a cookie.

Then she looked upward, and Giselle leaned down to kiss each cheek.

"Bonjour ma puce." Nora had not expected Marie-Louise to greet her niece in a such a strong voice, which was also filled with deep affection.

The tiny woman extended her hand to Nora, saying, "Enchantée, Madame Bennett. I have heard so much about you."

As Nora offered her hand, the woman gently pulled her close and gave Nora a bise. "We must not waste time with the North American handshake, ma belle. We are meant to be good friends, Giselle has assured me of that. I am delighted you are here."

Nora was shocked to hear her speak in almost perfect English. Giselle flashed her a grin.

"Then please call me Nora. Enchantée, madame. It is such a pleasure to meet you."

"Eh bien. If you are Nora, I am Marie-Louise."

Yvette placed two wrought-iron chairs with soft cushions next to a small table in front of Marie-Louise. "I have prepared tea. Are you all comfortable out here? Is it warm enough?"

Giselle looked at Nora, who nodded it was fine for her. "Yes, it's quite lovely here. So protected and the sun is strong. Ma tante, are you fine to remain here?" Giselle asked.

Marie-Louise smiled and said in clear English spoken with a most elegant accent, "Absolument. I have not even turned on my blanket today. The day is so beautiful." She raised a hand and gestured to the heater. "And Bernard is doing his job well, keeping me warm."

Nora chuckled as Giselle explained. "Tante likes to treat objects such as the heater as though they are handsome Frenchmen catering to her, as they should. Hence the name."

"A fine idea," Nora agreed.

Yvette appeared with a pot of tea, a plate of petite patisserie, and small china plates.

"Merci," Giselle said. "I will pour, and you can take some time off if you like, Yvette. It's a lovely day for a walk and we will probably be here for an hour."

"Bon idée. Merci beaucoup," Yvette said, and asked Marie-Louise if she would like anything else before she left.

"Oui, s'il tu plaît. Please put Nora's contact information in your phone, if Nora does not mind."

Nora nodded her assent, and Marie-Louise slid her phone across the table to Yvette.

"Giselle added your information to mine already," said Marie-Louise, "and now we can both keep in touch with you. Nora, do you mind if I text you? This is as techy ... as they say ... as I get. But I do know how to do it, and I quite like it."

"With pleasure," Nora said, hiding her smile. "It really is such a convenient way to keep in touch."

When Yvette was gone, Giselle apologized to her aunt. "I should have given Nora's number to Yvette. Good for you for thinking of it."

She told Nora that Yvette had been her aunt's caregiver for two years and was like a member of the family.

Marie-Louise added how fortunate they were to have found her and what good company she was. "She doesn't hover and lets me have plenty of time to myself. But I know she is nearby if I need her. I still try to do so much myself, but some days are better than others. Let me assure you, getting old is not for sissies!"

Giselle refreshed their tea, and an hour passed quickly. Nora paid attention as Giselle gently probed her aunt and encouraged her to talk about her life during the Occupation.

"Ma tante, you have kept so many details of your story inside your heart for a lifetime. Now I hope you will consider sharing everything with Nora and perhaps allow her to put it in writing for you. For all of us. No pressure, but now you have a unique opportunity to spend time with someone who truly can be of assistance."

Marie-Louise looked into Nora's eyes with a gaze as clear as a young girl's. Nora could almost feel the woman's experiences that were meant to be shared.

"Nora, I'm certain you have discovered our Giselle is a special woman with a unique ability to make things happen … in all the best ways. It is a delight to know we will spend time together while you are here. Let's talk and see where it leads."

Nora leaned over and covered Marie-Louise's hand with hers. "The most important aspect of us talking together is trust. When we have that, then your words will flow and together we will create the story you wish to tell. Or not. I look forward to whatever happens. I'm happy to be here."

Chapter Ten

Six weeks with Atticus begins.

Nora sat with Giselle as she closed her suitcases after having taken Atticus for a short afternoon walk. "I wanted that little memory on the plane with me. It will be a long time before I can do it again."

Luc arrived to take Giselle to the airport at one p.m. As she said goodbye to Nora, she added, "I can't tell you how excited I am that Tante Marie-Louise might share her story with you. This change in her has been a long time coming. Nora, you feel like family… There seems to be such a genuine connection with you. Some things are meant to be."

Nora looked into Giselle's eyes. "Thank you. I feel it too. But I also sensed your aunt's hesitancy and I certainly respect her privacy. We shall see. Nevertheless, I'll enjoy spending time with her."

Giselle took Nora's hands in hers. "You will do that, ma belle. My heart tells me you are the right person to reach her, if anyone can. She took to you immediately, which does not often happen. She is a very discerning, private woman."

Nora nodded. "What a gracious woman too … with a spark, even at her age! I see where you get it from!"

Giselle grinned. "The best compliment I could ask for! I hope I always have that spark."

Luc made them laugh when he said, "And Giselle's spark bursts into flame on a regular basis!"

"You can believe so did ma Tante's back in the day," Giselle said, giving his cheek a pinch.

Giselle leaned down and planted a kiss on Atticus's head. "Be the best boy for Nora, mon coeur. Nora, he is now about to become your devoted companion and is allowed on all the furniture. There is nothing to worry about here. This is your home for the next six weeks. Enjoy every moment. Au revoir!"

Nora waved as they disappeared down the hall. She closed the door and looked at Atticus, who lay next to the sofa.

"Well, here we are, boy. It's you and me for the next little while. Let me unpack and then we will go out."

Atticus cocked his head and studied her intently, as if contemplating her words. She tried her French and repeated what she had heard Giselle say to him. "Vas y, mon chien."

He leapt up and followed her into the bedroom, where he jumped up on the bed and got comfortable.

Nora took his actions as acceptance of her. She gave his back a good rub and felt all the happy memories of when she'd had her own dog.

As she organized her clothes, she appreciated how Giselle had taken such care to make her feel at home. The French woman had made plenty of room in the closet for Nora's belongings and left several lovely oils and creams in a gift bag in the bathroom.

Nora had already decided to set up her workspace in the studio. "I can't think of a more inspiring ambiance," she said to Atticus as she set up her computer, chargers, and notebooks. He cocked his head again and made her laugh.

Once she had everything just the way she wanted, she clapped her hands and said, "Okay, let's go! On y va."

Atticus dashed to where his leash hung on a peg by the door

and Nora congratulated herself on the fact that he'd understood her French.

More likely it's dogs' intuition. She chuckled as she put on her warm jacket and grabbed her gloves from the kitchen table.

They walked the streets of the neighborhood at a good clip. Nora put in her earbuds and started a French lesson.

She was thankful for good cloud cover as her body temperature began to rise before long. Walks with Atticus were going to be good workouts, she decided. Today he seemed to be very focused on the journey and didn't take much time out to sniff around. She remembered how Maggie paused at every tree and bush to check out who had been there before her.

Nora was also aware of how differently people reacted to a sleek Doberman than they had to a shaggy Wheaten. Walking Maggie always seemed like an act of public service, as everyone wanted to stop and pet her, which the dog loved. Sometimes people avoided Atticus or looked at him with suspicion or fear.

After an hour, they stopped at a café, and a waiter brought a bowl of water for Atticus as he came to take Nora's order of a café crème.

"Bonjour, Atticus," he said as he took the time to give the dog a scratch between his ears. Then he looked at Nora. "You must be the Canadian. Madame Tremblay told me Atticus would have a new friend with him for the next while. I am Joseph. Bienvenue en France." His smile lit up his face.

He's treating the dog as important as its owner—so French, Nora thought, and grinned back as she told him her name, pleased to have not spoken English.

On their way home, she stopped at the boulangerie down the street from her building. After greeting the shopkeeper, she asked for a "baguette jambon et fromage, s'il vous plaît." The thought of a ham and cheese baguette sandwich had been on her mind since she'd arrived. She paid for her lunch and said, "Merci. Bonne journée." The essential French courtesies had not been forgotten. She hurried home to savor her treat.

Much later that evening Nora relaxed on the sofa, answering emails on her phone. She was enjoying the same panoramic view that Chloe's apartment had. Atticus napped in his bed by the window.

She snapped a photo of him with the lights of Paris streets behind and sent it off to the Girls.

She had promised herself she wouldn't open her computer until the next morning, knowing full well she'd never get to bed early if she did.

Chloe and Olivier had to work late at their studio. But Chloe texted Nora several times to ask about her day and make certain everything had gone well with the move into Giselle's apartment.

Nora was drawn into the view of the twinkling city lights. Into the magic.

A quiet night was just what she needed after the whirlwind few days since her arrival. She knew she would be in bed early. A frisson of happiness tingled through her about having made the decision to come to Paris. About being impulsive. She had done it.

A moment later, her cheeks were wet with tears.

Jeremy. It was still all about him. If she was honest, every one of her visits to Chloe in Paris had been about him. This time, though, after meeting with the counselor and talking to Cynthia, she thought she might be able to keep him tucked in her heart and move forward. *It might not be easy though.*

She pushed back her thoughts, dried her eyes, and resolved to make this time different. It was way overdue. She simply had to get a grip and figure out how to do it. Tomorrow she would get back to writing and see if she could lose herself in that.

If Paris couldn't cure her writer's block, nothing could.

Chapter Eleven

On Nora's first morning alone with Atticus, Chloe dropped by for an espresso before leaving for the studio.

"Here's an apartment-warming gift," she said as she handed Nora a saucer with what looked like a bunch of seeds lying atop a damp cotton cloth. "This is how we celebrate la Fête de Sainte Barbe at the beginning of the December festivities. The holiday season is also called la Calendale. The celebrations start now and go right through to February second."

"What on earth is it?" Nora asked, looking puzzled.

"It's a mix of wheat and grass seeds, and you have to keep them watered so they grow tall and strong to ensure the harvest will be good in the new year and you'll have good luck. At Christmas, we will put the plate with all the sprouts on the table with our feast ... that is, unless it goes all droopy. Then we'll toss it! So make sure you water it just right."

Nora thought it seemed like a rather odd challenge but was determined to get the seeds to grow.

For the next two days, she fell into a comfortable pattern of catching up with work, walking Atticus, and spending time playing with him. She also made plans for things she wanted to do in the city.

She listened to her French lessons during each walk. Hearing the language all around her made it easier to absorb what she learned.

The number of excellent exhibits showing at museums and galleries was so large, they could keep her busy every single day. She needed to be organized with her planning, or she'd easily have no part of the day left for work.

And she was writing. Sitting in the square at Place du Tertre each afternoon with Atticus, surrounded by artists plying their craft, a glimmer of an idea had settled in her imagination.

On her first afternoon there, she had noticed a young man at a nearby table sketching a waitress who had taken a break outside a restaurant. Her hair was piled on her head, and she drew long pulls on her cigarette as she sat in the sunshine.

Nora's imagination took her to the portrait of Agostina that Vincent had painted in the Café du Tambourin. Was it a coincidence the young man at the other table also had reddish-blond hair and stubble, just like van Gogh? It was enough to fire her imagination. She quietly recorded thoughts into her phone to be saved for when she was at her computer.

The length of those recordings grew effortlessly and she hesitated to stop, not wanting to break the spell. She was aware of some strange looks as she spoke into the end of her phone and she chose carefully where she sat so as not to annoy anyone. Poor phone courtesy was a pet peeve.

She hoped her words would spill as easily onto the pages of a manuscript. To her relief, that was happening.

Chloe and Olivier worked late into the night for several days, but they finally all had dinner together. Conversation revolved around everyone's current projects. Nora was fascinated with their bold creative ideas, and she shushed them as they apologized for not having been available very much.

"Stop it. I appreciate how busy you are with all you plan to exhibit in Nice in February. It's exciting."

Olivier said, "Thanks for understanding. It's keeping us occupied trying to arrange to ship everything by the end of December. We're about to finish."

Chloe dropped by for an espresso again the next morning and continued to apologize for not being more available. Nora made clear it was not an expectation.

"Simply being next door to you brings me great satisfaction. I know we will do lots of things together at some point. And besides ... I'm writing."

Chloe screeched with delight and pulled Nora into her arms. "I'm so happy!"

"That makes two of us!" said Nora with a laugh.

"You knocked the block."

"Apparently, I did."

Nora's plan was to visit with Marie-Louise that afternoon. She texted to see if *13h* would be convenient, remembering to use the European time.

When she arrived at the woman's house, Nora knocked once and waited. Yvette answered after a few minutes, saying "Please feel free always to come in after you knock. The bell lets us know you are inside."

She ushered Nora into the parlor, commenting the cloud cover made it too cool for Marie-Louise to sit outside today.

Marie-Louise greeted Nora with a bise and a gracious smile. Atticus waited politely but with a concentrated stare at the elderly woman. Both ladies chuckled.

"You see, ma chérie. He knows a special treat is waiting for him." She beckoned him to her for a scratch on the head and gave him a large bone-shaped biscuit. He lay down on a mat by the door and began to work on it.

"That will keep him busy for a while. I'm so happy to see you. Please, tell me how you are and how you have been spending your time. Are you happy in Giselle's apartment?"

Nora filled her in, and Marie-Louise continued to ask engaging questions as Nora relayed the events of the previous days.

"When Giselle told me you are a writer, it gave me much pleasure. I spent a number of years in England after the war writing documents for the government. Very different from your chosen craft, but satisfying at that time."

"I can imagine it was extremely important to be involved in such work then. Living in England explains why you speak the language so well," Nora said, complimenting her host.

"That and an English lover," came the response as Marie-Louise's eyes sparkled. "It really is the best way to learn. If you wish to be fluent in French, I highly recommend it."

Nora smiled. "It's not on my agenda. But I hear you."

"Agendas should always be flexible," Marie-Louise teased back.

Nora was intrigued about the affair but didn't ask any prodding questions. Instead, they spoke of authors they admired and their favorite books.

"The library was my safe place, my comfortable place for most of my life," Marie-Louise told her. "Of course, during the Occupation they were under strict control by the Germans and there was much censorship. But even so, the spirit of resistance lived in the libraries."

She paused and Nora noticed a faraway look in her eyes before she continued. "I will have to tell you about that when we begin our work together."

Nora felt a wave of encouragement knowing that Marie-Louise was committed to telling her story.

They chatted easily, and Marie-Louise asked Nora about her writing history and what inspired her to help others with their memoirs. She was also interested in the novels Nora described writing.

"I still enjoy a good romance from time to time. Particularly these days, with so much disorder in the world. There is such satisfaction in getting lost in a good, uplifting story."

Yvette knocked at the open door and Marie-Louise beckoned

her in. She held a tray with an enticing warm cherry clafoutis and two plates, along with a fresh pot of tea.

"Just in time, ma belle. I was beginning to feel it was time for a treat."

Nora and Marie-Louise became engaged in a discussion about baking as they enjoyed the warm cake. When they finished eating, Nora saw that her host looked a little tired, so she and Atticus said their goodbyes.

"Promise to come again soon. I so enjoyed our conversation. Shall we say next Monday?" Marie-Louise said after they bised.

"With pleasure."

As she strolled home, Nora wondered if she would have to broach the subject of Marie-Louise's life during the Occupation or whether it would be brought up organically. She hoped the latter. There had been several hints Marie-Louise desired this too.

In the early evening, as Nora, Oli, and Chloe sipped apéritifs in Nora's new surroundings, Chloe chuckled as Nora repeated Marie-Louise's advice about taking a French lover.

Sitting next to Nora on the sofa, Chloe slipped her arm around her mother's shoulders and pulled her close. "Who knows, Maman. It's not such a bad idea."

Nora laughed. "À coup sûr! For sure! I'll add it to my list of activities while I'm here."

She gave Chloe a stern look. "At the moment, Atticus provides all the love I need. You were right, he is excellent at cuddling and keeps me company every night. I'm becoming very fond of his sweet nature."

Chloe shook her head and rolled her eyes. "Time will tell... Give yourself permission to feel the full French Effect."

Nora gave her a questioning look.

Olivier grinned at them both with amusement. "Chloe

believes in something she calls the French Effect. It's all about séduction et plaisir ... seduction and pleasure."

"The two most important words in the French language," Chloe said dreamily, softly drawing her finger along Olivier's jaw as she gazed into his eyes. "It caused me to fall so in love with this Frenchman."

She looked at Nora. "Just you wait, Maman, just you wait."

"She is right, you know," Olivier said, addressing Nora with a slow, knowing look. "Séduction has long been a philosophy in France in every aspect of life."

Nora looked from one of them to the other, not knowing quite how to interpret their words. "Fine, my children. I think that's enough of that. I do believe you both are trying to brainwash me." She laughed nervously as a vision of Luc filtered into her thoughts... Was he part of the French Effect? He just might qualify.

At the same time, Giselle's words of a similar nature came into Nora's head. Seduction and pleasure, the appreciation of beauty in everything down to the smallest details, passion... She radiated the French Effect.

"Enough already. On another topic," Chloe said, "how would you like to go to Strasbourg on the weekend? We've been working so flat out, Oli and I feel like we need a break."

"You must be making good progress," Nora said.

"Yes, but only because we've been so focused. Olivier has some Zoom meetings on the weekend and said he would keep Atticus with him, so you and I can play and immerse ourselves in all things Christmas."

Nora's face lit up. "Oh, bless you, Oli! You know I would love to go there again with you, Chloe. Will we take the train as before?"

They chatted enthusiastically about the day trip. Nora had never forgotten the day they'd spent there two years previously, in October. There had been an Octoberfest celebration throughout that stunning town and they enjoyed an unforgettable day of tasting wine, cheese, and local delicacies.

Nora had read about how the Alsatian town, with its two thousand years of history, had the very best Christmas markets, and she had seen Chloe's photos from past visits.

"Très bien! Sunday it is!" Chloe exclaimed. Nora wondered how she would manage to sleep for the next two nights, she was so excited.

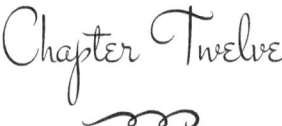

Chapter Twelve

Friday morning, Nora's phone rang. She was in the studio doing research on Paris during the Occupation. Hoping Marie-Louise would want to speak with her about it on her next visit, she wanted to be more prepared than what her long-ago history courses had taught her. She was surprised to hear Luc's dulcet tones on the line.

"Bonjour, Nora." His deep voice caressed her name, smooth and deliberate. It sent a ripple through her – not entirely unpleasant and Nora felt a slight discomfort hearing it, even though she was flattered.

"Do you have plans this evening?"

Being the polite Canadian, she replied without really thinking about it. "No, I don't."

"Are you brave enough for a little tango tonight? We can begin much earlier than our last dance party. You will have to settle for me as a partner instead of Frédé, however."

Nora hesitated. She turned away from her computer screen and looked out across the rooftops, wondering how to respond to such a surprise request..

"Please say you will."

"Well..." Nora began. His French accent was hard to resist. And he had seemed such a gentleman both times she saw him.

"Giselle made me promise to take you to dance the tango at least once a week while you are here. And you know Giselle cannot be refused."

Trying not to laugh, Nora exclaimed, "Really?"

"Vraiment! Really! So I will pick you up at nine o'clock. Non? This club begins dancing at ten and maybe we don't have to have so much champagne. Unless you wish to, of course."

"So I don't have a choice about going?"

"Non, pas du tout! Not at all! But you do have a choice about the quantity of champagne you want to drink." He was teasing and Nora knew it.

Nora couldn't help laughing. She knew she did have a choice but ... why not go? She would be impulsive again. She asked Luc about appropriate attire and said she would come down when he arrived.

Luc said, "You will like it. We are going to a very nice tango club. I will see you this evening. A tout à l'heure, ma belle." And he clicked off.

Nora stood gaping at her phone, momentarily stunned. Had that really just happened? The casual confidence, the unexpected invitation ... and that "ma belle". It was all so unexpected.

Going out for the evening at nine o'clock was also unusual for Nora. After showering and drying her hair, she stifled a laugh as she put the finishing touches on her makeup. It occurred to her that she was getting ready to go out dancing with a man who might be almost twenty years younger.

It seemed her life in Paris was becoming all about being impulsive. And she appeared to be dealing with it. At least she hoped she was.

She had decided her little black dress was just the thing to wear and paired it with the only heels she had brought—black and strappy. Checking herself in the mirror, she took a deep, bracing breath and prayed she would fit in.

While she waited, Nora thought about her new fascination with tango. She had actually watched a few videos recently and delved into its rich history. Everything about the dance had taken her by surprise and stirred something in her. She was eager to learn more.

A few minutes before nine o'clock, Luc buzzed her apartment and Nora said she would be right down. She usually wore running shoes on the stairs, but tonight as she started down the steps, it didn't occur to her she might have to walk differently in her heels. After rushing down the first flight, she turned the corner to go down the next. The heel of her shoe wobbled, and she just managed to grab onto the railing to avoid hurtling to the bottom. She stopped to catch her breath and make certain she hadn't hurt herself. Then she carefully took one step after the other to the bottom.

She fluffed her hair, hoping she didn't appear too frazzled before she stepped into the foyer.

And there he was. Luc, with his flawlessly sculpted French features, looking as gorgeous as he did in the occasional fantasies Nora had had of him since the first night she met him. He gave her a friendly bise and held the door open. "You look lovely, Nora. I hope you enjoy tonight. I believe you will."

How could I not? she wondered. A flutter of butterflies rose in her stomach.

On the way there, Luc gave her a brief history of the dance club. "This is a private club with a large membership. As you know, we love to dance in France. During the week there is dancing of all kinds here, and also lessons. Swing dancing is still extremely popular. Friday nights from ten until three, it is only tango. They bring in a live band, who are so good!"

"It sounds serious." Nora felt a twinge of nerves.

"Non, non. Pas du tout. Not at all. You will see, there are

dancers of every level." His voice was calm and reassuring, without any hint of expectations.

Nora's case of nerves was soothed somewhat by Luc's words and his easygoing personality. She couldn't help thinking how nice it would be to share the company of someone like him, but closer to her age. She promised herself to try and relax and enjoy whatever was to come ... as unusual as that was for her.

It wasn't difficult to enjoy being in Luc's company. His dark hair was slicked in a style reminiscent of a romantic tango dancer, and some of his unruly curls managed to escape just enough to show a hint of playfulness beneath his polished surface. His bright eyes, easy humor, and impeccable manners gave him an undeniable lived-in charm.

Nora looked at him in quiet moments, inwardly shaking her head at her good fortune at being able to spend time with someone so charming. *If only the Girls could see me now.*

Nora felt Luc's hand gently on her arm as the doorman greeted them. His description of the club had been accurate. The spacious music-filled room featured low lighting and gleaming wood floors. A lively crowd sat at tables and chairs lining the walls, which were festively decorated with pine boughs and red ribbons.

They were welcomed with warm enthusiasm, and Nora saw Luc was well known as people greeted him by name and affectionate gestures.

After being seated at a prime table with a view of the dance floor, a waiter immediately appeared with a bottle of champagne. Luc grinned at Nora's look of surprise.

"Nora, may I present Henri? He will be our waiter, and your wish is his command."

The waiter, in traditional white shirt, black trousers, and long black apron, bowed to Nora and, with a refined accent, said, "A pleasure to meet you. I will help make your visit here one to remember."

Nora smiled graciously. "Merci beaucoup."

Luc turned to Nora, "Do you mind champagne, or would you prefer something else?"

"Champagne is lovely, thank you. I'm becoming quite accustomed to it," she said with a hint of amusement in her voice.

Luc gave a slight nod and a smile to Henri, who returned it with a polite bow before retreating.

"You seem to know the waiter well," Nora observed.

"Yes, I do. But really it's not usual, we've known each other a long time. Here in France, we consider our waiters as professionals. Traditionally, they remain with their employer for their entire career and are well remunerated. It is a different situation than in America. When we see each other often, like this, we become friends."

The band began to play a piece Nora recognized, and Luc held out his hand. "This is our cue. It's one of the pieces we danced to at Au Lapin Agile. Shall we give it a try?"

Nora gulped and Luc grinned at her expression. "Remember, just lean into my abrazo and trust me. I won't disappoint you."

The dance floor was filled with diverse couples of all sorts of pairings. Everyone moved with quiet elegance to the music—some smiling, others solemn, and a few lost in the spell of something hopelessly romantic.

Despite her nerves and a few hesitant missteps, Nora found herself leaning in, as Luc had gently advised. The motion seemed like a dream to her, as she floated along guided by the quiet assurance of his subtle tutelage. She was acutely aware of his scent—light and intoxicating, a mere whisper of cologne, faint hints of vetiver and spiced citrus. Fresh yet undeniably seductive.

The evening was a blur of dancing and fascinating chats, at times in English and others in French. Luc was a charming companion in every way. He conversed easily, displayed a quiet refinement, and had a sense of humor that kept them both laughing. For the first time in many years, Nora felt like an attractive woman out with a handsome, intelligent man who enjoyed her company.

Luc was open about his friendship with Giselle, and offered their history without any prodding from Nora. She was surprised to learn that Giselle was a Professor of Philosophy at the Sorbonne. Luc had previously been a student of hers, and their friendship spanned many years.

"Giselle enjoys the company of younger men, and I love her joie de vivre! She is gracious, wise, and great fun. I'm never aware of our age difference. I also know she has many male friends, and I'm glad I am one of them."

Nora was dying to know more delicious details, but Luc was respectful, and she knew the rest would be left to her imagination.

The evening ended up being more delightful than anything she could have dreamed. Luc brought her home at one in the morning, and said goodnight at her door with a sweet bise. Friendly and affectionate. Nora felt no awkwardness at all and thanked him for another remarkable adventure.

"We will do this again. If you wish, of course." Luc's voice was low and inviting but not inappropriate in any way.

"I would love to," she said, the glow in her eyes still lingering from the hours they had spent together.

"Magnifique. Why not the same time next week?"

Nora twirled around like a schoolgirl after she closed the door. She flung her shoes off and flopped on her back on the sofa, closing her eyes and grinning as if living in a wonderful dream. Had the evening really happened?

Spending time with Luc was wonderful and bewildering. If she had ordered a perfect date, he'd fit the bill. He seemed to genuinely enjoy her company and, in his gaze, she felt more confident and attractive. Their conversation was relaxed and filled with laughter. And the tango? What could she say to this new, exciting experience?

There was no need to question where their friendship was

going. It just was what it was: effortless, natural, and undeniably enjoyable. She didn't have to overthink it. At least not yet.

Knowing she would be unable to sleep, she changed into her nightgown and settled at her computer in the studio.

She listened to her recordings from her terrace stops, which vividly described the young man and the waitress who had spurred her imagination. She wondered if those ideas would resonate with her now. To her amazement, they gently unfolded into words on the paper. Her thoughts, which had been so fragmented recently, began to flow without coaxing.

She wrote far into the early morning. Did she dare think her muse was back? Hopefully it would stay.

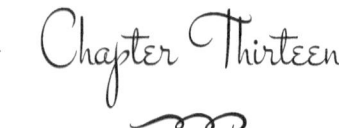

Chapter Thirteen

A LIGHT MORNING MIST HUNG OVER THE STREETS AT six thirty Sunday morning as Nora and Chloe climbed into an Uber to go to the Gare de l'Est. Olivier waved them off with a grin.

"We're having a guys' day! I'm looking forward to it," he'd said after Nora had given Atticus a kiss on his head and instructed him to be a very good boy.

At the station, they went straight to the renowned pastry shop, Maison Pillon, and picked up a croissant for Chloe and a pain aux raisins for Nora to eat on the train. They had time for a quick espresso before they needed to board the highspeed TGV, Train au Grande Vitesse, in time for its seven o'clock departure.

"We can relax with another espresso on the train," Chloe said. "And we could get things to eat, but they won't be as good as these pastries."

The seating on the train was spacious and more than comfortable for the two-hour-and-twenty-minute ride. After leaving the industrial area outside Paris, it wasn't long before they were watching the countryside of Champagne and Lorraine whiz by. Fields, small towns, and forests became blurs as the train picked up speed.

Chloe was eager to hear about Nora's tango evening with Luc.

Nora laughed as she described how she'd felt like a young woman in Luc's company. "Honestly, it was kind of crazy, but I just rolled with it. Can you believe that?"

Chloe shook her head. "Incredible. So not like you to roll with it! What's happening, Maman? You're falling under the French Effect, just like I hoped!"

Holding her hands up in surrender, Nora grinned and rolled her eyes. "I never would have believed it… And my tango dancing is not bad at all. Still basic but not bad. I love it."

After they had gone over every detail of Nora's date night, Chloe kept her entertained with a full description of the beauty of Strasbourg in December and the fabulous Christmas offerings in the markets. "OMG, Mom. You are going to love it! I predict you'll be right back in your Mrs. Claus persona within minutes."

Shaking her head, Nora said, "I don't know. I think those days belong in my 'been there, done that' compartment. It was fun while it lasted…" Her voice trailed off and Chloe noticed she had a nostalgic look in her eyes.

Chloe put her arm around Nora's shoulders. "Hmm. You've been saying that about a lot of things in your life in the last couple of years. Turning fifty did a number on you, and I want you to stop it! You aren't old! Keep remembering how you felt last night with Luc!"

"Advice from my optimistic young daughter," Nora murmured, leaning into Chloe and giving her a kiss on her cheek. "But I assure you, spending evenings dancing tango with a handsome man who may be twenty years my junior is not going to become a habit."

"You never know, Maman…" Chloe said with a sly grin.

"Well, he did ask me to go again next Friday," Nora said softly as a bit of a blush crept up her face.

Chloe gave her an exaggerated, wide-eyed look and patted her cheek.

They soon began to pass through small villages and the surroundings changed entirely. Ancient, half-timbered dwellings with their oak frames and plaster infill, added to the cultural charm of the region. Nora commented how even new houses were being built in that old style and Chloe explained how the building codes were very strict about preserving traditions.

Rolling hillsides were dotted with vast vineyards at rest for the winter. The bare vines stood in neat, endless rows, their twisted silhouettes etched against the sky.

Nora shot photos through the window and Chloe was absorbed on her phone before they pulled into Gare Centrale, a ten-minute walk from the centre of Strasbourg.

"Oh yes. I remember this so well," Nora exclaimed as they strolled through the district of La Petite France, with its charming architecture from the sixteenth and seventeenth centuries, winding canals, and cobbled streets. It once was a district for tanners, fishermen, and millers.

Almost every house was decorated to the nines with lights, carvings, tinsel, wreaths, and even teddy bears.

"What's with the bears?" Nora asked.

"I honestly don't know. I've even googled them and there doesn't seem to be a clear explanation. But as you can see, they do love them here!" Chloe said. "Do you remember that some of this was rebuilt after the war? I'm always so impressed at how true to the original architecture and city plan they stayed. The place has such a unique history through two thousand years starting with the Romans in 12 BCE. It's all part of a UNESCO World Heritage Site now, preserved forever."

"Thank goodness," Nora said. "Imagine if this had been redeveloped in a modern fashion. I love how France preserves its history and culture. Wow! I had forgotten how many canals there are! It's even more beautiful in winter."

Chloe nodded. "Too bad there isn't much snow yet."

Holiday lights had been strung across bridges and along balconies of the houses that lined the water. A dreamlike mist rose from the surface of the canals as white swans glided by, seemingly unbothered by the morning chill.

Chloe took them on a slight detour so Nora could see the famous Ponts Couverts from the thirteenth century. Originally wooden bridges with roofs, centuries later their structures had been replaced by stone bridges. The three stone towers fortifying each of them also dated from the thirteenth century and were covered with intricate carvings.

They paused often so Nora could take photos. The streets were filling with tourists, and she sometimes had to wait to get her shot.

"'Tis the season," Chloe said. "Today is going to be busy, but fun! And you will practise your French too. I'm proud of how you're doing."

Nora and Chloe used a view of the unique bell tower of Notre Dame de Strasbourg as their guide and reached the main square before long. The pinkish sandstone cathedral, richly adorned with sculptures and flying buttresses, along with the elaborate lace-like openwork of the spire was breathtaking.

"I'd forgotten how ornate and gorgeous it is," Nora said, taking it all in and shooting photos from all angles.

"It's the second tallest after Rouen. Victor Hugo described it as 'prodigy of the gigantic and the delicate,'" Chloe told Nora. "Do you remember the stained-glass windows inside dating back to the twelfth and fourteenth centuries? A tour guide told us they had been removed and hidden from the Nazis during World War Two."

"Right! I remember we watched the movie *The Monuments Men* together after our October visit."

"Good memory, Maman! Now let's go inside before we hit the market stalls ... and we have to get to the Christkindelsmärik, the oldest!"

They lingered inside the light-filled cathedral, admiring the vibrant colors of the windows and the stunning organ and artwork. "Let's stay and watch that amazing Astronomical Clock," Nora suggested. "It's almost twelve thirty, and I've never forgotten the show it puts on with the procession of the apostles and Christ and that mechanical rooster."

Chloe laughed. "Yes, we must hear the cock crow. Let's get a spot now because quite a crowd gathers."

"Great! And then let's give those 322 steps to the top of the tower a pass," Nora suggested.

"Oh darn, are you sure?" Chloe said, with a small pout. "We didn't climb them last time either, and the view is to die for."

"I'm sorry, but I'm getting warm just walking around in here, and by the time the clock performs, I'll be boiling. In fact, I need to take my jacket off while we watch."

Chloe's pout faded. "I seem to remember I showed you photos of the spectacular view on my phone the last time you didn't want to climb up ... and you were much younger then," she teased.

"Ha, cheeky girl," Nora said. "We can look at them again if you like, on the way home."

After the clock's performance, they both breathed a sigh of relief back outside in the fresh air.

They had dressed for a crisp day, so were fine taking their time browsing the diverse offerings at the stalls spread throughout the streets. Every aspect of the experience filled the air.

Aromas of cinnamon, cloves, and orange wafted from vats of mulled wine. Scents of spicy gingerbread, roasted chestnuts, and other exotic baked goods floated out from stalls and combined with the songs of carolers sauntering the streets. Friendly vendors offered samples of bredeles—quaint, traditional bite-size Christmas cookies. Church bells chimed on the hour. Laughter and conversation were everywhere as sellers called out their wares.

Nora stopped from time to time, exhilarated by the surroundings. She breathed in deeply, closed her eyes, and imagined the same experience through the centuries.

"Mom, are you feeling okay?"

"Never better," Nora replied. "In fact, I was thinking how I could write about this. It is so vibrant and alive. It's impossible not to feel festive ... and it's also making me very hungry!"

Chloe laughed. "The more times I hear you say you want to write, the happier I am. See, I knew coming to France would break your writer's block. There's just so much to inspire you."

Chloe agreed she was hungry too and led them to a special place she knew located on a narrow side street.

"Olivier always insists we eat here. He loves the food and the ambiance."

The dark, wood-paneled walls and all the carved wooden chairs, tables, and booths showed an obvious Germanic influence, as did the beamed ceiling.

They ordered sauerkraut and German sausages, which they washed down with a pichet of local Gewürztraminer wine. A slice of Munster cheese was a must to finish off the meal.

"This place is so rustic and definitely feels like we are somewhere different from Paris," Nora said.

"That's another reason I love living in this country. You can experience such different aspects of culture without going very far. There's always an adventure waiting nearby. So as much as I love Canada and the life we had there, I wouldn't trade living here."

Nora gazed lovingly at her daughter. "There's nothing better than seeing your child find happiness and satisfaction in life. It makes my heart sing."

"Well, I wish the same for you. You have a lot of living still to do." Chloe reached over and took Nora's hand, giving her a stern smile. "Don't give up on life, Mom. Don't just settle for what's comfortable." She paused for a moment and then added, "Mon Dieu! Now I sound like a mom!"

After lunch, they walked to the nearby Place Kléber to see the famous Grand Sapin. Each year, the town looked for the tallest tree, always around a hundred feet tall, and brought it to this square for the Christmas markets. Adorned with a thousand lights and beautiful decorations, it was a sight to behold, even during the day. The square was filled with stalls overflowing with every festive item imaginable, tempting to even the most serious Christmas Scrooge.

"Of course, I need to buy a tree decoration for each of the Girls back home. The problem is making a decision. These are all so sweet!" Nora said. Finally, she made her first purchases. "Oh, and they would love these tea towels too!"

Once she began shopping, it was difficult to stop. The variety and excellent quality of the items for sale were not to be denied.

At one of the last stalls they visited, she chose some colorful handmade decorations as gifts for Olivier's family and a few for Chloe and herself. She put them in her tote bag and announced she was not making any more purchases.

Chloe snorted. "Highly unlikely. We still have to get to Christkindelsmärik, the oldest heart of the markets here. From 1570! Imagine!"

When they reached their objective in Place Broglie, Nora stood and stared at their surroundings with her mouth open. Chloe poked her in the ribs. "Oh, just around three hundred stalls spreading out from here. Do you still say you are through?"

"How can I resist? What if I never get back here?" Nora muttered, as they dove into the crowd. "But I'm just looking ... admiring ... I don't need anything..."

But it appeared there was something she needed. A foot-tall, hand-carved Santa painted in such imaginative detail with vivid colors, Nora could not resist it. Nor could she resist more Christmas tea towels and a table cloth.

The vendor was thrilled with her purchases. She put them in a large, colorful, embroidered cloth bag, which she gifted to Nora and refused to listen to her protests.

"Wow, this was so kind of that woman. The Santa is definitely a necessary addition to your Christmas trunk, Mom! You have to promise you'll put him out every year from now on."

Nora gave her a noncommittal nod and moved on to another stall, but her heart was bursting with the generosity of spirit that she felt everywhere. She hugged Chloe, saying, "It's so special to be sharing all this with you."

They bought matching knit hats, adorned with pompoms and traditional Alsace embroidery. "We'll wear them in Provence!" Chloe said, choosing a bright-colored beanie for Olivier. And they bought socks. Socks for everyone in numerous colors and unique, eye-catching patterns. Plus a sweet, glass-blown angel for Marie-Louise. And an irresistible Christmas-themed collar for Atticus.

"Let's get a couple of jars of Nut'Alsace, Mom! It's even better than the regular Nutella," Chloe said.

By the end of the afternoon, they gave in to fatigue and their bags had become heavy. Before heading back to the station, they sat on a terrace by the cathedral and watched skaters gliding around to the sounds of traditional and contemporary holiday music.

Chloe ordered mugs of creamy hot chocolate topped with Chantilly from a nearby kiosk. "We can't leave without having this," she said as she brought them back to their table. The cream melted into the sweet beverage as they sipped. "No wonder Alsace is the champion chocolate-exporting region in France."

They toasted with their mugs and applauded wandering buskers as they relaxed. Chloe commented that Nora seemed to be rediscovering her Mrs. Claus persona thanks to all her purchases.

"If coming here doesn't do it, nothing will," Nora agreed. "It's impossible not to feel the Christmas spirit in these surroundings. If I'm really honest about it, I've missed being more festive even though I tried to convince myself I didn't. And all these brilliant handmade gifts and traditional decorations were irresistible." She finished with a happy giggle.

They stayed just long enough for dusk to fall, and they gasped as the town came alive with all the Christmas lights.

"It was a Christmas dream to be here during the day, but these lights put our trip into the category of magical," Nora murmured. "I'm so glad we were here to see this."

Chloe bought a foie gras sandwich for them to share on the ride back to Paris. "Strasbourg has had a reputation for exquisite foie gras since the 1700s. We can get a small glass of local beer to go with it on the train."

Nora teased her. "All the knowledge you've been sharing tells me you are definitely becoming French. I feel like I have a personal tour guide and I love it."

"It's one of our favorite places to visit for a day trip, and we've taken so many tours I feel like I know it inside out and backward. So easy to get to, and every season has festivals, food, and drink so different from Paris. Or Provence, for that matter."

On the way back home, Nora wondered aloud about Atticus, saying she hoped Olivier had enjoyed his day with him. Chloe teased her about worrying about the dog and not Olivier.

"It's obvious it hasn't taken long for you and Atticus to bond. And after all that worrying about how you would be able to handle him."

Nora grinned wryly. "Of course I worried. It's what I do."

Chapter Fourteen

FIVE WEEKS TO STAY WITH ATTICUS

Nora felt happy to be back with Atticus after just one day away from him. She smiled when he greeted her with excited bouncing.

"We had a fine day together," Olivier said. "He is very good company. Any dog who likes to snooze when I do is a friend of mine."

Nora texted Giselle to let her know Atticus was doing well and included a short video of the two of them sitting by the window. Giselle replied how happy she was but also just a little bit jealous.

On their walk the next morning, Nora was aware that her surroundings felt increasingly familiar. And having a canine companion brought back good memories of walking Maggie for so many years.

Everything felt surprisingly right.

Nora was also aware she was thinking incessantly about van Gogh as she explored the streets and alleyways of Montmartre. She stopped at a terrace for coffee and visualized the surroundings as they must have been in the late 1800s and could picture him there.

She thought about the young artist whom she saw around the neighborhood from time to time. He looked so much like van Gogh it was uncanny.

As she ordered her café crème, she was startled by the coincidence of seeing the young man at a nearby table, with his sketch book in hand. His face was etched with concentration as his hand moved deftly across the paper. She wondered if she would in time be bold enough to speak with him about his work.

Her imagination was fired up. This was the story that had found her so easily early Saturday morning after her evening with Luc.

She wondered what had stirred her desire to be open to the words in her head again. She finished her coffee and briskly walked Atticus back home. She was on a mission.

Back in the studio, she listened to more of the thoughts she'd spoken so softly into her phone during her walks and her coffee stops on terraces.

As she saw her thoughts turn into words on the paper, she felt the young man's love story with the waitress take shape. But she also was uncontrollably drawn back to 1887 and the passion between Vincent and Agostina. A dual timeline story was coming alive in her mind. She just had to keep writing it.

From time to time, she put her palms against the shared wall that divided Giselle's apartment from the one in which the van Gogh brothers had lived. Closing her eyes, she willed her imagination to take her back 150 years to picture where Vincent might have stood as he painted. It was thrilling to think of such brilliance having been so nearby.

As she had many times when she felt a connection to Vincent in the building, she played the song "Vincent." Over and over.

Her fingers flew across the keyboard for hours until her alarm interrupted her. She had forgotten to stop for lunch, but now it was time to visit with Marie-Louise.

She jumped in the shower for a quick one. She'd planned to

do it when she returned from her walk with Atticus, but once she sat at her computer everything else had been forgotten.

Elation was all she felt now as she stood in the shower. It was so good to experience the joy of writing again.

The door to Marie-Louise's little house was ajar, but Nora used the knocker anyway before she entered. Yvette was dusting a mirror in the foyer and paused to greet her with bright smile. A delicious aroma wafted from the kitchen.

"Bonjour, Yvette! You have been working your magic in the kitchen?"

"Bonjour, Nora. It is so good to see you. Yes, I made some apple beignets and coffeecake. They're almost ready. Fresh Normandy apples from the market."

"Mmmm, what a treat!"

"Marie-Louise is out on the terrace and eager to greet you. She has been counting the minutes to your visit since she arose."

Sunlight filled the enclosed terrace and warmed the stone walls, making it more like spring than mid-December. Marie-Louise's face lit up as Nora approached her.

"Bonjour, ma belle amie. I am very happy to see you again."

"And I you, Madame."

They exchanged bises and Marie-Louise rewarded Atticus.

"Tell me everything you've done since I last saw you," Marie-Louise asked as Atticus made himself comfortable by Nora's feet with his special biscuit.

Nora gave her a rundown of her busy few days.

The old woman was intrigued by the tango story. "This makes me so happy. To dance tango is truly French. How wonderful that you enjoy it. I did too."

Marie-Louise was thrilled to hear of the trip to Strasbourg. "Everyone should visit there at this time of year. The magic there is palpable. And how lovely to have a special day there with your daughter. She must be delighted to have you in Paris for a while."

Nora's face lit up. "We are both enjoying being neighbors. It's a special experience."

Quite a bit of time was spent talking about the charming architecture of Strasbourg and the beauty of the Alsace region. Marie-Louise's face glowed as she spoke of her favorite dishes there. "Choucroute garnie is their famous sauerkraut, and I loved it served with knackwurst and smoked pork belly. Oh... And I cannot forget flammekeuche! A tarte flambée with crème fraîche, onions, and lardons. Simple foods but so delicious!"

Yvette laughed as she came out to the terrace with the baked treats and plates on a tray. "Mmmm, I think my timing is just right!"

After Yvette served the warm apple coffeecake and delicate beignets, Nora asked Marie-Louise if she would like to go for a drive after dinner to see some of the Christmas lights. "Chloe and Olivier would like to take us."

Marie-Louise beamed at the suggestion. "Oui! Bien sûr! That would be lovely."

"We will collect you around seven. Olivier doesn't think the traffic will be bad then. His plan is to take us all the way down the Champs Elysees and go around some of the smaller streets in le Marais. We will bring hot chocolate too."

Marie-Louise's face lit up with anticipation at the mention of chocolat chaud.

Then the elderly woman became serious. The look in her eyes pierced Nora's heart. She realized the woman wanted to tell her story, and the emotions she was about to experience would be like no others she'd ever felt.

"Nora, I have been thinking a lot about Giselle's desire for me to tell you about my childhood during the Occupation. I have searched my soul. This will not be easy, but it must be told, and perhaps this is the reason I have lived so long. Who knows how much longer I have."

She paused and looked at her hands folded in her lap.

As if he sensed comfort was needed, Atticus left his cozy spot and nuzzled her hands as he sat beside Marie-Louise. She smiled and rubbed his nose. "Such a sweet boy. He seems to understand."

"It's amazing how sensitive he is," Nora agreed. "There have been moments when he's come and sat next to me right as I felt the need for comfort or a hug. I'm finding him quite a remarkable companion."

Nora looked away to collect her emotions. She didn't want to lose control before they even got started.

"As you know, it will not be a happy story, but I believe Giselle is correct. It needs to be told. And I would like to tell you so you can then write it for me."

Nora cleared her throat. "It would be my honor to hear your story and write it in some form. I appreciate how difficult it must be for you to recollect those painful years. I admire you for your desire to do so."

Marie-Louise looked so seriously at Nora that she had to avert her eyes once more. The depth of their undertaking was now becoming real to her.

She brought herself back into her professional role. "I would like your permission to record our conversations, so I don't miss anything important. I'll also take notes, but the recording would be a major help, if you don't mind."

Marie-Louise shook her head. "Not at all. It's a good idea. I don't know how much I will be able to talk about those days. We will simply have to cross our fingers and hope for the best."

"There is no pressure. We'll go slowly and stop whenever you wish."

A smile softened Marie-Louise's face. "Eh bien, let us begin on your next visit. Shall we say tomorrow afternoon?"

"Perfect! But we will see you this evening for our tour of the Christmas lights."

Olivier had thought of everything. At the appointed time, a shiny Mercedes pulled up in front of their apartment. The driver emerged and opened the back doors for them.

"It's the best way to tour the city," he said.

Chloe added, "This way we can all enjoy the lights and not worry about other drivers."

They drove to Marie-Louise's to collect her. She was happy to sit in the front with the charming chauffeur. The back seat was spacious for the other three. Chloe passed a mug of hot chocolate to everyone, driver included.

All the little boutiques and cafés in Montmartre had been sweetly decorated with boughs, snowflakes, lanterns, and fairy lights. Carolers and musicians strolled along the street. The effect was quaint, artistic, and romantic. Pedestrian traffic was busy around the wooden chalets in the small, festive marché de Noël in Place des Absesses.

Marie-Louise was delighted when they had to go slowly every now and then.

Softly she told them, "The whole city shimmers, and I cannot deny it is beautiful. But what touches me most is not the brilliance itself—it is the way it awakens the child in me, the memory of cold fingers wrapped in wool mittens, of roasted chestnuts on the corner, of my father lifting me to see the lights above the crowd. Paris has changed but its heart still knows how to sparkle at Noël."

Soon they were cruising Boulevard Haussmann and admiring the elaborate windows of the big department stores. More than once they were able to pull over and park to get a better look for a few minutes before a security guard tapped on the window for them to keep moving. The mood was light and festive.

They continued to Place Vendome and on to the ritzy luxury shops and designer boutiques on Avenue Montaigne, where the festive decorations had everyone gasping with delight. It seemed no expense had been spared to turn their surroundings into a stunning spectacle.

Finally, they drove up the Champs Elysees, sighing at the display of a million lights adorning the trees from Place de la Concorde to the Arc de Triomphe.

Marie-Louise clapped her hands as they made their way home, clearly delighted with the evening's entertainment.

Chapter Fifteen

THE NEXT AFTERNOON, NORA TOOK SOME DEEP breaths as she and Atticus came to a stop in front of the little home tucked away in the cul-de-sac. This would be Nora's first conversation with Marie-Louise about her life as a child during the Occupation.

In all her years helping people write their memoirs, nothing could be compared to what she suspected she would hear from this fragile woman, who still possessed a razor-sharp mind.

She didn't want to doubt her own ability, but she needed to believe she was truly up to the task. *I know this will be tough. It makes sense that I feel some pressure about it, but I've got this.*

Yvette was outside sweeping the front step as they approached. She took a treat from her pocket for Atticus and greeted Nora with a somber expression. "Bonjour, Nora, our dear lady has much to share with you today. She has been speaking about it all morning. I think this is a very good thing she is doing. Thank you for helping her."

Nora thanked her for being so supportive. "I'm sure Marie-Louise is grateful for your encouragement. I am honored that she's entrusting me with her story."

They stepped into the salon, where Atticus went straight to

Marie-Louise and snuggled next to her feet with a quiet certainty. Nora felt a familiar warmth in her chest. He always seemed to know where his presence would bring the most comfort.

Marie-Louise's hands, thin and papery, rested clasped in her lap. "Some things I still cannot say aloud to anyone," she murmured, almost to herself. "But perhaps they can be written."

Nora reached for her notebook, her pen hovering just above the page. She turned on her recorder. "We'll tell it as truthfully as we can."

Marie-Louise gave a small nod—partly as an assent, partly as a farewell to the silence she had kept for decades. She then spoke in a hushed tone.

"Eh bien, Nora, let us begin."

The beginning unfolded as the minutes passed.

"I was born on 11 July, 1933. My family lived in the Pletzl quartier of the Marais, the traditional Jewish neighborhood since the Middle Ages. Pletzl means little square in Yiddish. I remember it as a magical, vibrant place to live, even though my family was not Jewish. My father was a printer and took over the printshop from his father and grandfather. It had been there through many generations."

She paused to take a sip of tea that Yvette had discreetly brought in on a teacart for them.

"Many of my friends were Jewish. Nobody cared what religion someone was. Sometimes I went to synagogue with my friends. Sometimes they went to church with me. It was all fun. I knew all the Hebrew blessings for Shabbat and I remember I thought for years that the blessing for the bread ended with Minnie Horowitz."

She looked at Nora, her voice tinged with amusement, as she explained the phonetic misunderstanding of a child. "One has to laugh."

Nora listened with fascination as she made her notes, glad that she was also recording. There was much she would have missed as Marie-Louise's voice filled with vivid emotion recalling her daily life. She shared rich descriptions of the shops, bakeries, traditions, and the general culture that had endured to various degrees in spite of the war.

"I and most of my friends went to the public school, Hospitaliers St. Gervais. Monsieur Joseph Migneret was the principal. I can still see him so clearly and sometimes I think I hear his voice. He was loved by everyone and all of us kids loved going to school."

Her eyes darkened and her voice often broke as she described how life changed once France surrendered to Germany.

"The Nazis ordered Jewish students to be expelled from our school, but Monsieur Migneret refused to do it. We did not know this until after the liberation, but he hid some Jewish families and arranged for forged documents so others could escape. After the shocking roundup of most Jews, the Val d'Hiv in 1942, there were very few students left at our school. I was one."

Nora asked if her principal had been arrested. "Non, amazingly enough he was allowed to keep the school operating even with a bare minimum of pupils. I don't know to this day how he was not caught for his clandestine activities. He was incredibly brave, and he helped us to be brave. He is honored forever now as Righteous Among the Nations."

Marie-Louise spoke much longer than Nora expected. Giselle had definitely been correct in her assumption about her aunt having an important story to share. Nora would text her an update.

Nora made a note to visit the Memorial de la Shoah in the Marais, the national museum honoring the memory of the Jewish victims of the Holocaust as well as those who risked their lives to save others.

Marie-Louise continued. "I did not understand why Jewish people were treated so inhumanely. We were all kids together, families, friends. My parents became involved with the Resistance and some of us kids did too. We had to keep secrets."

She stopped and closed her eyes, as if allowing herself to be carried back to those terrible times.

"Some of us children became couriers, runners, agents de liaison. Delivering messages, forged papers, although we did not know what we were taking with us. We could sneak around, and we learned how not to get caught.

"The Germans tried to be friends with kids. But they took away my Jewish friends and their families. We didn't know why or where they were going. We hated the Germans."

Nora could see that Marie-Louise was becoming upset and emotional.

"Perhaps we should stop for today. You have shared so much information and feelings. Why don't we continue another day?"

Marie-Louise took Nora's hand. "Please, could we meet every day? You have opened something inside me, and I want to get it all out."

"Whatever you wish. You have helped me realize I want to do this as much as you do, and I feel honored as I listen to you."

After dinner, Nora went back into the studio going over her notes and transcribing recordings. The more she wrote, the more she was aware it was going to be a long process. To honor the story Marie-Louise was sharing with her meant additional hours doing research and looking at photos online and in museums.

The project was turning out to be much more detailed than either woman imagined. Both of them expressed satisfaction that the story was coming alive. Marie-Louise's memory seemed to become clearer the more her story unfolded.

Chapter Sixteen

NORA'S WEEK TOOK ON A DAILY ROUTINE OF EARLY morning sessions with Marie-Louise, followed by transcribing notes into a rough draft. Once Marie-Louise got on a roll with her reminiscences, she didn't want to stop. Both women shed tears as they were immersed in the past horrors of the Occupation.

Nora felt compelled to put her thoughts into her rough draft after every conversation. She was caught up in the brutal emotions of the memories Marie-Louise shared. The words insisted on being seen, and Nora didn't want to risk losing any of it by delaying her writing.

Some afternoons, Nora explored the parts of the Marais Marie-Louise spoke of. She wanted to absorb the atmosphere.

One afternoon, she left Atticus at home and approached the Pletzl neighborhood with trepidation. Vivid memories were stirred as her imagination took her back to the days of the war as Marie-Louise described them.

She read from her research that in the late 1800s and early 1900s, Eastern European Ashkenazi Jews had fled persecution and settled in the Pletzl part of Paris, where there had been a Jewish presence since the 1300s.

Nora wandered the narrow streets. She discovered a thriving

community of synagogues, kosher shops, bakeries, and schools. Conversation and children's laughter could be heard everywhere.

She tried to picture it without the modern shops that had slowly crept in among the others after the war. Still, the streets offered a rich tapestry of Jewish life. After stopping for a bagel and coffee, she wandered over to the nearby Musée d'Art et d'Histoire du Judaïsme.

There she found a solid source of information on how the Jewish quarter was a focal point of German persecution and, despite the dangers, clandestine resistance.

Groups of residents, including children, as Marie-Louise had told Nora, were involved in intelligence gathering, sabotage, and hiding individuals and families. They were known among themselves as "les poches de résistances"—pockets of resistance. Marie-Louise's mother had been very involved, particularly in creating and distributing printed materials. Her father had joined the Maquis in the countryside and seemingly disappeared.

Her mother's friends called Marie-Louise "La Petite," not just for her size but also for how easily she melted into crowds and ducked soldiers' gazes. She was a runner, carrying tiny slips of paper in the lining of her blouse, the heel of her shoe, or inside a carved-out wooden dreidel. Since she wasn't Jewish, she had no yellow star on her clothing and attracted less attention.

On Mondays she bought bread from Madame Stein's boulangerie. The old woman wrapped the bread with rough brown paper and hid a message inside the crust. Eleven-year-old Marie-Louise hurried past shuttered shops and synagogues and across the quartier to M. Abromavich's tailor shop.

She never read the notes. That was the rule, she told Nora. But she knew they saved lives.

She told Nora she would relate her more harrowing experiences the next time.

In the meantime, Nora became deeply involved in her transcriptions. She wanted to keep everything in draft form until she went back to Canada, where she would flesh out the story, keeping it true to Marie-Louise's memories.

The romance Nora had been working on about a painter and a waitress had been set aside for now. She wanted the story Marie-Louise was sharing to be a priority.

At dinner in Chloe and Olivier's apartment on Friday, Nora said, "It's so good to have some downtime with the two of you. My goodness, we've all been going flat out. How is your work coming along?"

Chloe blew out a long breath and Olivier put his arm around her shoulder, giving her a comforting squeeze, as she said, "It's been crazy with a capital C, for sure! But we're making great progress, and I'm positive we will have all our pieces ready to ship by the first week in January."

Olivier nodded. "Yes, I'm amazed we are on schedule. We will still have quite a few late nights to go, but that's not a problem. We have until the end of the month to finish up. So, we'll be in good shape to travel to my family's farm in Provence for the fête de Noël. It's going to be lovely to have you there with us."

Chloe said, "You'll adore the farm and the traditions of celebrating the holiday there. I'm so excited to have you experience all of it. Olivier's grandparents, aunts, and uncles are the most wonderful people."

Nora turned to Olivier. "I remember your grandparents were unable to attend your wedding because your grandmother had a hip replacement at that time. I am so looking forward to meeting them and spending the holiday at the farm. Your father was not around much after the ceremony, as I recall. I only have a dim memory of him."

"Well, perhaps my dad is not included in 'the most wonderful people category'," Olivier said, scrunching his face in disgust. "But maybe he will be better this year. We can always hope."

Chloe patted his hand. "Mon chou, he's not so bad. He just has his moments." Then she changed the subject and talked about their travel plans.

It was clear Chloe didn't want to discuss Olivier's father any more at that moment. Nora let her natural curiosity go, and they went over some plans for the weekend.

Olivier offered to spend time with Atticus so Nora and Chloe could visit the most popular Christmas market in Paris, La Magie de Noël in the Tuileries Garden. Chloe had described it as a huge carnival with stalls, rides, and yummy festive treats. "It's very different from what we saw in Strasbourg. We'll ride the Ferris wheel for sure!"

An alarm on Nora's phone buzzed, and she realized dinner had gone on much longer than she'd expected.

"Yikes! I've got to get ready. Luc will be coming to pick me up in an hour."

"Luc? Again?" Chloe asked with a twinkle in her eye.

Nora got up from the table and began to clear her dishes. "Yes! I told you last week he made a date for us to dance tango again tonight. We're just friends. I mean ... I'm almost old enough to be his mother."

"Well, hardly. But whatever you say, Maman. I'm glad you are having such a good time dancing tango with him. I think it's very cool. Just leave the dishes, we will clean up."

Luc texted Nora there was absolutely no place to park.

> Luc: Would you mind coming to the front of your building? I will drive around the block and then pull up to collect you. I'm sorry.
>
> Nora: That's absolutely no problem. I will come right down.

She had laid her clothes out during the afternoon, and her

naturally wavy hair was always ready after a quick comb-through with her fingers and a dash of product.

Now, she took a quick look in the mirror. The mid-calf, soft aubergine-colored silk-blend dress had a low-cut back, and the filmy chiffon overskirt would move in just the right ways for the tango's sensuous spins and turns. Her outfit was graceful without being flashy.

She had spotted it in the window of a vintage clothing store down the street a few days earlier and knew it was meant for her. It had been a long time since she'd had put so much thought into what she wore for a night out with a man, and she felt pleased with the result.

She picked up her black cashmere shawl and draped it around her shoulders with an easy grace. It would be warm enough, she figured, since she'd be in Luc's car and the club most of the time, and not outside more than a minute or two.

Since she wore her strappy black stilettos again, she chose the elevator—taking the stairs the previous week had been nothing short of life-threatening. She felt a twinge of nerves thinking about another evening with Luc. But he was such a gentleman and had made their previous Friday such relaxed fun ... even with her tango anxiety. She shook the nerves off.

Exiting the elevator, she almost bumped into a man carrying a large box who was waiting to go up. He excused himself in French. Nora hoped she wasn't staring too hard because she thought he might be the most intriguing man she had ever seen. Salt and pepper, short-cropped hair streaked with silver framed his striking, chiseled features and a light stubble only added to his quiet magnetism. His deep blue eyes, seemed to be looking straight into her soul. And he appeared close to her age. An older, more lived-in version of Gabriel from Emily in Paris was her immediate reaction.

She stuttered an apology, "Ex-excuse me... Er... Excusez moi." She blinked to stop staring.

Then she saw Luc standing right inside the door. He strode

over to her. "I found a spot," he said as he gave her an affectionate bise.

She noticed the man who had stepped into the elevator was still looking at her. His eyes darted to Luc as he slid the glass door closed.

Luc took her arm and guided her to the car. "What a crazy night! Everyone is out on the town. I'm very happy to see you. How was your week?"

While she updated Luc on her activities since she last saw him, she could not stop thinking about the stranger at the elevator and wondered if he lived in the building. One thing for certain: she hadn't seen him before. He was not a man to be forgotten easily.

Luc told her he and Giselle had a couple of video chats during the week. The weather had cleared up in Mexico and she was enjoying her visit. She had invited him to join her, and he was thinking of going for the week of Christmas.

"What are your plans for the holidays?" he asked.

"I will be going to Olivier's family home, an ancient farmhouse in Provence. It sounds like a very special place, and his extended family will be there so I'm excited. I haven't visited that region before."

Luc told her of some of his visits to that beautiful countryside, and said he particularly enjoyed the Luberon, where she was headed. He said he loved its vast vineyards, winding roads, and enchanting villages. "You will love it too," he assured her.

At the dance club, they were greeted like old friends and invited to join a lively table of people of all ages. Nora stumbled with her French and others stumbled with English, but everyone spoke the same language on the dance floor.

The evening slipped by in a blur of music and movement, the hours melting into one another as they danced nearly every number. Luc, ever attentive, offered Nora warm praise, marveling at how effortlessly she seemed to grasp each new step they tried. His encouragement was steady and sincere, and with each graceful turn and playful pivot, Nora's confidence grew. The tango, once intimidating in its intensity, now began to feel like a language she was learning to speak—with rhythm, with flair, and with a quiet thrill that lingered long after the music paused.

It was pouring rain when they left the club at one in the morning. They hurried along, Luc with his arm around Nora to help keep her dry, as the doorman escorted them to the car with an umbrella.

When they drove off, Nora was shocked by how much energy she felt. "How can I not feel exhausted? My feet are saying they're tired, but the rest of me is so alive!"

"Ha!" Luc exclaimed. "It's the music! Studies show it releases endorphins. One would think the dancing would be exhausting, but it becomes energizing."

He went on to describe some scientific articles he had read about how music activated the brain regions involved in pleasure and reward. "The reward system is rich in dopamine and other neurotransmitters that relieve stress and pain and lead to a sense of well-being."

He laughed as he parked the car. "I'm sorry if I sound like a psychiatrist now. The subject fascinates me."

Nora said, "Not at all. I've read the same information about how music helps us, but I've never put it into practice so much as I have at the dance club. I think I'm a believer!"

Luc picked up her hand and kissed the back of it lightly. "Nora, I will report this to Giselle, and she will be delighted. The world is so messed up right now, we need to spend time in these happy pursuits. I'm so glad you are enjoying our dance nights. Shall we plan for next Friday?"

Luc's casual yet, to her, romantic gesture when he kissed her hand surprised Nora. For a moment, she wondered if something else might come next. But he just smiled and got out of the car. He ran to the passenger door and opened it for her, holding an umbrella. He put his arm around her waist to keep her close and dry as they walked into the building.

"Next Friday would be lovely. Thank you so much, and—"

Before she could say anything further, the elevator door opened and a rather inebriated couple stumbled out, wishing them a "bonne nuit." Nora and Luc laughed on the way up at that surprise and about the fun of the rest of the evening. At her apartment door, Luc kissed her cheeks and touched her face gently. "Bonne nuit, ma belle. Á la prochaine!"

Nora felt a flicker of something unexpected stir within her—a quiet response to the tenderness of his gaze and the warmth in his touch. Her breath caught slightly and when she finally spoke, her voice was soft as she said, "Mille mercis, Luc. Á la prochaine!" The words lingered between them, like a promise.

She closed the door and floated in, just as she had the week before. As she flopped on the sofa, she wondered if all French men were like him. She told herself she would never be involved with such a young man... *Or would I?* He certainly knew how to awaken feelings she had missed for a very long time.

She wasn't complaining.

Atticus gave her a joyful welcome home, and Nora was happy she had arranged for Chloe and Oli to take him out for his walk earlier.

Chapter Seventeen

AT DINNER THE PREVIOUS EVENING, NORA HAD WARNED Chloe not to come early for coffee, as she expected to sleep in after her tango date with Luc.

She found Giselle's bed extremely comfortable with good support. It was also very cozy, and she snuggled under the fluffy duvet, which felt like a warm cloud draped over her.

Atticus nudged her awake close to nine o'clock. With a loud yawn and luxurious stretch, she got up to give him his breakfast. Then she threw on her jeans, a light sweater, and her down jacket and took him out for a quick potty break.

"You've been a patient boy," she told him, scratching his back.

At ten o'clock, Chloe texted.

> Chloe: Crêpes with us at le Moulin in half an hour. How does that sound?

In exactly half an hour, they were seated. The waiter brought Atticus a treat and bowl of water and chatted with the dog for a moment. Then he took their order.

"So! Another exciting evening with the oh-so-handsome Monsieur Luc!" Chloe teased. She gave her mother a sly look, implying Nora might be keeping secrets.

Nora knew she was blushing. Laughing, she gave Chloe a light kick under the table. "You and Olivier should come with us next week. I can't describe how much fun it is. Everyone is so welcoming and just loves to dance. It's like a drug! And yes, Luc is undeniably so goddam good-looking, but he's good-looking inside too and just the best company. Giselle has excellent taste in companions."

"Or whatever you call him," Chloe said, laughing and not trying to be disparaging at all.

"Chloe, let's go next time," Olivier said. "I know people who frequent that club and they describe it the same way as your mom. We need to have some fun like we did at Au Lapin Agile when your mother first arrived."

"You're right, mon chou. Especially now," Chloe said as her mouth turned down in a frown.

"What's wrong?" Nora asked, feeling concerned as she reached for Chloe's hand.

"Pierre. Monsieur Morceau. Mon beau-père. My father-in-law."

"My father is in town" Olivier said, giving a classic Gallic shrug.

"Oh! Were you expecting him now? What's the problem?"

Olivier shook his head, his lips firmly pressed together.

The waiter arrived with their crêpes. Savory, with ham, cheese, and eggs for Olivier, sweet for Chloe and Nora, with Nutella and banana and a dab of Chantilly on the side.

"Are we going to order these together for the rest of our lives?" Nora asked as she cut into hers and dipped the bite into the whipped cream.

"Oui! Bien sûr!" Chloe said, and then they both sang, "Tradition!" like the song in *Fiddler on the Roof*, which made them laugh. Olivier grinned and gave them an amused look as he shook his head. Atticus stood up, surveying the room with his ears perked, unsure of the commotion around him.

Nora laughed and gave his back a rub before he lay down again under the table.

"Okay, back to Monsieur Moreau. If you recall, I only met him briefly at your wedding. He had long hair and was always talking with his friends. In fact, I felt he ignored me, and I truly wondered if he even spoke much English. Remember?" Nora said as she dug into her crêpe.

"Oh yes," Chloe said, letting out a long sigh. "Oh, how we remember. But his divorce was still raw and we knew he would not be the life of the party. I think I had warned you."

"And!" Nora added, "He wore sunglasses practically all the time! That I remember. It was a sunny day, but that was ridiculous."

Olivier gave Nora an apologetic look. "I've always felt badly about his behavior at our marriage. But our dear friends made up for his lack of hospitality. I was also sorry that my grandparents were indisposed with Mami's hip replacement surgery."

Nora said, "Your friends were so delightful. It was a lovely casual and intimate wedding lunch ... so refreshing compared to most over-the-top North American wedding extravaganzas."

Chloe piped up. "Getting back to my beau-pére, here are the quick details as I know them. I guess we were so wrapped up in ourselves, we never did tell you the whole story. This happened before I came on the scene. Ever since his divorce five years ago, he's been angry and bitter. Seriously. He's so mad at his ex-wife and just can't get over it. She was Oli's stepmom.

"As you know, Oli's mother died in a car accident when he was just ten." Her voice trailed off, and she paused, her expression clouded with sorrow. She reached out and gently took Olivier's hand, holding it in a silent gesture of shared grief.

Nora stopped eating and put down her fork. She felt a knot in her stomach as she saw the strained look on Olivier's drawn face.

Nora's expression grew solemn. She understood and she knew that Chloe did too. They both carried the quiet pain of such a loss. "Yes," she said softly. "It's so sad. I'm sorry, Olivier."

Olivier closed his eyes and nodded. "Merci. It was a very long time ago. Her name was Annalise, and I have happy, loving memories of her. She encouraged us to speak English and French. Those years of our family are the most important part of who I am. And it's the same for my father." He nodded for Chloe to continue.

"Angelique is quite nice, just ... um ... flighty might be a good word. She lives in Costa Rica now with her new, and I might add younger, husband. So, we don't see her at all."

Olivier's face was overtaken by an expression of chagrin. "The divorce was messy and, truthfully, they had never been happy. My strongest memories of them together are of their loud shouting matches. They never should have married."

"How sad for your father ... and you," Nora sympathized.

"Pierre is actually very nice when you're alone with him. He has always been very sweet ... and funny ... with me. Well, most of the time. He's just not great in social situations. It's as if he's unhappy about being alone or something. We can't figure it out," Chloe said, shrugging her shoulders.

Olivier agreed. "Yes, deep down he is a nice man, good-hearted, but can't let go of being furious with Angelique."

"An unfortunate name, under the circumstances," Nora commented.

Oli and Chloe snorted.

"You will get to see him soon. He went out early this morning to deliver something to a friend," Olivier said. "He texted to say he's coming to take a look at our artwork this afternoon. So, you can come to the studio with us if you like."

In spite of their comments about Pierre's demeanor, Nora looked forward to meeting him again. It would feel like the first time. He owned a small art gallery in Nice, and she always thought he sounded interesting the few times the kids had mentioned him.

"Perhaps he'll be in a better mood when we're all together at the family farm for the holidays. Crabby and Provence are two words that just don't go together," Nora said.

Chloe shrugged. "Let's hope. Right now, he wants to make certain his van is the right size to drive the art down to Nice in January. We're amazed he came here in advance, because he always says he hates Paris."

"Yes, but it seems he is concerned whether everything will fit," said Olivier. "It makes sense for him to see what he will have to load in. We hadn't really given it much thought."

Nora said, "Well, I would love to go to the studio with you this afternoon. I'm meeting Marie-Louise soon. Yvette is going to text me when they've finished lunch. I think I'll be there for about two hours. Does that timing work?"

"Pretty sure it will be fine. We'll confirm with you later, okay?" said Chloe.

Nora's session with Marie-Louise ended abruptly after a particularly emotional outpouring which lasted for more than an hour. Nora called out to Yvette, and they gently helped her to bed.

"Don't worry, chérie. I'm all right," Marie-Louise told Nora. "Just ... tired in my heart. I'm grateful I could finally speak about that story—it mattered more than I realized."

Nora felt equally drained as she and Atticus made their way back to the apartment. The day had turned chillier, and the sky a pale, indifferent gray. A heaviness pressed against her chest—the weight of all those young lives, fractured and bruised during the Occupation. It was almost too much to carry. The sadness didn't just settle over her, it seeped in, quiet and relentless, like the cold creeping through her coat.

She stopped in at the little flower shop, Les Fleurs de mon Coeur, knowing it would lift her spirits, if anything could. Nora dropped by every few days to choose fresh blooms. Not because she needed them, but because the charm of the shop and the ever-changing selections were impossible to resist. Fresh flowers had been a constant in her life ever since Jeremy had given her a china vase the day they married. She continued to fill it weekly.

Garlands of cedar and fir framed the outside of the door, and were threaded with dried orange slices, cinnamon sticks, and tiny brass bells that chimed softly whenever the door swung open.

Inside, the air was a comforting mix of warmth and wood smoke from an old iron stove in the corner and the heady fragrances from the seasonal blooms that filled every corner of the tiny space. Buckets of amaryllis, freesia, holly, and cream-colored winter roses stood in quiet rows under soft lighting.

Wrapped in a woolen shawl, Claire, the young owner, greeted Nora like an old friend after Nora said bonjour. "Bienvenue! Baf! Il fait froid aujourd'hui!" They always conversed in French, and Claire answered all of Nora's language questions about flowers.

Nora shivered and agreed it was definitely cold. They chatted about the weather for a minute and Nora complimented her on the flower selection. Claire explained she had been to the flower market at the crack of dawn and had gotten first selection of her favorites. She praised Nora on her choice of three stunning white amaryllis stems.

"I had no idea amaryllis stems could be found as cut flowers. I only knew them as potted plants that fill our shops at home at Christmas. My mother would purchase one very year and we would all wait excitedly for it to bloom ... hopefully by Christmas Day. I love them individually like this!"

After Nora paid for her choices, Claire carefully wrapped them in waxed paper and tied the parcel with a green velvet bow. She tucked in a small bouquet of pink freesia. "This will give you the fragrance the amaryllis will not," she said with a smile, refusing Nora's insistence on paying for it.

She reminded Nora there would be vin chaud simmering on the stove starting the next day, and Nora assured her she wouldn't miss it.

Atticus calmly accepted his treat from Claire, and Nora resumed their walk home with a lighter spring in her step.

She texted Chloe to say she would be ready anytime to go to the studio with them.

Chapter Eighteen

JUST AFTER FOUR P.M., OLIVIER DROVE THE SHORT distance to Rue des Martyrs with Chloe and Nora. The street was noticeably less congested with pedestrians than their street, Rue Lepic.

"I didn't realize your studio was so close," Nora said. "What is this area called?"

"This is South Pigalle," Olivier said. "Or, as the cool folks call it now, SoPi. You cannot imagine how many artists' studios there are behind the facades of these ancient buildings, although some have been taken over by galleries. In the time of van Gogh, Degas and friends, it was a creative hotspot known as La Nouvelles Athènes. I've got a few good books about those days, if you want to borrow them."

"Love to!" Nora replied.

Chloe told her about some of the excellent patisseries and fromageries as well as specialty shops. "Locals shop here, and you can see it is far less touristy. We love working in this environment."

"That's dad's van," Olivier said, pointing to a white van with a few dents in the back.

"Do you mean the one with the boot on it?" Chloe asked.

Olivier swore, seeing what she pointed out. "Merde! Oui! Now he will be really pissed!"

"What are you talking about?" Nora asked.

"Do you see the yellow clamp on the front wheel?" Chloe asked.

Nora nodded.

"Well, it's called a sabot de Denver here, don't ask me why. It means a Denver boot. Police put it on illegally parked vehicles. Mon Dieu." She ended with a groan.

Just then a police vehicle arrived. The officer stepped out with a good-looking man Nora recognized. She did a double-take and gasped with surprise.

Chloe moved Nora and Atticus toward the door of the building while Olivier spoke with his father, who was scowling.

Olivier came back and explained his dad had just stopped in the no-parking zone for a few minutes. "In fact, he left his flashers on. Then he went inside to ... um, uh ... use the bathroom. He came back out and found the clamp. He said he was furious. He looked up the closest police station on his phone and saw it was a block away, so he walked there to get someone to remove the clamp."

"TMI," Chloe muttered.

"You two should go inside and not watch. It's not going to help his bruised ego, and it's too cold to stand around anyway," Olivier said.

As they left to go into the studio, Nora took a backward look to confirm what had shocked her. Pierre was the man she'd nearly bumped into on Friday evening as she exited the elevator on her way to meet Luc.

She told Chloe what had happened.

"Hmm, I wonder if he remembers."

"He absolutely did not look like this at your wedding," she added in a lower voice. "The Girls would say he's a hottie."

Chloe rolled her eyes.

Nora continued, amazement on her face. "He looked

completely different at your wedding ... long hair and a beard. And what's funny is that when we nearly collided at the elevator I thought he looked like an older version of the boyfriend from Emily in Paris ... Gabriel."

Chloe rolled her eyes again. "I didn't know you watched that."

"All the Girls did!" Nora replied.

Chloe chuckled and said, "Right. Well, he was still struggling with his divorce and not a happy camper when we got married."

She put an enormous key in the keyhole on a tarnished brass escutcheon. The tall wooden door with faded green paint looked like it had many stories of its own. She opened it and they walked into a spacious courtyard.

"Wow, what a secret space," Nora said, gazing at the surrounding ivy-covered stone walls. A bicycle rack was full and a young couple were standing next to it smoking.

"One of the few places smoking is allowed, from what I read these days," Nora said.

Chloe nodded. "France has rigid non-smoking laws with more coming. The country is serious about the health issues. Pretty good, huh?"

They walked through the quiet space to a paneled door with a sign that said, "Atelier Moreau ~ entrez doucement."

A soft light poured in from north-facing windows and a skylight above. Canvases were on easels or leaning against the walls—some unfinished and others covered in layers of rich color. There were strong smells of paint, turpentine, and coffee.

Nora smiled with pride at Chloe, who said, "This is where the magic happens."

Nora gave her a quick shoulder squeeze. "I am so happy that you love what you are doing. It's what parents hope for."

When the two men came into the studio, Olivier explained the police had removed the clamp and didn't give Pierre a parking ticket.

"He got lucky with that!" Chloe said.

"Mon père, you remember Chloe's mother, Nora, from our wedding. She arrived a week ago from Canada, as you know."

Nora stepped forward, extending her arm for a handshake. "It's lovely to see you again."

Pierre glanced at her, then his eyes widened with a flicker of recognition as he shook her hand.

"Enchanté, Norma," he said. His expression revealed nothing and she wasn't sure what to make of it. She wondered if he was thinking of the wedding or their near collision at the apartment.

"Nora," she corrected him, as did Chloe and Olivier all at once. Pierre bowed his head stiffly and looked embarrassed.

Awkward, Nora thought. *He is hard to read—completely inscrutable.*

Pierre shifted his gaze from one to another as he spoke with Chloe and Olivier in very fast French. They turned to walk to the back of the studio. Nora stood rooted to the spot, certain Pierre was saying something less than complimentary about her.

Chloe returned to her mother's side and grabbed her by the arm, sensing Nora's concern. "Come on, Mom. Don't be so judgmental. I know you think he was talking about you, but he wasn't. He said he's in a hurry, as he has other things to do. We're going to take a look at the pieces to be transported. You can help."

After an hour of looking at the artwork and measuring a few larger pieces, the task was completed. Pierre only grumbled a little bit and even laughed some, although he avoided looking at Nora.

Olivier drove back to the apartment in the van with his father, while Chloe drove Nora in their car.

When Chloe and Nora arrived at the apartment building, Nora said she had to take Atticus for a walk.

"Will you join us for dinner? I know things didn't get off to a very good start. I'm sorry Pierre was kind of rude. Sheesh, what else could have gone wrong?"

"Of course, I'll come for dinner. He was probably just upset about the clamp situation. I'm sure everything will be fine."

"Excellent. I made a daube de boeuf this morning. Beef stew, your recipe, from when you liked to cook..." She gave Nora a little punch in the arm.

"Haha, very funny. Those days are gone, all right. I would much rather write than cook."

"Well, Olivier loves your stew as much as Dad did, and it's been simmering on the stove. Should be just right. We'll have drinks at seven, dinner at eight."

"Sounds like the perfect meal for a chilly day like this, sweetheart. That should win over Mr. Grumpypants. Atticus and I will see you then. I'll pick up a fresh afternoon baguette."

Nora and Atticus took a brisk walk and when they arrived home, she breathed in the perfumed fragrance from the freesia. She thanked Claire silently for her thoughtfulness, which was a perfect touch, and although unbeknownst to the shop woman, had come on a day that had caused Nora such heartache earlier with Marie-Louise.

Thinking about it, she texted Yvette to see if Marie-Louise was feeling better now and was relieved when the reply was affirmative.

Atticus settled in for a nap while Nora transcribed the day's notes.

After a few short minutes she stopped, and tears streamed down her cheeks. This day's transcription proved to be even more emotionally demanding than she had anticipated. She decided to leave it for the morning.

The last thing she wanted was to arrive for dinner with her eyes puffy and red. Pierre already seemed to think she was strange, and she didn't want to add to that impression. Wiping her face with the back of her hand, she reached for the tissue box, which was a recent addition to the table she used as a desk.

She hoped the dinner would provide good family time, although it might be too much to ask. Her first impressions of

Pierre had not indicated there was anything warm and fuzzy about him.

Now she needed to compose herself. A long soak in the tub would be just the answer.

Just before their scheduled cocktail hour, Chloe knocked on Nora's door. She tried not to laugh as she explained the reason for her visit.

"I had to come and tell you before you came to our place. Pierre does recall almost bumping into you at the elevator on Friday evening." She snorted. "He was quite indignant that you were dressed to the nines to go out with a… What did he say… 'Un homme beaucoup plus jeune,' a much younger man. Emphasis on the 'much.'"

"Oh my God," Nora said, shocked. "Why would he care?"

Chloe shook her head. "Who knows? But it did seem to affect him. Maybe it reminded him of Angelique leaving him for a much younger man. Dunno. Oli agreed it could be a factor, in a bizarre way."

Nora looked perplexed. "Well, I hope it won't make things uncomfortable this evening. I don't know what to say…"

"Just ignore it. I thought it was hilarious and wanted you to know in case he acts weirdly." She sighed loudly. "Adults!"

As an afterthought she added, "At least he thought you looked gorgeous. He said you were 'sur son trente et un,' which is a big compliment. Crazy, huh?"

"Well, that's something positive, I guess. Probably just a slip of the tongue on his part. I'll wait a few minutes before I come over," Nora said. She gave Chloe the baguette she had picked up on her walk.

Chloe told Nora there was a surprise addition to the dinner, which she thought would create a welcome diversion. A family friend of Olivier's had called on them, as she'd heard Pierre was in town.

"I've met her several times, and she's very nice. You'll like her. I insisted Oli invite her to join us."

When Nora arrived, the young woman, named Celeste, was already there. She looked to be in her early thirties, with highlights in her brown hair and a friendly, sporty appearance.

Her parents were great friends with Pierre, and she had known Olivier since childhood. She explained she taught school but was also an artist, and Nora liked her instantly. There was much laughter as the others reminisced about family experiences, and the mood remained light.

Celeste was interested in writing and spoke English well. With a writer in the group, the conversation turned to that topic and Celeste asked many questions in English so Nora could give her long answers. Nora was happy she had something to contribute to the evening without having to converse with Pierre, who avoided looking at her except to frown if she said too much in English.

Again, Nora thought Pierre spoke more in French on purpose, to annoy her. She knew his first wife had studied in England and raised Olivier to speak both languages. Nora was aware Pierre spoke English very well ... and with a delicious French accent.

She was reminded all evening of how a dog can be an instant socializer, as Atticus made the rounds with everyone and always brought smiles. She was happy to see Pierre was a dog-lover, so he couldn't be all bad.

Chapter Nineteen

Nora lingered in bed, watching the sunrise. The first light slipped in quietly. The night softened from inky black to lavender before a pale-gold hue spread eastward and the morning came alive. Smoke from the narrow chimneys in Montmartre rose straight up, signaling a cold day. Good conditions for writing.

It was going to be a difficult day of transcription, but it had to be done while the feelings were still raw.

Nora dressed quickly in her down jacket, wrapped a long, green scarf several times around her neck, and pulled on a woolen toque. Atticus waited patiently while she searched for her gloves and put them on.

"It's going to be a quick, chilly walk," she warned him. "You won't like it any more than I will." She opened her French app and went out, listening to words about the weather.

She felt badly that Atticus didn't have a warm coat to wear, but Giselle had told her he refused to move when she put one on him. Nora thought perhaps she could persuade him, but when she tried, he had the same stubborn reaction.

They were back in fifteen minutes, after a quick pause at the park for a doggie pit-stop and a visit to the boulangerie for the usual warm greetings and her pain aux raisins and baguette traditionale.

While Atticus ate his breakfast, Nora made a café au lait and took it to her computer.

She played the recording, beginning where she had left off. Atticus was soon snuggled at her feet, comforting in his quiet, strong way.

Marie-Louise gave a great deal of detailed description of how the streets in her neighborhood in 1941 had changed in just over a year. Many businesses and apartments were shuttered as their occupants had either mysteriously disappeared or been rounded up. Most of the missing people were Jewish and included many of Marie-Louise's friends.

Sometimes it was French police, who were all under the control of the Nazis, and other times Gestapo who arrived on doorsteps early in the morning, before sunrise. Sometimes they came quietly and other times not. They demanded identity papers and then said the family in question had to go with them to have the documents verified. Marie-Louise's family learned of the routine from one man who had hid with his brother's family and hadn't been discovered.

"As a ten-year-old, I could never understand why being Jewish made our friends so different or terrible from us that they had to be taken away to go to work in Germany. We were told that was what would happen. I worried all the time it would happen to us too. I missed my friends. Especially Rachel."

Marie-Louise's descriptions of the streets of her neighborhood were dark and somber. Cafés were full of Germans, for the most part. Few people wanted to share space with them. The heavy footfalls of the black-booted German soldiers who patrolled the streets day and night echoed in her head for years.

Most people who went out did so to line up for hours at the bakery or food markets with ration cards. Marie-Louise continued to attend school.

"I was happy but scared when Maman told me I had a delivery

to make. I was a year older and knew it was serious, dangerous even, but I was a brash kid, and I despised the Germans. They made everything awful. It made me feel good to fool them."

She described how she always mussed her hair and looked disheveled and dirty on purpose. Her school uniform had holes in the skirt and her cardboard-soled shoes were worn. The use of cardboard wasn't ideal, but it was how it was.

The people her mother met with said Marie-Louise was perfect for the job of agent de liaison, like a courier. She was too young to be questioned. Too small to be suspected. The rules for her were simple: Carry. Nothing else. Don't read. Don't question. Don't speak. Be brave.

Her routes were never the same, although the destinations often were. They took her to a small bookshop near the Latin Quarter, the back door of a café by the Seine, or a rundown bakery in Montmartre. Each place was a lifeline, a point of contact where the Resistance could safely exchange information. But the locations frequently had to change without warning.

She knew every delivery was extremely important and could be lifesaving. At times she was given posters, or leaflets printed in secret basements and backrooms. Carefully hidden in the pages of newspapers or school books, or in laundry baskets or the hollowed-out frames of bicycles, they would be distributed discreetly. Kids could appear to be going to school or ride past checkpoints without suspicion, particularly in the early years.

On the way home, her task complete, sometimes she took it as a challenge to change things up. Sometimes she dawdled, played hopscotch, looked in windows, went the wrong direction, had secret shortcuts.

For the most part, she learned to move fast, to stay alert. The streetlights cast long shadows, and every face seemed to carry the weight of suspicion. The Germans had begun raiding homes more often, rounding up anyone they suspected of Resistance activity.

Although so young, she could feel her neighborhood suffocating, the walls closing in around them all. Quiet was taking over. No one made eye contact. She tried to blend in, sometimes walking at a normal pace, sometimes not. Always with her heart pounding. She sensed danger around every corner.

Messages were often hidden in her school satchel or sewn into her clothing by her mother's skillful hands. Notes from the bakery might be inside buns or a loaf. Before her shoes fell apart, in the heel or insole. From time to time, all she was given was a coded scribble in her notebook.

She had described her first frightening interaction to Nora.

One night, snow had begun to fall. Not soft, fluffy flakes but sharp, icy pellets that hurt her face. She tightened her coat against the wind and pulled her scarf higher. Her fingers, red and cracked, gripped the strap of her satchel.

Her mother had carefully stitched the message into the hem of her coat.

She walked with her head down against the elements. Then she heard someone say, "Halt."

Two German soldiers. Young, with cold eyes and rifles across their backs. One was already stepping toward her, his palm raised. He demanded her identity papers. "Papière."

She reached into her coat pocket, hands shaking slightly. She'd memorized this routine: present forged papers, smile politely, don't run. Running was death.

The soldier looked her over—first her face, then her worn-out shoes, then her bag. He didn't give the papers back.

He pointed to her satchel, and she told him it was for bread she was to pick up at her aunt's shop.

She passed him the satchel slowly, eyes on the ground. Her heart thudded in her ears, loud enough she thought they might hear it.

Bread crusts in a wrapped handkerchief.

He dug deeper, felt around the seams.

She held her breath.

"Nothing," the soldier grunted to his comrade, shrugging.

But the first man wasn't done. He passed the bag back to her ... and pointed to her coat.

"Take it off."

Her blood turned to ice.

"What?"

"Off. Now." His hand went to the strap of his rifle.

She unbuttoned her coat slowly, each button taking an eternity. Her scarf came loose. Her thin frame shivered in the cold.

He looked her over, arms folded. Then he inspected her coat but didn't see anything. Not under the torn lining near the hem of the coat, where the message was hidden—carefully stitched inside.

He stared at her. For too long.

Then, behind them, a siren howled—the shrill wail of a truck turning onto the Quai. The soldiers turned. Just for a second.

They turned back and waved her on her way.

Nora thought back to when Marie-Louise had finished relating this tale. Her delicate hands had trembled as she reached for a tissue. She apologized for getting emotional.

Nora hadn't been able to say anything at that moment. She had sat there, feeling hollowed out. So many emotions for then. So many for now. She'd looked with heartache at fragile Marie-Louise, who was once that brave, frightened, eleven-year-old child.

Marie-Louise had finished the story by telling how she'd arrived at the old bookshop and went through the door, where the bell no longer worked.

She handed her coat to a silent man with ink-stained fingers.

He didn't speak, just nodded as he locked the door and freed the tiny slip of paper from its hiding place. He gave her a book to carry home for her mother.

Marie-Louise had said she was never more frightened than in those moments. But somehow by the time she'd returned home from the bookshop, she realized she was even more determined to continue to carry out her tasks. She didn't tell her mother what happened, as she knew if she did, that would be the end of it.

Nora wrote until midafternoon, completely lost in the world Marie-Louise had painted for her with words and emotions. It caused Nora to feel, once again, guilty, sad, and helpless.

On a sudden whim, she dressed warmly and headed to the nearby Metro Blanche station with Atticus. She knew where she needed to be.

One transfer and a half-hour later, Nora and Atticus turned off Rue des Rosiers onto a narrow, cobblestone lane and stood in front of the address Marie-Louise had given the day before. She stared at the weathered, cream-colored building and looked up to the second floor. She pictured a young Marie-Louise, in happier days before the war, at the open French doors looking over the simple wrought-iron railing.

Then the image switched to the closed French doors. A curtain edge moved slightly and a frightened Marie-Louise peeked out over the street she loved, which had changed horribly during the Occupation.

After all she'd written that day, Nora tried to capture some of the feelings of fear, anxiety, and sadness that existed during those four years of the Occupation.

She and Atticus walked one street after another, along cramped laneways and wider streets with busy traffic, passing Hasidic Jews and orthodox wives. She imagined some of the routes the young carrières must have taken.

Nora and Atticus went into a café, where she ordered a café crème and Atticus had his bowl of water. Sitting at the window, she had a view of the corner of Marie-Louise's apartment building. She closed her eyes and took herself back to the terrible years as much as she could.

Later, back at her computer, Nora felt an even greater connection to the words she had been writing. The smells, the colors, the sounds… All of it was alive in her thoughts and poured onto the pages as she typed.

She stopped writing when she suddenly realized Atticus was waiting patiently by his leash. They left for a walk. It had started to rain as they came back from the Pletzl, and the cobblestones were slick. She trod carefully now, her hood pulled over her head, and it was Atticus who indicated the walk would be short by making a beeline for the front doors after a quick circuit around the square.

Emotionally drained and thankful for a dinner of leftovers dropped off by Chloe, she sat on the couch and watched the evening news. But really, she just stared blankly at the television, her mind lost in the nightmare of the horrors from eighty-three years ago.

Right after taking Atticus for his last walk of the day, she had another long soak in the tub and fell into bed, hoping to read a few chapters of her book about Vincent van Gogh's life. Her imagination still worked overtime knowing he had lived next door.

Nora also wanted to get back to the manuscript she had begun about the young painter in Montmartre and the waitress, but her focus was all on her talks with Marie-Louise now. There was absolutely no possibility of her mind being able to go anywhere else until they were finished.

She felt frightened she might not do the story justice, but she was committed to writing it from her heart to honor Marie-Louise and all who had survived those terrible times.

She reached down and gave Atticus a good belly rub and they both fell into a deep sleep.

Chapter Twenty

FOUR WEEKS TO STAY WITH ATTICUS

Nora and Atticus were managing to visit many of the Christmas markets dotted around the city. They went early in the morning or later in the afternoon, depending on Nora's schedule with Marie-Louise.

She'd never become very familiar with the Metro system, but taking Atticus gave her the confidence to explore, and she was happy to discover how easy it was to get around.

She had even managed two FaceTime visits with the Girls at home while she visited the markets, in spite of the time difference. She made one call from a very small market across the Seine from Notre Dame.

"It wins best prize for setting," Nora told them. "Look at that view! I've been to this Square René Viviani before because it's minutes from the Shakespeare & Company bookstore and just down the street from Odette, the best place ever for cream puffs!"

That market was known for its focus on locally crafted merchandise, excellent food products, and a lovely setting, thanks to lots of evergreens around the vendor stalls. Nora couldn't resist the beautiful choices of jewelry and bought earrings as a

Christmas gift for Chloe from a particularly impressive vendor. The Girls helped via video with her choice, much to the amusement of the young woman who had designed and crafted the jewelry.

The other market Nora shared with the Girls was in the Tuileries—La Magie de Noël. She and Chloe went in the evening because it had "the best ambiance, then, with all the lights," Chloe had told her. Atticus stayed home with Olivier.

This market was big and noisy and crowded, but that added to the fun of it. Chloe took selfies of the two of them on la grande roule, the Ferris wheel, and when they reached the top, Nora couldn't stop taking shots of the spectacular view over the city.

There were a dozen other midway rides, and Chloe insisted they also ride the bumper cars as they often had at the autumn fairs when she was growing up. They laughed until they both had tears streaming down their faces and staggered off to find a food hut for a snack and a rest.

Steaming copper vats of traditional onion soup, served with fresh baguette and mulled wine, called to them, and they were happy to take a break and watch the masses enjoying themselves.

With over a hundred wooden huts offering French-produced food products, artisan handiwork, crafts and gifts from around the world, there were endless distractions. Nora sent a few videos along with more of Chloe's selfies to her friends in Canada. After a few hours, they declared themselves exhausted, and as soon as Nora purchased fresh gingerbread, the tantalizing aroma of which she could no longer resist, they'd hopped on the Metro for home.

One thing the Girls at home all decided was that they needed to plan a friends' trip to Paris over Christmas the next year.

The closest market to Nora was a few minutes' walk away from her apartment in Montmartre, by the Place des Abbesses metro station. It was small, with only twenty vendors. Nora had discovered it by chance on a walk with Atticus. There was a stall with the most delicious escargots and raclette, and she found herself stopping by near lunchtime more often than she ever imagined she would.

She'd chuckled the first time she noticed the champagne bar. *How French is this?* she'd texted to the Girls at home, accompanied by a selfie.

On Wednesday, after Marie-Louise told more of her story for two hours straight, Yvette and Nora bundled her in her wheelchair and took her to the small market.

The sun shone brightly, and the temperature was reasonably mild. It was a perfect day for browsing. The atmosphere was that of a small town—many people stopped to greet and chat with Marie-Louise. The conversations were often accompanied by laughter. Nora was touched to see what a well-loved local personality she was and the reverence with which she was treated.

After a while, Marie-Louise suggested they all go and enjoy some escargots. The tantalizing combination of butter and garlic was irresistible, and the owner of the stall placed a small table and three chairs in a spot warmed by a heater. He bowed with great respect and recognition to Marie-Louise as he helped with her wheelchair.

Marie-Louise closed her eyes as she took her first bite and sighed, "Délicieux! It tastes heavenly." They all agreed the infusion of parsley, garlic, and butter, mixed with the slightest hint of an earthy flavor, was divine. The baguette dipped in the sauce was the crowning glory. The conversation was all about food as they savored theirs.

Nora looked from her friends to the lively market, then back to her food, as though trying to hold the whole moment in place... The warm feelings, the flavor, the shared indulgence. *It's just so French*. She couldn't stop grinning.

The owner of the stall insisted there would be no charge, as it was his honor to host such fine women. They all knew he referred to Marie-Louise and were touched by the dignity he accorded them. Nora discreetly asked Yvette if she should leave a tip. Yvette looked horrified and said the owner would be enormously insulted if she did.

"It was his way of honoring Marie-Louise," Yvette whispered to Nora as they walked back home. "Everyone in Montmartre, indeed in France, knows her and her family's history with the Resistance. It is never forgotten."

Nora understood and again thought, *Just so French...*

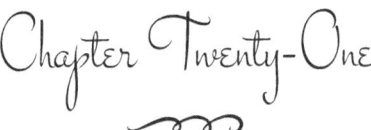

Chapter Twenty-One

ON FRIDAY MORNING, NORA JOINED CHLOE, OLI, AND Pierre for crêpes at le Moulin and the atmosphere was almost convivial.

Without thinking, when their Nutella crêpes arrived, Nora and Chloe burst into singing "Tradition" again, while Pierre stared at them with a quizzical expression. Olivier laughed and explained to Pierre what it was all about. Nora thought Pierre didn't quite get it as he still looked at them strangely and then changed the subject.

Pierre had been away most of the week visiting the galleries of some friends in Normandy, so Nora hadn't seen him since the dinner with Celeste.

She listened as they talked about his trip. Pierre insisted on speaking French most of the time and Nora thought he enjoyed making her feel awkward about it. In spite of that, she found his voice—low, steady and unmistakably alluring—incredibly attractive ... in French or English.

He explained he was pumped about the success of his trip, since he'd discovered a new young artist who showed interest in exhibiting at his gallery in Nice. Nora was impressed with his enthusiasm and couldn't blame him for wanting to express it in his own language.

My bad, she thought, as she still stumbled in French ... particularly with him. *I need to keep improving.*

After sneaking a peek at her translation app in the loo, Nora asked Pierre in hesitant French about his drive. She added she was thinking of going to Normandy for a couple of days in January, but probably by train.

Apart from the fact that she said she was going to *drive* the train, which had them all laughing, including Pierre. They congratulated her on her effort.

"It will be quite cold then," he told her, switching to English. "But coming from Canada, you are no doubt used to that kind of weather."

She wasn't certain if he was being disparaging, as he gave no hint of a smile. But she agreed, and Chloe made some comments about not missing those cold Canadian winters.

Pierre shook hands with Nora when he left, after giving warm bises to Chloe and Olivier.

He wished them all a good trip to Avignon, saying he would see them in Provence. Then he climbed into his van and drove off.

"No bise for me," Nora said to Chloe and Oli after he was gone.

Oli apologized and Chloe raised an eyebrow as she shook her head in disappointment. "He can be so nice when he wants to be."

"I'm joking. Honestly, it's fine. But I hope he won't hate me all throughout our Christmas visit," Nora said.

Olivier kicked at a pebble on the sidewalk. "Even if he is still crabby, you will love the rest of my family. Don't judge us all based on my dad's current behaviour, please. There really is another side to him."

"Oli, dear. I'm not judging anyone. I feel sad that your dad is so unhappy. But perhaps all the festivities of the season will cheer him up. I'm so excited! I can't wait to go!"

Olivier smiled at her. "We can't wait too. We thought we would leave a little earlier. Like next Monday instead of Wednesday. Is that okay with you? We will take the TGV—Train à Grande Vitesse—to Avignon, and one of the family will pick us up there. It's less than a half hour to our farm. There are lots of cars for us to use when we are there."

"It's entirely up to you, but it sounds like a fine plan. Atticus and I can be ready any time."

Chloe jumped up and down, performing her usual ritual of excitement. "We're taking the extra days off! We decided there's so much to show you we didn't want to rush the visit."

Nora gave her a big hug. "That's so wonderful! Thanks!"

Then she looked concerned. "Oh, but what will I do with my blé de Sainte Barbe? It's growing so thick and tall. I don't want to lose the good luck it promises."

Chloe chuckled. "No worries. Give it a good drink before we leave, and I'm sure it'll be fine when we get back. Trust me, there will be a healthy crop at the farmhouse. I only gave you one saucer, but normally each household has three, and they are placed in the crèche. You'll see."

Friday night promised to be extra special. Chloe and Olivier planned to join Nora and Luc at the dance club, and suggested they all meet there a little earlier to catch an hour or two of swing dancing.

Nora put up with being teased by Chloe about it all week. Chloe knew her mom loved to jive, as they called swing dance back in Nora's younger days. Chloe had vivid memories of her parents jiving around the house to golden oldies and often joining in. Nora had been thrilled when Chloe first met Olivier and learned he loved 'le swing'.

"Just wait until Luc discovers you're a wild one on the swing floor! I can't wait," Chloe chortled, as Nora waved her away.

Luc insisted on picking them up. Nora and Chloe both brought an extra pair of shoes so they had a different pair for each session. "I definitely cannot jump around in stilettos," Nora said. "But I bet there are French women who can."

"Pas de question. No question," Chloe agreed.

Nora laughed at Luc's look of surprise when she leapt up first and took his hand to go to the dance floor. The music was mainly classic swing from 1930s and '40s big band orchestras. Tunes by Count Basie, Benny Goodman, Fats Waller, and others kept them hopping.

"Nora," Luc exclaimed, "you are the best! This is your style, no question!"

Nora laughed. "I love this! I'm happy to show you I'm not just a beginner with this kind of music. It makes me feel better after stumbling around at tango at first."

"You did not stumble for long, ma chérie. But this is such fun."

They switched partners with Chloe and Olivier from time to time, as often as they switched speaking French and English. Nora's comfort zone was growing because of it, as well as her vocabulary. The laughter-filled time passed quickly. They had all agreed to have just one glass of champagne until the swing time was over and planned to pop a bottle when tango began.

When Chloe and Nora were alone for a few minutes, Nora said, "I have to admit, I had no idea my time in France would involve so much champagne. Now I've come to expect it, and I truly enjoy it."

Chloe nodded. "It's just one of those French 'things,' I agree. I had only consumed champagne at New Year's and weddings until I moved to France. It just seems to go with everything."

Nora raised her glass. "Now I understand that F. Scott

Fitzgerald quote, 'Too much of anything is bad. Except champagne–too much is just right.'"

They were both laughing when Luc and Olivier returned to the table with an impressive cheese platter. "We have probably worked up a bit of an appetite," Olivier said.

As they relaxed, the conversation turned to Nora's meetings with Marie-Louise. They were all interested in how her project was going.

"It's definitely the most meaningful writing I have undertaken. To be in Paris and spend time on the streets where her story unfolded just brings it all to life for me. I've never felt anything like it, and I hope I can do her story justice."

She received encouragement from all three. Luc shared some stories from the Occupation, as some of his family had lived in Paris and Normandy during that time, as well as in Provence. Nora was once again touched by the dramatic history experienced by past generations of so many French families.

"In North America, we simply haven't had our lives impacted by anything even remotely comparable. Hearing such personal memories in the places they were experienced is adding a different dimension to my stay."

After they'd relaxed for a bit, the tango music called to them. Chloe and Olivier went home after an hour, claiming exhaustion.

"But it was so much fun! Let's do it again after the holidays," Chloe had said.

When Luc excused himself for a few minutes Nora took out her phone and sent a message off to the Girls:

> This evening is so much fun with a capital F!

She also sent along a video Chloe took of her jiving with Luc to "Crazy Little Thing Called Love."

Nora and Luc danced for another hour and then became absorbed in a conversation about life and choices and things that weren't choices. He was intrigued by Nora's writing history, and her suspicion he was well read was confirmed.

Luc suggested they go to a quiet lounge across the street. The night had become bitterly cold and the wind cut right through their heavy coats. Luc put his arm around Nora to shield her as they hurried along.

In a dim, amber-hued corner of a dark bar, they were served a fine cognac as they settled into leather chairs, which were warmed and softened by a long history of use.

For the first time Nora learned about his personal life, which wasn't at all what she expected.

"I am forty-three... Not so young as you thought, non?"

He did look younger, Nora agreed. There were only eleven years between him and Nora. The next disclosure was a shock.

"And I am married."

Nora hoped her face did not register the reaction she felt at those totally unexpected words.

As he spoke, something in his voice shifted. The easy cadence slowed and a quiet gravity crept in. He explained he had been wed for twenty-one years. His wife, Mathilde, had been seriously injured in a car accident fifteen years ago.

The light in his eyes darkened even more.

"The doctors call her condition a 'persistent vegetative state.' For me, it is something more abstract—grief with no clear end."

Nora's heart leapt into her throat as he continued. She felt such sadness for this man, who obviously loved so much about life.

"She suffered severe brain damage and lives in an elegant nursing home an hour outside Paris."

Luc was not uncomfortable sharing the story of his wife's accident, and Nora listened calmly now as he continued to reveal more of his story.

"Our daughter's name is Dominique, and she is in her second year of university in Switzerland. We try to see each other once a month either here or there, and she is my pride and joy."

He described how he had brought up Dominique on his own and when she was little, they visited her mother every Sunday. Nora's heart broke for all of them.

She apologized for dabbing at her eyes throughout the conversation. Luc held her hand at one point. "Nora, do not cry for me. I am devoted to my wife and daughter and also have learned how to enjoy a very happy life."

Nora nodded. A tear slipped down her cheek and she sniffled, squeezing his hand gently. "But this is such a painful story you are telling me. It's impossible not to feel sad. Please tell me more, but only if you wish."

They both took a long slow sip of cognac. The warmth of it lingered, delicate and smoky.

"Everyone has a story, Luc. I'm so sorry yours is such a tragedy."

He gave a small contemplative smile. "Oui. D'accord, it is a tragedy that lives on. But it happened many years ago and is part of my life. I do not carry it as a weight but rather as a shape. Part of the shape of my life, my love."

He showed her older photos on his phone of his wife as a beautiful young woman with long golden hair and stunning turquoise eyes. Then he showed others of an equally beautiful older woman. "Still as beautiful today but caught in a cruel limbo between existence and absence."

"She's lovely," Nora whispered.

"She is. Time has softened her features but not taken them. She is tenderly and respectfully looked after by a dedicated and skilled staff. Better care could not be found anywhere, no matter the cost."

"And Dominique looks just like her."

"She does," Luc said, his eyes glowing, "And her personality is the same. It really is quite bizarre. She is a brilliant young woman in every way. Her mother would be as proud of her as I am."

Nora nodded, unable to find words.

"So, you're probably wondering what's going on with me.

Fine dining, dancing with beautiful women ... living the high life."

Nora gave him a quiet, compassionate look and slowly shook her head. Before she could speak, he went on.

"After Mathilde's accident I worked very hard for a small IT company I had started with two friends. We became successful beyond our dreams, and a few years ago sold the business. Now I work as a consultant and only when I want to."

"It's a very fortunate arrangement for a young man," Nora said.

"Trust me, I feel blessed in that regard. I have many friends, male and female, and live life as I wish. The longer you are here, the more you will understand: We French see life very differently from North Americans. It's one of our defining traits."

"In what way?"

"We live for pleasure. Le plaisir ... the art of seduction. Men and women. It has been this way for centuries. But not the way you might think of it. It is not only about romance or desire. It is in how we speak, how we dine, how we argue and agree. It is everywhere. It is about savoring – food, conversation, beauty, even melancholy. There is no rush. "

Nora was intrigued. "Go on..." she said, her voice, low and thoughtful, as if she were weighing every word.

"This is our culture. Passion with restraint. I see it as the French way. There is a book I recommend to all my non-French friends because I believe it captures very well the essence of what I have said. I insist on giving a copy to you as well. It is *La Séduction* by Elaine Sciolino, an American journalist who has lived in France for decades. She gets it right."

"Thank you, I believe this is part of what Chloe keeps talking to me about ... the French effect. I look forward to reading it. You talk about pleasure like it's something you live, not something you chase."

"Yes, I think you get what I'm saying. Until you read the

book, I hope you will not judge me and the way I live my life." He looked at her intently.

Nora returned his gaze. "First of all, know this about me: I am not judgmental. Believe me, I have no intention of judging you in any way. I enjoy every moment we spend together, and although it was probably painful for you, I respect your willingness to share something so very personal with me."

"Giselle said you have been a widow for some time, so we have a journey with grief in common. That, in itself, colors the way we live."

"Yes, it does. Although my husband passed many years ago, he's still very much alive in my heart."

They talked quietly about grief, the weight of past choices, and the uncertain path forward until, surprised by the bar lights flickering to indicate closing time, they went out into the cold night.

As he drove to Nora's, Luc said, "We should not part on a sad note. I know you are going to Provence for the holidays, and I am going to Mexico for a week to see Giselle. Dominique is coming too. She knows Giselle well."

"Fabulous. What a good time you will have."

"And I'm certain you will as well. Provence is magic at any time of year, and especially with all the traditions and food... Mon Dieu, the food! Prepare yourself!"

Nora sighed. "I'm still trying to sort out exactly how many meals I will have over those three days. Dining is going to be a marathon, from what I am told. But a delicious marathon!"

As Luc went up in the elevator with Nora, he said, "Why don't we plan to see each other two weeks from now for more tango? But rather than wait so long, would you like to meet earlier in the week for a tour of the newly reopened Notre Dame?"

"I would love to!"

"Fantastique. I will arrange it for perhaps the Tuesday after we both return. How does that sound?"

Nora touched his arm as Luc leaned in to give her warm bises.

"I am already looking forward to it. Thank you and enjoy your time away with Dominique. Please give Giselle my love."

Before she could think twice, her emotions still stirred from their conversation, Nora slipped her arms around Luc and pulled him into an embrace. He held her just as tightly.

They stayed like that for more than a minute, wrapped in silence. When they finally stepped back, their eyes met and no words were needed. A simple nod passed between them, full of understanding.

When she went inside this time, Nora didn't pirouette around the room, but she did flop on the cushions. She was overwhelmed by a tangle of feelings. The evening had been such fun, but her heart hurt as she considered Luc's story.

She thought about how life could be unspeakably cruel. Not necessarily in loud, violent ways but in the slow unraveling of everything one believed was safe. A time in life which one thought might be the happiest suddenly could turn into the most painful. And over that, one had no control.

And despite the pain, life continued. Nora remembered how she felt in the early days after Jeremy was gone. How could the sun still rise, birds sing, people laugh? It didn't seem right.

But slowly life expanded... New people, new stories, new memories. One never forgot—ever—but grief became part of one's being, and one learned to live with it.

It seemed like Luc had found a way to live with his. It was such an unusual and unexpected story. And yet he made it sound right.

Perhaps I am finding a way to live with my grief too, this time, thought Nora. *On my other trips here, I've brought Jeremy along with me. This time I feel I'm creating more distance and making my life here my own. It's different and it feels right.*

Rain was forecast for the entire weekend, and Nora welcomed it as an opportunity to get ahead with Marie-Louise's story. The grey skies and dull light helped bring her into the grim darkness of life during the Occupation.

As she made sense of her notes and recordings, the powerful story of the innocent young Marie-Louise began to take shape. Nora had already drafted a substantial number of pages.

Reviewing what she had so far, she thought how the memoir was also in many ways not just the life of the little girl and her neighborhood, but it also represented a quiet elegy for the tragic suffocation of the city.

She went back to the beginning of her notes of Marie-Louise's story and reviewed. She knew this would occur many more times.

At ten, Marie-Louise and her friends initially thought the soldiers were exciting, in their neatly pressed uniforms and shiny boots that clacked when they marched past their windows. They gave the children candy.

Her mother would pull her back from the window and hiss, "Don't stare. Don't watch." But she didn't understand why. Then, as the streets became so quiet, so strangely still except for the heavy thud of the soldiers' boots and the chaos of arrests, a fear set in.

Her neighborhood had never been without voices, without laughter. There had always been someone singing, someone arguing, mothers calling children, neighbors chatting to each other across balconies, children running in the street, radio sounds drifting out windows. Now that was gone, replaced by a silence that didn't belong.

As time went by, the soldier's novelty wore off. Swastikas were everywhere. Food was scarce and her mother would send her to line up at stores for whatever scraps could be had. Her father had vanished. She saw her Jewish friends forced to wear the yellow star and their families pulled from their apartments and loaded into army trucks. She had to learn to say nothing.

Her mother's eyes showed a new kind of tired, and she often

disappeared for much of the day ... and sometimes the night. Marie-Louise began to understand the importance of her message-carrying.

The posters on the walls of buildings changed, and so did the looks people gave each other in the streets. Mostly they looked down at the ground. She stopped seeing her Jewish friends at school. When she asked about one of her friends, her teacher just said, "She moved."

By fourteen, she knew better. But still not where they had been taken.

She knew who watched too closely and who no longer spoke. She saw how some women laughed too loudly at German officers and how others spat at their feet when they thought no one was looking.

She learned to carry silence like armor. But she also noticed the quiet heroes—the baker who passed secret messages hidden in his bread to the tailor, the old man on the corner who fixed radios and whispered news from London, the older boys who pretended to be going to school and instead slapped posters on the walls around the neighborhood. Some acted as lookouts and whistled warnings to their friends.

Her fear didn't disappear—it grew roots. But something else took hold too: the spark of defiance. Her mother explained she would not tell Marie-Louise anything, so if she was questioned, she'd know nothing.

"Someday the stories will be told, ma puce. But for today we must resist quietly."

There were moments Nora felt she was living it, breathing it, right there looking out over the same rooftops that others had looked over years ago. It became all too real. And she cried.

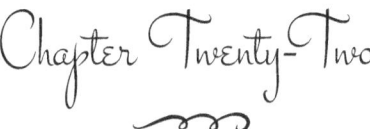

Chapter Twenty-Two

THREE WEEKS STAYING WITH ATTICUS

After a weekend of pouring rain, which Nora spent at her computer, they departed for Provence, and she was excited.

At the Gare de Lyon, Nora reminisced about their dinner at the iconic Le Train Bleu on one of her previous visits. "I'll never ever forget that magnificent restaurant and the outstanding meal we had there that summer. Let's go again next year!"

"When we save enough money," Chloe joked. "But the cost was definitely worth the evening we had. It's such a special place. A treasure in Paris for sure."

Nora got Atticus comfortably settled on the train. Because they had reserved a four-seat carré famille, or family square, Atticus was allowed his own seat. Nora had brought a small blanket to cover the plush upholstery and a special harness to keep him safe. After checking out the other people passing by for a few minutes, he curled up for a snooze.

Olivier moved to a vacant set of seats to make a business call.

"Okay, Maman," Chloe said in a hushed voice. "I really hope you'll give Pierre another chance while we're in Provence. I honestly think you two could be good friends ... and maybe even more." Her eyes lit up expectantly.

Nora attempted not to sound annoyed. "Why on earth would you say such a thing? You saw for yourself he wasn't impressed with me in any way. I mean, really, he could not have been ruder most of the time we were in each other's company."

"But you really didn't spend so much time together. Maybe you're being too defensive. I thought I saw him warming up to you. How could he not?"

Her daughter's suggestion of the possibility of romance got Nora's back up. She was the parent, not a girlfriend wanting to be set up. "Chloe, sweetheart. I know you want me to fall in love again, but I've told you many times it isn't something I need in my life. I had a happy marriage cut short, and I have learned to live with that. Some people never have as much as I did. You need to accept this."

Chloe sighed heavily and threw up her hands. "Mom, you keep saying that. I understand you and Dad had the best marriage, but you've been on your own for so many years now. Pierre does have a good side. He can be kind and funny. Give him a chance ... please."

She seldom got angry with Chloe but was definitely losing patience now. "Well, I haven't seen that good side and don't care if I do. Please. I'm asking you to let it go!"

Nora put her earbuds in, opened her French app, and gazed out the window. French grammar still drove her crazy. Chloe pouted.

For lunch, they ate the baguette sandwiches they had picked up at their local patisserie and espresso from the cart that came through their train car.

"Almost as good as Le Train Bleu," Oli wisecracked.

He looked surprised as neither Chloe nor Nora laughed and had probably noticed both women were giving off unusual negative vibes.

The trip was quick on the high-speed train, and they would arrive in Avignon in three hours. Chloe and Olivier promptly fell asleep after eating and Nora was overjoyed to have uninterrupted reading the rest of the way.

After they disembarked, Chloe and Olivier were immediately greeted with warm bises by a fit-looking, older couple waiting for them on the platform.

Olivier's grandparents had the effortless poise of people long comfortable in their own skin. The man, tall and lean with a shock of silver hair neatly combed back, had a firm handshake and a smile creased at the edges by good humor.

The woman beside him radiated energy. Her eyes sparkled a sincere welcome, and her white hair framed her face with soft waves. Nora had an immediate impression they were a couple who shared a quiet love and understanding forged over decades.

Before Chloe could say anything by way of introduction, the couple gave the same sincere bises to Nora. In strongly accented English, they said how thrilled they were to have her come to their home for the holidays.

Pointing to each other, they indicated Nora should call them Mami and Papi. "Comme notre famille. Like our family. Grandma and Grandpa."

Nora's heart swelled with affection at their heartfelt welcome. Chloe grinned.

"They are the sweetest people. I adore them," she whispered to Nora.

Olivier had taken charge of getting Atticus off the train, and the dog sat politely as he was introduced to Mami and Papi. Petting him, they told him their dog Fântome was waiting for him at the farm. Nora smiled at the suggestion and their obvious immediate affection for Atticus.

As they walked to a small SUV in the station parking lot, Olivier said to Nora, "Atticus is going to be exhausted by the end of your visit. The dogs will be running through the fields and vineyards nonstop."

Olivier and his grandfather chatted briefly about the route home. Then he explained to Nora that there was an evening market going on in Avignon and the traffic was not conducive to driving into the city as he had hoped.

"Unfortunately, you won't see much of Avignon from here except the outskirts, but we will come early the day we leave to show you the highlights," Olivier said.

On the drive to the farmhouse, they spoke excitedly, much of the time in French with Chloe translating.

Nora promised, "Et je vais pratiquer mon français. Je vous promets." She knew it would take her a bit of time to feel comfortable speaking French with Mami and Papi. It never failed when she was with new French-speaking friends. But she would do it.

Chloe pointed out aspects of the peaceful landscape along the way. The Provençal countryside unfolded into a patchwork of small villages, vineyards, orchards, and olive groves dressed in their winter wardrobes.

The grapevines, stripped of their leaves, stretched in neat rows, and earthy tones of brown, rust, and ochre dominated the fields. Silver-green leaves on the ancient and gnarled olive trees shimmered in the sunlight.

Seeing the grayish-brown mounds of lavender plants gave Nora a good idea of how stunning it would be in late June when they boasted their glorious, sweet-smelling, purple-hued blooms.

"You must come back in lavender season," Mami said to Nora. "It's a sight to see, and we can take you to private fields where there are no tourists. Chloe, you must promise to bring your maman back then."

"I'll do my best," Chloe replied, nudging Nora and beaming at her. "We're stopping on the way to choose le sapin, the Christmas tree, at a neighbor's farm. That was part of the discussion you missed a minute ago. So, the festive fun is beginning. The serious food stuff won't be for another day though."

As signposts indicated they were near Saint-Rémy-de-Provence Chloe pointed out the rocky outline of Les Alpilles in the distance. The small range of limestone peaks dominated the landscape in that region. "Hopefully we'll have some time to spend on a hiking trail or two. There are tons of them."

Soon they drove down a long gravel lane ending in the middle of a thick forest. Nora breathed in the smell of wood smoke she loved so much.

They climbed out, leaving Atticus, as Papi gestured down a row of tall trees and handed Olivier a saw. In front of a small wooden hut with a welcome sign, a cast iron pot hung over a wood fire, and a young girl approached with a tray of steaming mugs.

"Mulled wine to sip while we choose the perfect specimen," Mami told Nora. "Also, a relatively new tradition because le sapin de Noël was not part of our fête de Noël until after the Great War. My parents were the first to embrace the tradition of an entire tree in our family. Before that, we just collected branches and made garlands to hang on the doors and in hallways."

After a stroll through the woods and much discussion among everyone as to the height, fullness, and shape of their ideal tree, the perfect choice was made. When it was paid for, the men tied it to the top of the SUV and they continued on their way to the farm.

Chapter Twenty-Three

Vineyards, pruned for winter rest, lined both sides of the narrow dirt driveway. Everything was awash in the increasing silvery moonglow.

Nora sat in the passenger seat of the SUV and watched through the windshield as the view suddenly opened onto a vast field, neatly tilled. To one side of the property was a long, two-story, yellow-gray limestone farmhouse with a terra-cotta roof and wooden shutters painted a weathered blue, which protected small windows on the back side.

Dark outlines of goats dotted a field on the far side of an olive grove and chickens pecked in the gardens that surrounded the house.

Nora gasped as she took it all in. "Be still my heart. It's like photos I've salivated over for years on France real estate websites."

Chloe explained the French word for this type of stone farmhouse was "le mas," pronouncing it as 'mahs.' "It's pretty much a classic, as you will see when we show you around this week. Wait until you see what's in those outbuildings on the property." She pointed to two smaller barns a short distance away.

When they pulled into a parking area around the side, Nora's jaw dropped even more as she took in the broad terrace that ran across the front of the house. It was inviting and elegant in its simplicity, even with chickens wandering the length of it.

She recognized some large, green-glazed Anduze pots on the terrace, with dried remnants of summer plantings still in them. A bare, thick wisteria vine clung to the walls of the house and wound its way across the entire front façade, secured by wire in some places. Vintage wrought-iron tables and chairs were bathed in sunshine.

"I can just imagine how glorious this is in the spring," she said to Chloe as they followed Olivier, who had piled their bags on a small cart, into the house through wide, thick oak double doors. "These were hand carved over two hundred years ago when my ancestors began farming here," Olivier told her proudly.

"Aren't they something, mom? And you are so right. Spring is the most beautiful time here," said Chloe.

Nora stood still in the entry hall and breathed in the delicious smells of simmering spices that filled the air. Mami had slipped in before her and was waiting with a warm smile. When Nora breathed out a quiet, "It smells amazing in here. Ça sent incroyable ici," Mami's grin widened, pride flickering in her eyes.

Chloe said Nora should get used to it. "Mami's house always has the best smells coming from the kitchen."

Olivier laughed as he agreed and then pointed to the bags. "I will take care of these. Dad and Fantôme are off on a hike. He texted me a while ago saying they should be back before too long."

Nora was somewhat relieved by Pierre's absence. She could get organized in her room and become familiar with the surroundings before worrying about his appearance. She felt like a schoolgirl hoping her crush would like her. She gave her head a mental shake; she wasn't interested in getting romantically involved with anyone. But it still would be nice to be friends with him.

Chloe led Nora and Atticus up the uneven wide stone steps of the main staircase to the bedrooms on the upper floor. They entered Nora's cozy room, and Chloe flung open the shutters of the French doors, which led to a narrow balcony. "Check this out, Maman! Picture-perfect or what?" she said.

Before she walked to the French doors, Nora's eyes fell on the bathtub of her dreams in a corner of the room. The glossy, white porcelain finish and brass claw feet gave off a vintage charm that took her breath away. "Chloe, you put me in this room on purpose, right? It's my fantasy tub."

Chloe gave her a knowing look. Then she opened a door at the end of the room to show her the sink and toilet.

After freshening up at the sink for a moment, Nora joined her daughter at the balcony. Gazing out over the moonlit rows of grapevines, she breathed in the earthy scent of the crisp air. "Honestly, sweetheart, when are the dreams going to stop? This is straight out of a French romance for me!"

Chloe chuckled. "I hear you. I felt the same the first time Oli brought me here. It's pretty special to us, but run of-the-mill to the locals. Although, don't get me wrong, they appreciate the history of their homes and farms. In many ways, life goes on as it has for centuries ... just with a few more modern conveniences. Oli's family has farmed this land and lived in this house since 1750. It's a peaceful life."

"That's before the French Revolution!" Nora exclaimed.

Chloe nodded. "Exactly. The way centuries of history live on here is all part of the French Effect for me. You feel it everywhere."

Atticus stepped up to the railing and began barking. Not far off, a man walked toward them, accompanied by a sturdy dog about the same size as Atticus but with a dense coat. Returning the barks, the dog ran toward the house.

"It's Fantôme with Pierre!" Chloe cried. "Let's go downstairs so the dogs can meet each other!"

"I hope they get along," Nora muttered, concerned.

"Mom! Don't worry until you have to!" Chloe cautioned and gave her a light punch on the arm. "Remember how social Maggie was? Dogs love to hang out with other dogs. I bet these two are going to be besties right away. Let's find out."

Nora followed Chloe downstairs, muttering, "If only it were the same for people."

Chloe mumbled, "I heard that."

Atticus was way ahead of them, and when they got to the kitchen, he was nowhere to be seen. Papi stood by the open door, laughing. It seemed everyone had gathered around to see how things were going to work out.

Pierre stood outside, leaning on a gnarled, well-used walking stick. Nora couldn't help but think he looked like the epitome of French rustic charm: from his weathered leather boots to his worn, brown, waxed canvas coat topped off with a battered, wide-brimmed felt hat pulled low over his brow. He looked like he had spent time shepherding in a field and had been through many rainstorms, market trips, and harvests.

She felt her writing muse arrive, almost uncontrollably, as she stood looking at him ... trying not to stare. *He is a picture. Composed, textured, the kind of face a story could rest inside.*

She caught herself smiling and quickly turned her attention to Atticus.

Atticus and Fantôme faced each other, stiff-legged, ears perked. For a moment, there was a staring contest and then tails began to slowly wag.

Atticus stretched his front legs forward, with his backside up. His 'play bow,' as Nora called it. She held her breath. After a second, Fantôme replied in kind and in a flash the two dogs were chasing each other around the driveway.

"Voilà! L'amusement a commencé! The fun has begun!" Papi announced with a wide grin.

Pierre waved to them and walked over to where the pine tree was tied to the roof of the SUV. Taking a knife from his pocket, which Nora thought indicated he was in 'farmer' mode, he began to cut the ropes.

Olivier called out from the kitchen that he would be right out to help bring the tree into the house.

Mami and Papi had an intense discussion as to where the tree should be placed and then turned to Chloe and Nora.

"Qu'est-ce que vous pensez? What do you think?"

With Pierre and Olivier impatiently holding the tree at each end and urging a decision, it was agreed it should be placed in the great room, between the sitting and dining areas. "We can begin decorating while we have our apéros in an hour," Mami suggested.

"Bonne idée," Chloe agreed. She checked her watch, noting they should be gathered by seven o'clock.

Mami asked if everyone would like to have some time to freshen up beforehand. "You have had a busy day with travel."

Nora agreed without hesitating. She had one thought in mind.

The dogs were called into the house, and everyone chuckled at the cloud of dust as the two animals raced up to the door for their treat. It appeared they had already become fast friends.

Nora took Atticus up to her room. She tried to control the urge to bound up the steps, since the deep claw-foot bathtub was calling to her.

While Nora ran water in the tub, she added a drop of essence of lavender from the bottle sitting on a small pine table nearby. The room filled with a divine scent. Relaxed and happy, Nora gave Atticus a long hug and climbed into the tub. As she soaked, Atticus snuggled into the dog bed thoughtfully placed in her room.

So far, Provence is proving to be as magical as promised, Nora mused as she sank up to her neck in the soothing water with a long sigh.

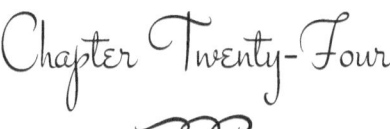

Chapter Twenty-Four

COMPLETELY REFRESHED AN HOUR LATER, NORA WENT downstairs and headed toward the great room. She heard voices coming from inside, so knew the others were already there and champagne—of course champagne—was ready to be served. She smiled to herself.

Casually dressed in a light-blue silk blouse, black tapered jeans and ankle-high boots, she breathed a sigh of relief when she saw her choices fit right in with everyone else's attire.

Pierre came over to her and extended his hand. *Hmm, still no bise for me. No acceptance yet.*

Nora gave Chloe a pointed look as if to validate her comments on the train. Behind Pierre, Chloe widened her eyes in return and held back a chuckle, reading her mother's thoughts.

"Bienvenue. Welcome to the home of my parents. It is where I enjoyed a very happy childhood." Nora was pleasantly surprised to see his smile seemed almost warm.

"Thank you. It's a lovely home. I'm honoured to be here."

Once champagne flutes were filled and toasts shared, Mami produced two large wicker baskets filled to the brim with the family's treasures wrapped in tissue paper for protection.

Stories and much laughter were shared, mostly in French with

Chloe translating when needed, as le sapin de Noël was dressed in traditional decorations of pine cones, dried fruit, small bundles of cinnamon, and simple paper ornaments tied with red string—many obviously created by a young child. The family lovingly teased Pierre and Olivier about them.

They all took part in weaving red and gold ribbons through the branches, the colors of Provence, Nora was told. Finally, vintage stamped tin candle holders were attached to a few boughs.

"Little white candles will be lit tomorrow evening when we feast on les Treize Desserts ... the Thirteen Desserts after our Christmas Eve dinner," Chloe told Nora.

Olivier looked proudly at his wife. "Chloe has embraced our traditions and become *une vraie femme Provençale*. Truly a woman of Provence."

Nora was startled when Pierre asked if she would like him to explain their crèche and the santons to her. In English! She thanked him but requested he speak French, and she would see if she could understand everything. He gave her a look that seemed to her like respect, for a change, and agreed to only speak English if she needed explanation.

Nora thought maybe she'd made a positive inroad with him. She hoped so.

Arranged across the wide oak mantle of the deep fireplace sat small, hand-painted terra-cotta figurines. In the center a nativity scene had been set up, and spread out from there lay a village with a few buildings and many other santons, acquired through decades by the family.

"They represent a whole Provençal village of everyday characters," he said as he pointed out a few. "The baker, the farmer, the lavender seller, the butcher, the shepherd..." The list went on and Nora became enchanted.

As he spoke, Nora sensed his demeanor toward her soften and she heard his affection for the crèche in his voice.

Papi said, "There's an excellent santon market tomorrow

morning in the village, and we will go to buy a special one to celebrate Nora's visit."

It was just past ten o'clock when Papi gave the quiet signal Mami was ready for them to sit down to dinner. A wave of relief—and hunger—washed through Nora. The rich aroma that had teased her for hours heralded a simple meal of coq au vin simmered slowly in red wine with vegetables and garlic.

"This is one of Mami's specialties," Chloe told Nora as they went to the long pine dining table. "She buys an old rooster at the market to give it that special flavor." She laughed at Nora's questioning look. "I know it sounds a bit weird," she whispered. "But everyone swears by it."

The deep-burgundy-hued sauce pooled around the tender meat, covering pearl onions, parsnips, and chunks of winter carrots, which Mami explained were much sweeter than those harvested in summer. They ate it accompanied by crusty bread and velvety mashed potatoes, and Nora lingered over each bite. The rich flavors convinced her, without a doubt—this was comfort food.

When she climbed into bed that night, snuggled into the soft mattress and warm duvet, bittersweet thoughts of Jeremy quietly filled her mind. How lovely it would have been to share this experience with him. But also, she thought about how wishes like those had to stop. He was gone. Forever in her heart but not part of whatever lay before her.

Remembering again the counselor's advice on her last visit, she told herself it was well past time to stop inflicting sadness into her new experiences and move on. "You are more than overdue on living your new life. Embrace it," the counselor had said.

Easier said than done, was her final thought as she drifted off to sleep.

The market the next morning was a celebration of community and season. Stalls were draped with evergreen boughs, and the chilly air was filled with a pleasing blend of the fragrances of mulled wine, roasting chestnuts, fresh gingerbread, and other festive treats.

Nora was glad she had packed a few warm sweaters. One of those, along with her down jacket and woolen toque, saved her from unnecessary chill as she walked through the market.

They had left extra early to stop first at the santons vendors' stalls. The variety of the terra-cotta figurines mesmerized Nora. Papi took charge and gave Nora an elaborate description of many of the santons, encouraging her to choose a special one for herself. Nora felt awkward as he obviously meant to buy it as a gift for her.

Chloe poked her in the back and gave her a look that said, *Just do it*. When Nora settled on the figure of a woman with a basket of lavender, Papi picked up a woodsman with a bundle of kindling on his back to go with it.

"You must have two santons, so they can keep each other company," he explained. He asked the vendor to wrap them as a gift and then paid for the figures and put the package in a canvas bag he'd brought. "I will save them for tomorrow," Papi said, smiling.

Nora graciously smiled back, hoping she didn't show her discomfort. She loved to give gifts but was not always at ease being the recipient.

Everyone seemed to know everyone else at the market, and voices rang in the air with happy greetings as shoppers filled their baskets with all manner of goods.

Mami had stayed at home with the dogs and was taking care of last-minute details.

She had sent Chloe and Nora off with a list. As they approached the food stalls, they were pleased they had left extra early as lines were already beginning to form.

"It's a good thing we have a list," Nora said to Chloe. "Otherwise, I would be filling up with all sorts of amazing temptations. How can you possibly make sensible decisions with all these enticing treats?"

Olivier and Pierre went off on an errand with Papi, saying they would meet the women later at the market café. When Nora questioned if they would be able to get a table, Chloe said with a giggle, "Pas de problème. Papi has his own table. He's been a regular for over sixty years. Next stop is the boulangerie next to the market. Mami had them set aside a pompe l'huile for her. It's a brioche made with olive oil. It tastes more like a cake to me, and it's part of the Thirteen Desserts we'll have tonight after Mass."

"We're going to Mass?" Nora paused for a moment. "Of course, we always used to go to Christmas Eve services at home, so I don't know why I'm surprised."

"This will be Mass like you've never seen or heard. It is so special. We will have le Gros Souper before we go."

"Le Gros Souper? To be trite, it sounds gross."

Chloe laughed. "That's the classic English response. It's actually not gross at all. It's a completely meatless meal Mami is working on while we're out. Then after Mass, we have les Treize Desserts."

While they chatted, they moved around to the various stalls to keep working their way down Mami's list. Several times Nora dawdled, tempted by the enticing food displays, and once Chloe had to text her to find where she was.

"Sorry!" said Nora when they found each other again. "Did you see the stall with all thirteen desserts laid out so perfectly? When you first mentioned Les Treize Desserts, I had to google the term. I couldn't picture all the cakes, cookies, and other rich goodies we would be served. I was surprised at what I saw."

Chloe said, "After our meal last night and with what awaits us tomorrow, we eat sparingly even though les Treize Desserts doesn't sound like it. As you saw at that stall, it's mostly nuts and fruit and sweets. Mmmm, yummy nougat and calissons are my favorite. But..." She stopped and spread her arms wide.

"On Christmas Day we have le Réveillon, and ooh là là! In the old days they started eating after Mass and went on into the wee hours. Fortunately, now we begin in the evening… And who knows when it ends. Mami and Papi will have several family friends join us and they bring dishes as well. It's truly a feast. So much fun!"

As Chloe expounded on the upcoming food challenges, they filled their baskets with lettuce, tomatoes, shallots, leaks, dates, pomegranates, persimmons, clementines with stems and leaves attached, and other fruit and produce.

"What does she do with persimmons? I don't think I've ever tasted one."

"Well, you'll get to taste and cook with them this afternoon. You and I will be making a cranberry and persimmon tarte tatin. It's a tradition with this family and very yummy."

They walked over to the café to join the men. Pierre noticed them walking up and quickly left his seat to join friends at the bar as Olivier waved them over.

Making their way through the crowded room, Nora asked Chloe, "Did you happen to see Pierre beat a hasty retreat as soon as we walked in?"

"Yeah, I did. Too funny," Chloe replied. "Never mind. It seems to be more relaxing without him when you're around. I still think you can find a way to change the situation. Maybe talk to him a bit more."

"I can't force him to talk to me. He simply doesn't want to. Although he was surprisingly gracious telling me about their crèche. I could tell how important it was to him. He went into so much detail about each santon and how its personality fit into village life. It was very considerate of him."

"Well, see?" Chloe said. "Cut him some slack."

"I don't think I've done anything wrong, but I keep putting my foot in my mouth. I feel badly that I've brought tension into the holidays," Nora said.

"Mom! It's not your fault he's being a dork. Who knew he

would act even more grumpy with you here? It's crazy. But you know Oli and I have our theory about him—he thinks you like younger men because he saw you with Luc. And that reminds him of Angelique and then he gets pissed off. We just ignore him when he's not being nice, and he usually comes around ... or not."

Nora let the subject go and indulged in a decadent chocolat chaud—avec chantilly—the latter at the insistence of Papi, who once again went out of his way to make her feel welcome.

Olivier explained Pierre had gone to have lunch with some friends who would drive him home later.

Chapter Twenty-Five

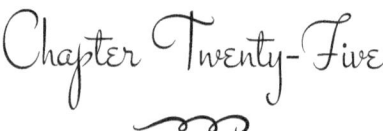

CHLOE AND NORA HELPED MAMI SET THE TABLE IN THE afternoon with three white tablecloths layered over each other, each representing a layer of tradition and reverence. On that they set three silver candlesticks representing the past, present, and future. Chloe continued to explain everything they were setting up. This trio not only evoked the passage of time but also reflected the Holy Trinity, blending Catholic symbolism. The shape of three round loaves of bread symbolized eternity and abundance.

Sprigs of fresh holly they had brought from the market were scattered about —adding a festive, natural touch connecting the sacred with the seasonal.

"See, mom?" Chloe asked. "I always was a good student, right? And I learned all that in French." She finished with a smug grin that made Nora laugh and reminded her of times past. She pulled her daughter to her for a warm hug.

Everyone, including Pierre, stepped forward to light candles on the sapin de Noël and they collectively gasped at the effect as lights in the house were dimmed.

"We gasp like this every year," Mami said as the others agreed. "But it is just so beautiful, and we think about previous generations who lived by candlelight. Imagine how that was."

They made themselves comfortable in the salon. The candles on the tree lit the room, casting soft shadows and creating such an intimate ambiance. Each took a turn handing out les étrennes—small gifts. Chloe and Nora had shopped for theirs together, and Nora understood that the gifts were not extravagant, just things like books, lotions, sweets, candles, lavender sachets, and santons.

Pierre had brought gifts from Normandy: mini bottles of Calvados, the famous local apple brandy, and the famous Caramels d'Isigny, which made everyone very happy. Nora watched as his stiff demeanor softened and became warmer every so often. She saw hints of something he seemed to keep hidden from her.

All gifts, no matter how small, were graciously received with warmth and laughter. It was the giving and receiving that brought everyone together.

Before they sat down to eat, Papi announced it was time for the cacho-fio. He, being the eldest, and Chloe, being the youngest, carried a log together around the table three times and then lay it in front of the fire. Pierre sprayed it with wine three times.

Nora was enchanted as the family, including Chloe, sang a Provençal song which, they explained later, celebrated the beginning of the festivities and wished good luck to all. The log was laid in the fire by Oli and meant to burn for three days. It would be removed each night so it would last.

Three saucers of le blé de la Sainte Barbe were placed on the table. A vacant chair symbolized that a guest was always welcome.

Le Gros Souper was exactly as Chloe had described, simple and reflective of the solemnity of Christmas Eve.

Papi asked them all to join hands once they sat around the table so he could say grace. Nora was between Pierre and Papi, and she noticed the difference between holding hands with each of them. Papi squeezed her hand warmly while Pierre held Nora's hand lightly with his fingers, as if it was a dead bird.

Nora knew Chloe was taking it in and didn't dare look at her, otherwise they would have struggled to hold in their laughter. She hoped Papi's grace would be brief.

"We give thanks for this meal and for the joy of sharing. It is our pleasure to welcome our dear Chloe's mother, Nora, to our home in Provence and we hope she returns often."

The 'amen' from everyone was hearty, except from Pierre who muttered his. Olivier shot him a look which went unnoticed by the others except Nora and Chloe, who smothered smirks.

They lingered over each flavorful dishes, making their way through vegetable soup, spinach omelette, au gratin potatoes, salt cod, escarole salad, and artichokes with anchoïade, an anchovy sauce that Nora discovered was also very good on bread. Everything was served family style.

Pierre seemed to relax and genuinely smile as wine glasses were refilled and they all relished the meal.

Mami explained they wouldn't remove the tablecloth until after Mass and the leftovers and crumbs were to be left on it.

"Another tradition," Chloe whispered to Nora. "Just like the vacant chair, this is left in case the spirits of departed loved ones visit while we're out."

They looked at each other for a moment, knowing her explanation had brought thoughts of Jeremy. Their embrace lingered full of unspoken meaning.

"He would have loved all of this," Nora said, "And been so happy we're together in your new life."

Their eyes glistened.

When Nora asked Chloe why they were leaving for Mass an hour early, her daughter gave her a knowing look and said, "You'll see."

They arrived at the ancient stone church, just minutes away, and already there was a hushed crowd of all ages by the front door. As they inched closer through the crowd, Nora saw a life-size crèche with people dressed to tell the story of the nativity.

"It's a great honor in the village to take part in this crèche," whispered Olivier, who stood next to her. "All of our family has participated through the years."

After a few minutes the gathering parted, and three men and one woman walked to the nativity scene leading a lamb. They took their places in the setting just as the three wise men arrived bearing their gifts. A donkey and two goats had been placed in the crèche. The choir gathered around with lit candles and sang Provençal carols.

Nora had never seen anything like it and was overcome by the solemnity of it all.

When the choir finished singing, the congregants entered the church, which was filled to standing room for the entire forty-five-minute service.

As they left, Nora told Chloe she had been moved to tears several times. "The a cappella singing of the choir was so emotional."

"I agree. The first time I experienced this, I couldn't stop crying. It was embarrassing."

Pierre had joined them in church and he looked at her just as she blew her nose. "Oh great," she muttered to Chloe. "He's caught me looking like an idiot again."

Back at the farm, the first white tablecloth was removed by gathering each corner. Chloe took it out the kitchen door to the field, where the crumbs were shaken out to ensure a good harvest for the new year. Nora loved all the traditions.

Les Treize Desserts were ceremoniously set out. For the final sweets, Nora's cranberry and persimmon tarte tatin held a place of honor next to Mami's traditional bûche de Noël.

The tarte tatin was a hit and Nora breathed a sigh of relief. Mami praised her for her first-time contribution, and included a compliment to Chloe, who had given Nora directions. Nora thought Mami's pastry dough was the crowning ingredient and she hoped to get the recipe.

The highest praise was for Mami's chocolate bûche de Noël,

stuffed with mascarpone whipped cream and tender chocolate sponge cake, all covered with whipped chocolate ganache. Chloe explained Mami had made it every year since she and Papi were married, without any change to the recipe.

Nora's mouth tingled with pleasure as the silky, smooth flavors rolled across her tongue. "Mami, this is truly the most delicious dessert I have ever tasted," she murmured. "I don't want it to end."

There were smiles all around the table. Olivier said, "Nora, we love to be here when a new guest is served Mami's bûche de Noël because the first reaction is always just like yours. We wait for it. It never fails."

As they began to tidy up, Pierre asked Nora if he could let Atticus go out with Fantôme for a quick run. It was almost two in the morning, and he said he would stay out with them. She agreed, confident nothing bad would happen to Atticus with Pierre watching.

When they'd first arrived, Nora had noticed how Fantôme responded immediately to Pierre's loud, sharp whistle and wished she could whistle like that too. When she'd mentioned to Pierre earlier in the day how much she admired his skill, he had given her a crooked smile, which made her slightly embarrassed, like she'd said something stupid to him.

If only he realized how honest she'd been. If there was one thing she had wished for her entire life, it was to be able to give a sharp, loud whistle through her teeth. Every attempt produced nothing but a sad little raspberry sound and a spray of spit.

Once the dogs were back in the house, wishes of Joyeux Noël were shared again, and they all went to their bedrooms.

Nora lay in bed contemplating the busy events of the day, overwhelmed by the emotions aroused by all the traditions she'd experienced. She felt full, not just of delicious food, but also of warmth, well-being, and pleasure. She was soon fast asleep.

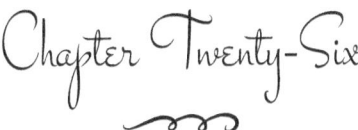

Chapter Twenty-Six

THE SMOKY, COMFORTING SMELL OF THE WOOD FIRE IN the kitchen wafted up the stairs. Nora awakened with a smile as she breathed it in. She loved the smell and the memories it evoked; it took her right back to her childhood cottage days.

She'd always been a fresh-air sleeper, so the French doors to her balcony were open slightly, and the sound of water trickling in the fountain on the terrace was pleasing.

Atticus gave a loud yawn as he stretched in his bed. Nora assumed he shouldn't sleep on the guest bed, but she couldn't help herself for just a quick snuggle. She patted the comforter beside her, and sensing her permission, he leapt up for a morning nuzzle.

He had become such a loving companion, something she hadn't considered might happen when she'd first arrived to stay with him. She had hoped they would be friends, but somehow a Doberman had never given her warm fuzzy feelings. How wrong she had been.

The sounds of clinking dishes and cutlery reached her ears, and suddenly the enticing smell of fresh coffee wafted into the room. The combination caused her to hop in the shower, dress quickly, and go to the kitchen to see if she could help. Atticus led the way downstairs.

Mami stood alone by the sink, and a roaring fire was going in the hearth. "Joyeux Noël, chérie," she said. "Papi and Pierre are down with the goats, and Chloe and Olivier have not been seen yet."

"Joyeux Noël, Mami." Nora sat down at the old wooden table. "The kitchen feels so cozy and inviting with that beautiful fire."

Placing a large ceramic cup of café au lait in front of Nora, Mami smiled and said, "I took a guess you might enjoy this with breakfast. I like to wait a while for my espresso."

"Merci! I do too," Nora said. "May I help you with anything?"

Mami sat at the table with her. "Non, merci. Everything is under control, and I want all of you out of the kitchen this afternoon. Usually there is a hike planned, and I believe I heard Pierre discussing it with Papi earlier. You need a big appetite for le Réveillon!" she finished with a chuckle.

"So I understand," Nora replied, wondering how she could possibly eat anything more.

"But this is it today! After this feast, we will return to our normal diets. Grâce à Dieu!"

Nora laughed with her, just as Chloe and Olivier came into the kitchen.

"What's so funny?" Chloe asked.

"Mami assured me they don't eat like this all year round."

"Wait until tonight!" Olivier said. "Then you will truly need a rest."

Mami had put a plate of warm Madeleines on the table, fresh out of the oven. The easily recognizable scallop-edged French butter cakes were a favorite of Nora's.

"Chloe, do you know Starbucks sells these at home? But they're no comparison to the real thing," Nora said. "Mmmm, Mami, these are so good!"

"I will give you my recipe, ma belle. They are easy to make."

Mami placed a bowl of fruit on the table, as well as a basket with fresh breakfast pastries and baguette.

"I see dad did his usual quick boulangerie run this morning," Oli observed.

"Bien sûr!" Mami replied, just as Pierre and Papi walked in the door, followed by the dogs.

The men spoke quickly in French and then Chloe burst out, "Ohhh, les chevreaux! Les bébés chevres! Oh Mom! You are going to go crazy when you see them!"

Nora couldn't quite sort out what the excitement was all about. Pierre explained in English, "We have some new baby goats in the barn. They are just a few days old and—"

Chloe cut him off and said, "And sooo cute and hilarious! You'll die laughing! Can we go down?"

Pierre glowered at her for interrupting, and she quickly apologized. "Désolée, Pierre. I get so excited when there are babies while we're here. I can't wait for my mom to see them."

"Of course. Have something to eat first," Olivier said. "I have to make some phone calls right now, but Dad said he will go to the barn with you. Right, Dad?"

Pierre nodded and turned his back to get some coffee.

Olivier continued, directing his words to Chloe and Nora. "And if it is all right with you both, we have a hike planned for this afternoon in les Alpilles. You know how Mami doesn't like us in the kitchen while she cooks for le Réveillon."

Chloe looked at Nora. "Also, Mami's two besties, Suzanne and Nicole, will be here in the kitchen with her. They're a fierce trio and the meal will be outstanding. Papi and Henri and Joseph will play cards, that's how they help. Trust me, it'll be a party waiting to happen when we get back."

Nora watched Chloe, who was hardly able to contain her excitement as she quickly ate her croissant and jam. Nora gave her a light kick under the table and discreetly nodded to Pierre, who sat at the other end of the table sipping his espresso. Chloe seemed to get the message that she had to wait until he said he was ready.

Nora timed finishing her café au lait to coincide with Pierre putting down his empty cup. He looked at their plates, checking to see if she and Chloe were through with breakfast.

"Eh bien! Allez zou! To the barn!" he said.

Nora was happy to hear a cheery tone to his voice.

Leaving the dogs inside, they walked to the first stone barn, not far from the house. The outer double doors were open and behind a wooden gate, which prevented animals from getting out, just inside the barn, chaos ensued.

"We have twelve babies," Pierre said to Nora. "They were born in the last few days and are just figuring out how their legs work. Chloe is right. They are very amusing."

In among the mother goats, the tiny, furry babies bounced and hopped around—on and off hay bales and into each other. They seemed to be leaping, twisting, and sprinting for no reason other than pure joy.

Often they got knocked over, and it took a moment for them to figure out how to get back up. Once they did, they went right back to being airborne again. Playful little bleats filled the air.

Chloe and Nora couldn't stop laughing and taking photos. Even Pierre looked entertained.

"They look like they have springs on their feet. I've never seen anything like it," Nora exclaimed when she caught her breath. "And what sweet faces! Oh, they are so cute!"

"Yes, they are pure delight. So innocent," Pierre agreed. He flashed what Nora thought might be the sweetest smile she had seen since she met him.

Pierre opened the gate and invited them to join him with the goats. They were immediately mobbed and spent the next half hour petting and cuddling the squirmy, lovable bundles of fluff.

"They're so soft!" said Nora.

They also got jumped on, and more than once Nora almost lost her balance. The nanny goats demanded their share of attention as well, with not-so-gentle nose bumps.

Laughing until tears rolled down their cheeks, Chloe and Nora took selfies and videos, many with goat noses pressed right up to the camera. The furry actors were endlessly curious and not camera shy in the least.

"Wait until the Girls see these! They are going to die." Nora couldn't wait to text her friends.

As Chloe and Nora played with the goats, Pierre busied himself at the back of the barn, organizing feed and other supplies. But from time to time, he came in to interact with the goats too. Nora thought it was sweet that he knew all the nanny goats by name and when he wasn't looking, she snuck a shot or two of him for the Girls.

While the kids began literally falling over and dropping off to sleep, Nora agreed with Chloe's suggestion that it was time to go back to the house and get cleaned up.

"Pierre, thank you," Nora said, brushing hay and dirt off her jeans. "This was the most fun I've had in years! What an experience."

He flashed a glimmer of a smile and nodded in acknowledgement.

"I loved every minute with those little cuties," Chloe babbled. "I'm so glad you were here to see the kids, Mom!"

Chapter Twenty-Seven

THE AFTERNOON HIKE TOOK THE GROUP OF SIX HIGH into the rocky pathways of the Alpilles. The sky was bright, the purest of winter blue, scrubbed clean by a recent mistral, Pierre explained. The temperature was just chilly enough to be comfortable.

Jean-Marc and Lucy, the son and daughter-in-law of Suzanne and Henri, had also come along for le Réveillon. They brought their little Corgi, ChouChou, and his efforts, thanks to his very short legs, to keep up with Atticus and Fantôme amused the group. It was hard to know whether the dogs or the humans enjoyed the hike more.

Olivier explained because the trail was not one of the official sentiers and only used by locals, the dogs were allowed to run free. Otherwise, they would have had to be leashed.

"We prefer these trails we know so well, where they can have fun too and we don't run into many people. The regular hiking trails are getting crowded," Pierre added.

"Atticus is going to miss all this freedom when I take him back to the city," Nora said. "It's so much fun to see how happy the dogs are here."

Lucy agreed, explaining ChouChou had to go to doggy

daycare several days a week, so coming to the country was a big treat for him.

At times, the trail wound through dense pockets of low-growing shrubs—thyme, rosemary, wild lavender—their oils laced the air with sharp, pleasing scents. Even more so, as dogs or people stepped on them.

"It's instant aromatherapy," Nora said. She plucked a few sprigs of the plants, squished them gently between her fingers, and lifted her hand to breathe in the sharp, earthy fragrance. "Mmmm, heavenly."

"Yes, those plants are called the garrigue," Olivier told Nora. "And watch out for those pointy-leaved boxwoods. They can give one a nasty scratch."

There were breathtaking panoramic views far across the countryside that demanded they stop to take photos and enjoy the beauty of the winter landscape. Like a vast patchwork quilt, vineyards, orchards, olive groves, and fields waiting for spring planting spread into the distance.

At the end of their two-hour walk, the hikers were welcomed back at the farm with a party scene on the terrace, which was warmed by propane heaters. Atticus and Fantôme rushed ahead to greet two new canine visitors.

The hikers had been invigorated by the exercise and the crisp clean air up in the hills, and there was no shortage of enthusiasm for food and drink. Everyone quickly blended together and animated conversation flowed and laughter frequently erupted.

A copper pot of mulled wine hung over a wood fire, and several adults sat and stood around it. Neighbors had dropped by, bringing platters of seafood, including one heaped with a glistening selection of oysters. The table became filled with an array of wooden boards: some offered homemade pâté and terrine forestier as well as fois gras and fig jam, alongside crisp crostini.

Others featured bowls of olives and an assortment of young and old local goat cheeses accompanied by honey and slices of baguette.

Nora was aware Pierre had been involved in organizing the appetizers and watched as he was helpful to his parents and hospitable to everyone. His short temper, gruff replies, and air of irritation were nowhere on display now. She made a point of keeping out of his way but wondered why he was such a conundrum, with his fluctuating moods. Although he only seemed to be grumpy around her, and not so much when others were around.

As the sun set, everyone went inside to enjoy le Réveillon. Two tables had been set in the dining room to accommodate them all, and the food was placed buffet-style on the long sideboard. Main dishes included roast turkey stuffed with chestnuts, rabbit stuffed with olives, leg of lamb with rosemary, and a daube provençal, a hearty red wine stew. Vegetables included gratin dauphinois, green beans with garlic, and roasted root vegetables. Guests had brought another bûche de Noël, and Nora swore the cheese board was the most abundant she had ever seen.

Nora had been to many dinner parties through the years, but none like this. She discreetly took photos to send to the Girls. Chloe hadn't exaggerated when she'd described it as a feast, and yet it did not seem extravagant, just one delectable dish after another. Good will and laughter filled the room, and Nora stumbled in French while others did the same in English.

The atmosphere seemed unhurried and grounded in tradition, reunion, and joy. Nora's heart was full as she observed how Chloe was embraced by the family and their friends. She loved her daughter's life in France and was grateful to feel welcomed into it.

She couldn't say she had warmed up to Pierre, but she saw his edges soften. He was relaxed and friendly with all the family friends, even if his interactions with her were infrequent.

Mami and Papi Moreau had brought her the greatest joy. They seemed to live each day so openly and honestly, as if it were second nature. The way they listened to each other, leaned in when the other spoke, and smiled like they'd been smiling at the same face for a lifetime and still hadn't tired of it—it was the kind of happiness that made her believe in lasting love. She had believed in it once, when she lived it with Jeremy. It just hadn't lasted as long as it should have.

She often reminded herself she was lucky to have lived it for as long as she had. Some people never got to experience it.

So now it was the kind of happiness she often wrote about in romance novels under her pen name. The kind of happiness she never expected to find in her own life again.

By the time all the good nights were said, and the dogs had been brought in for the night, Nora couldn't wait to sink into a hot bath before falling asleep. Her heart was full, not to mention her stomach.

She thought about a few quiet conversations that had occurred on Christmas Day, moments which unexpectedly revealed more about Pierre. It was fascinating to learn pieces of his history, each one adding depth and clarity to the larger picture of who he was.

Chloe and Olivier had had several conversations with Pierre about their exhibit at his gallery in Nice. It would be their first exposure in the south of France, and they were excited about it.

Mami and Papi were interested in hearing all about their work and the exhibit and promised to visit Nice when it was on. "It is just a few hours' drive from here, and we love going to visit Pierre, which we do several times a year."

"Always in the off-season," Mami explained. "We avoid those hot summer months and all the tourists. Although we loved taking dips in the Med and partying with the crowds when we were young!"

"But wait," Papi added, laughing. "When we were young, there were no crowds there!"

Nora learned from these chats that Pierre had been a serious artist in his youth but gradually had become more interested in discovering and supporting up-and-coming artists rather than promoting his own work.

Eventually he'd opened his own gallery, and his timing was perfect. The south of France had always been a haven for artists throughout history, and in the 2000s the arts life in Nice blossomed. Since the Covid years, it had virtually exploded with exciting new artists bursting onto the scene, and collectors made the Riviera the place to discover them.

Plans had been made for their departure the next day, and she drifted off to sleep thinking it would be nice to stay at the mas longer.

She, Chloe, and Olivier planned to take the train back to Paris the next afternoon. Pierre was also leaving at the same time, in his van, to return to Normandy for a week. Then he would go back to Paris to begin loading the artwork.

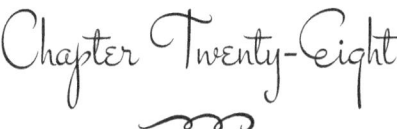

Chapter Twenty-Eight

NORA WAS SLOWLY AWAKENING THE NEXT MORNING, when Chloe knocked on her door and crawled into bed with her.

They both groaned and declared they would not eat for the rest of the week.

"Sweetheart, this was a Christmas to remember. Even after hearing about all the food and traditions from you in past years, it was truly something I could not have imagined. Thank you for convincing me to come to you for Christmas."

Chloe snuggled in as they held each other tightly. "It means so much to me to have you here. To Olivier as well. He often worries about having taken me away from our life in Canada, so it made him very happy to see how you've blended in with his family. He hopes you'll come more often."

They laughed when Atticus surprised them on the bed.

"I have to admit, I do feel right at home here ... and in Paris. Who knew dog-sitting could be so wonderful!"

As Chloe rolled out of the bed, she said, "Take your time this morning. Everyone will be moving a bit slower today. Pierre will drive us to the train. He said to be ready at three o'clock since the train leaves at four. See, I still prefer to tell time our way."

"Yeah, I have difficulty with that too. I hope we can go down and see the kids again," Nora said.

"Yes, definitely!" Chloe, so excited, let out a hushed shriek and threw her arms in the air. "Pas de question!"

Nora didn't feel right lounging about. She had a quick shower and packed her things, then went down to see if there was anything she could do to help clean up in the kitchen.

She stifled a chuckle as she saw Mami and Papi, both in aprons, busy wiping and sweeping.

"Please let me help. There must be so much to do after last night's wonderful feast."

"Ah, mais non, ma belle," Papi said. "This is part of my Christmas promise to Mami. Every year I am her assistant for the clean-up. In fact, I believe she made me promise it in our marriage vows."

He pulled out a chair and gestured for Nora to sit down in front of a place setting on the table. He moved the basket of breakfast pastries closer to her with a flourish. Mami was already preparing a café au lait for her.

Nora complimented them on their teamwork when they sat at the table with her. "You both are such inspirations."

Mami put her hand on Nora's and said, "It has been such a pleasure to have you here with us, and we hope you will return many times to enjoy the changing seasons of Provence. We love Chloe, and now we love you too. We are all family."

Nora squeezed back tears, not surprised at how emotional she was. "I cannot thank you enough for loving my daughter. I feel the same way about Olivier and am so happy they found each other. You have been so kind and welcoming. It's such a pleasure to get to know you as family and to share in the amazing traditions of Provence."

Mami's voice became solemn as she said, "Chloe and Olivier told us how you are helping an elderly woman in Paris record her memories of the Occupation. Olivier suggested we might describe to you how things were here in the countryside of Provence."

"Oh goodness. You are so thoughtful. But only if the memories don't cause you discomfort or sorrow."

Papi said, "The passage of time has eased the pain, and of course what we know we learned from our parents and extended family who lived through it before we were born. Two of my uncles were Maquis, killed fighting with the Resistance."

"Would you mind if I recorded our conversation?"

"Not at all. We are happy if this is helpful to you. We think it is wonderful you are helping the woman in Paris. These stories need to stay alive."

For the better part of an hour, Nora worked at keeping her emotions in check as these two dear people recounted what they knew. They told her stories of bravery and betrayal, which for the people of France were part of everyday life during those years.

Nora saw their eyes darken with memory. Papi's mouth tightened around words that still burned. She began to understand so much more about the scars that even the later generations carried.

They spoke of the strict rationing that began right away, and the ruthless treatment of Jews. At first, their region was under the rule of the Vichy France government—French officials who collaborated with the Nazis. They told her about their family's disbelief their own countrymen could turn against them.

They described how after 1942, Germany took over all control of the south, but this part of Provence was under Italian soldiers until Italy surrendered in November 1943.

"I remember my mother saying some of the Italian soldiers had souls and could actually show some kindness," Mami said. "But when German soldiers took over, cruelty one could never imagine became part of life."

Papi added, "Everyone was under suspicion, and no one was spared. Collaborators betrayed neighbors, sometimes with untrue stories, simply to gain protection. "

Nora saw grief flicker in the lines around their eyes. She looked down often and swallowed hard, fighting tears.

The stories continued. Farmers had to give over most of their harvests and animals to the German soldiers, leaving little for locals. Many schools closed, and children foraged in the forest to help feed their families.

The Resistance, the Maquis, grew strong in the forests and rocky terrain of the hills. Papi related a story passed on in his family of his grandparents hiding maquisards in one of their barns, beneath a trapdoor in a pigsty.

"It smelled so vile, they knew no one would suspect them of concealing anyone there. At times they even hid downed Allied pilots recovering from injuries, who were later led out of the country."

His voice trembled with pride when he spoke of how they risked death but felt it was their duty to fight back any way possible and defy the hated Nazis.

"It is difficult for us to feel the terror and despair of those years, but we know through these stories how brave they were, and our hearts still ache."

Olivier had come into the kitchen, and after listening for a few moments, came to the table and sat with his grandparents. He added some details of bravery he recalled being told as he was growing up. In particular, he told a story from a nearby village which featured a beloved statue of a drummer boy who had saved the town during the Napoleonic wars.

The Germans demanded everything metal, especially bronze, copper and brass. They looked for anything they could find, including statues, gates, and fences, to repurpose for war materials. Late at night over a period of days, at great risk, farmers dug a big hole in a field and the villagers joined together to transport the statue and bury it. After the war, it was recovered and joyfully returned to the village square.

"I've taken Chloe to that village square for coffee. You should ask her about it," Olivier said.

Chloe appeared in the kitchen, not realizing the serious nature of the ongoing conversation. "Pierre just texted that we should come to the goat barn now. The dogs are with him, and he's letting them go off for one more run before we leave after lunch."

Olivier opened his mouth as if to tell Chloe what they were discussing, but Papi motioned him to be silent. "For today, it is enough for all of us. Go now and enjoy laughter. Nora, we are grateful to you and appreciate your respect."

Nora's heart ached with a deep sadness. It wasn't just from the facts she'd heard, but also the overwhelming weight of the war's human cost. She'd had the same feelings when she spoke with Marie-Louise. It was almost unbearable guilt she existed in a world that had never suffered like this. There was a sense of helplessness in her. No words could bridge the gap between listening and having lived through it.

Mami took Nora's hands in hers. "Thank you for your desire to tell these stories, ma belle." Papi had his arm around Mami and nodded, his eyes reflecting his appreciation.

Nora had been working hard at holding back her emotions. Her voice was soft and reverent as she said, "Thank you for sharing this history with me. I am so humbled."

There was quiet in the room for a moment.

Mami and Papi shooed them toward the door. "We will have a light buffet lunch at noon with what you call leftovers from last night. Les restes is not part of our tradition, but Chloe taught us about it."

Mami gave Chloe a hug as she pointed her to the door. "You see, Nora, she has even taught me to hug."

Nora grinned.

As they walked to the goat barn, Nora took Chloe's hand. "Now, that conversation was seriously emotional. It was so good of them to talk with me about the past and so hard to hear it. To think this kind of horror went on everywhere we walked on our visit. To imagine what happened right here on this property."

Chloe said, "Yes, you are so right. It is so difficult to process.

I've heard stories through the years. It means a great deal to the French to make certain people from other countries, as well as the next generations everywhere, understand what happened. Thank you, Mom. I'm so grateful to you for helping in this."

The dogs appeared out of nowhere. Atticus ran up for some attention, and their mood lightened. A moment later, he and Fantôme headed off through the vineyard.

"He's going to find his walks back home terribly boring after the past few days," Nora said.

"No kidding! I don't think Giselle has ever had him out in the countryside before. She likes to stick to the city, but I know she takes him to parks a lot. Hardly the same as being wild and free here, though."

The kids put on their uproarious show for Chloe and Nora. "It's simply pure glee," Nora murmured. "I'll look at these videos when I need a laugh."

"You better send them to the Girls too," Chloe said.

"It goes without saying. Instant therapy is what this is!"

Olivier and Pierre had entered the pen and stood together behind the women. They chuckled at Nora's comments, getting the women's attention.

Olivier turned to Pierre and gave him a light punch on the arm. "I guess that's why we boys from Provence grow up to be such easygoing men. N'est-ce pas, papa?"

Chloe snorted, while Pierre knitted his brows and gave Olivier a questioning look. One of the nanny goats came up behind the men and butted each of them in the behind.

Then they all burst out laughing.

That's what goats do for you, Nora thought.

During lunch, it became obvious the dogs had not returned. Pierre went outside a few times to whistle for them but to no avail, which was most unusual.

As the time drew closer for them to leave for the train station, Atticus and Fantôme were still MIA. Chloe and Olivier stayed inside to clean up and bring down the luggage while Pierre, Papi, Mami, and Nora went outside to call the dogs. They walked in different directions to cover more of the area where the dogs might have wandered.

Nora became increasingly anxious about finding Atticus. There had been no reason to worry about him throughout their visit, since he had stuck by Fantôme, and they had always come home on their own or responded to Pierre's whistle.

The time came where a decision had to be made. Nora was now beside herself with concern. Atticus was her responsibility, and to think something might have happened to him was more than she could bear.

She told Chloe, Olivier, and Pierre they should leave for the train station because they had responsibilities back in Paris and Normandy in the next few days. Mami and Papi assured her she could stay as long as it took for the dogs to return.

She thanked them and promised everyone she and Atticus could take the train back to Paris on their own. She felt a bit of anxiety about the prospect, but quickly pushed it aside. Atticus had behaved very well on the trip down.

Chloe and Olivier were stressed about leaving without her. Nora put her foot down and insisted they let Pierre take them to the station.

Pierre said it wasn't urgent he go to Normandy right away, so once he took the young people to the station, he would stay as well. Then he offered to help get Nora and Atticus back to Paris on the train, or drive them himself. He insisted it wouldn't be a problem.

Nora tried not to show her surprise at Pierre's calm thoughtfulness. This was a reaction she had not expected.

Mami and Papi had planned to leave after everyone else to go to visit friends in Avignon for two days. It was decided they would leave now and drive Chloe and Olivier to the station, allowing Pierre to stay behind to continue the search for the dogs.

The four of them got in the car after assuring Nora all would be well, and Nora and Pierre waved goodbye to them. Pierre looked at her and suggested they think about a plan, but for now they should give the dogs another hour to show up.

For a while, Nora tried to read. Pierre busied himself around the yard and then asked Nora if she would like to go with him to collect eggs from the henhouse.

As well as becoming infatuated with goats, Nora had discovered she enjoyed the chickens too. She'd never seen eggs in such a beautiful palette of colors before; Mami's hens laid eggs in everything from dark brown to pale turquoise, plus soft green and olive green, in addition to the usual brown and white. The free-range birds wandered the gardens and had often followed Nora around when she was outside. She was surprised they paid no attention to the dogs, other than to occasionally antagonize them.

They opened each laying box to remove the treasures, and she was amused that Pierre knew all the hen's names. But still she couldn't stop worrying about the dogs.

As they walked back to the house with a full basket of eggs, Nora said, "I noticed you and Papi were having kind of a serious exchange before they all left. Obviously, I didn't understand a word either of you said, but I had a bad feeling about it. Was it about the dogs?"

Pierre looked hesitant but Nora held his gaze, unblinking. "I would like to know," she said, her tone calm but resolute.

"He reminded me that the neighbors two roads over used to hold a boar hunt every year at this time. He thought the dogs might have heard the barking of the dogs in the hunt and gone to investigate."

Nora stared at him, horrified. "Do the wild boars attack dogs?"

"Rarely."

"But it can happen?"

THE FRENCH EFFECT

"Please don't let your imagination get carried away. We need to be sensible," he said curtly.

Nora felt embarrassed ... again. "I just can't stop thinking of every terrible possibility." In her mind she pictured a horrendous scene and grew nauseous.

"You must stop. But I will go walk through the vineyard in the direction of the hunt and check things out."

"And I will go with you. I can't sit here alone."

He nodded. "I understand."

Dusk was beginning to fall so with flashlights in hand, they trudged through the fields and along paths in the forest. Pierre whistled every once in a while. After an hour or so, he said they should turn back.

"We can't really go any farther on foot. Let's go get the van and look down some of the roads a bit farther out."

Driving slowly in the gathering darkness, Pierre offered some other explanations as to what might have happened.

"People cooked outdoors over the holidays and the dogs might have been tempted by leftover food. We can't know. I'm certain there will be a reasonable explanation."

In his own way, he tried to reassure Nora, although she had a feeling he blamed Atticus, because Fantôme hadn't done anything like this before.

But he wasn't being unkind, and Nora decided she was paranoid and overly defensive.

For another two hours they searched, mostly in silence. They looked along the narrow country lanes, where they got out from time to time and walked into the forest to call and whistle. But there was no sign of the dogs.

As they drove through a small hamlet, Pierre pulled up in front of the local bar. "Come, Nora. We both need a drink."

Nora reluctantly followed him inside but said she would just have water. Pierre insisted. "Let me order something that will help you relax. Have you ever had pastis?"

She shook her head. "Never. I know of it, never tasted it."

Two glasses with an amber liquid arrived, along with a small jug of water and a bowl with a few ice cubes. Nora wasn't certain she had ever seen ice cubes in France. She watched as Pierre explained while he poured a bit of water into each glass, which turned the drink milky.

"Pastis is an anise-flavored spirit and is refreshing. As a writer, you would have read about absinthe, non?"

"Most definitely, particularly with van Gogh and so many of the artists of his time. I thought it was forbidden."

"It was and, much later, this is the replacement, similar but legal. I do not usually put ice cubes in, as I believe it dulls the flavor. However, some people prefer it. Try it and see what you think."

Nora put the glass to her nose. "It smells like black licorice, which I happen to love."

"Yes, it contains anisette. When it turns cloudy like that, we call it 'louche,' and it is ready to drink. Sip it slowly. I hope you find it soothing."

He touched his glass to hers and looked into her eyes. "To the dogs. We will find them."

The intensity of his gaze startled Nora, in a good way. Her voice caught as she softly repeated, "The dogs."

Black licorice had been a childhood favorite, and the velvety taste of the liquid as it slid down her throat appealed to her. In fact, it tasted delicious. "I'm a fan."

She couldn't stop saying how badly she felt and how she was responsible for Atticus, and how terrible it would be telling Giselle something had happened. She didn't want Pierre to think poorly of her—again—but she was having a difficult time holding herself together.

Pierre tried to comfort her, but she detected some impatience in his voice. "They will come home. I guarantee it."

The waiter arrived with a plate of ratatouille and crispy baguette for each of them. Pierre explained, "I thought we should eat something, and this is their specialty."

"Thank you for being so thoughtful. I really appreciate it," Nora said. A faint flush crept into Pierre's cheeks, and he looked away, as if awkward in his kindness.

Nora hadn't given any thought to food but realized she was hungry. The slowly stewed blend of eggplant, tomato, bell peppers, and zucchini was flavorful and soothing. Each spoonful tasted to her of something lovingly tended. *It's no doubt just my imagination, but that's part of why this dish is so enjoyable to me. I can picture the chef humming while he stirs.*

Once they finished eating, they agreed they would return to the farm and get up early to continue searching, if need be. Nora felt sad and discouraged but accepted they had done all they could for the time being.

When they drove up the lane to the farmhouse, Nora hoped with all her heart the dogs would suddenly appear in the headlights. But it didn't happen.

It was a dark, moonless night, which didn't help, and getting late. They got out of the van and stood on the terrace, perhaps both of them unwilling to go to sleep quite yet.

Pierre looked worried and paced back and forth. Then he said he had an idea and made a phone call. He spoke in French, then waited for a reply. After a minute and a terse goodbye, he hung up.

"I had a thought and called my friend, Jacques Delaurier, just one farm over. I know they roasted a lamb on an outdoor spit yesterday because we were invited to join them. Mami wanted us to stay here so you could experience our family traditions, and we all agreed. But it occurred to me that the dogs might have wandered over. He is getting his brother to help him check around their property. It's worth a shot."

When there was no response from the neighbors right away, Pierre said, "Let's go inside and wait. If we don't hear soon, I will drive over."

"Please don't go without me. I couldn't stand to wait by

myself." A tear trickled down her cheek, and she quickly wiped it away.

In the kitchen, Pierre poured them each another pastis and pulled out a chair for Nora to sit at the table. "Here, this will help ease your tension. I'm sure they will call back soon."

Chapter Twenty-Nine

NORA TOOK A LONG SIP OF HER DRINK AND SAVORED again how it was cool and velvety on her tongue. Then a sensation spread slowly across her chest—deep, warm and slow. Soothing. But not enough to quell her anxiety. Her feet shuffled nervously under the table and she took another long swallow.

"Pas trop vite, Nora. Not too quickly," Pierre cautioned her. "You need to lean into it. Let it calm you."

They sat quietly. Both phones pinged.

Chloe and Olivier and Mami and Papi had all texted to see if the dogs were home yet. Nora felt more and more despondent.

Then she lost control and burst into tears. "Oh Pierre. What if something terrible has happened? How will I ever be able to tell Giselle? How will she forgive me? How will I live with myself? I love Atticus too and..." Her voice trailed off, caught in deep sobs.

She wept, and Pierre looked at her uncomfortably from across the table. Getting up, he came around to her side and sat on a chair beside her. He put his arm tentatively around her shoulder.

"Là, là... Ne pleure pas. Tout ira bien ... je te promis. Don't cry, everything will be fine ... I promise you." His voice was soft and low, as if he cared.

Nora put her head in her arms on the table, and her shoulders shuddered as she tried to pull herself together.

"I'm going outside," Pierre said, giving her back a gentle pat.

Soon, Nora heard his whistles out on the terrace. She wasn't certain how long it was before he returned, but it felt like forever. She had wiped her face and blown her nose, thankful to be alone for it.

When Pierre came in, he said they probably should go to sleep and see what the morning brought, but Nora knew sleep would be impossible for her.

Suddenly the sound of a vehicle crunching on the gravel came from outside the house. Pierre leapt up and ran to the door. He shouted, "It is Jacques!"

There was shouting and a commotion, and seconds later Atticus and Fantôme burst into the kitchen, yelping and barking. Tails wagged in a frenzy of joy.

Nora got down on the floor with them. Her tears flowed freely as Atticus climbed on her and licked and nuzzled her, almost knocking her over. Fantôme joined in the celebration as Pierre knelt with them. It was clumsy, messy, and overwhelming, a tangle of fur and arms and happy chaos.

When he finally stood up, Pierre spoke to Jacques and a woman at the door who looked on in amazement. He invited them in and introduced them to Nora, who was still on the floor with tears pouring down her face.

Nora blubbered, "Merci, merci, merci," and tried to pull herself together as Atticus continued to climb all over her and cover her face in sloppy dog kisses. The thought did cross her mind briefly she might be embarrassing Pierre, but she didn't care.

"The dogs were shut in one of the outbuildings," the woman, Janine, explained to Nora in English. "I think they ate a lot of scraps at our place and lay down in there to sleep. Our brother did not see them when he closed everything up. We are so sorry!"

Pierre's face glowed with happiness as he bent over again and hugged both dogs. The corners of his shimmering eyes crinkled and his mouth curved into a gentle smile. He looked at Nora with an expression she hadn't seen before.

He gave her his hand and helped her to her feet. Caught in the moment, they threw their arms around each other ... and quickly parted. Nora continued to repeat her thanks to Jacques and Janine as she wiped her tears.

Pierre invited the couple to join them in the salon. He explained to Nora that he and Jacques had been close friends since childhood. Jacques' wife, Janine, was originally from Quebec and spoke English well.

Pierre stirred the embers in the fireplace and laid on kindling and a log. They settled comfortably and enjoyed easy conversation about the holidays. Pierre poured more pastis. The dogs collapsed on the floor.

When Jacques and Janine left, it was well past midnight. They exchanged warm bises with Pierre and Nora and insisted Nora visit them the next time she came to the Moreau's.

Nora took a moment to sit back down on the couch and respond to texts from Chloe. Pierre had sent everyone short messages to say the dogs were home and fine, but Chloe wanted details.

Pierre refilled their glasses and sat with her on the couch. He seemed as relieved as she was that the evening ended well, and told Nora some amusing stories about adventures with Jacques from when they were growing up.

To her surprise, he even asked about Nora's life in Canada.

That was the last thing Nora remembered until she awoke on the sofa in the early hours of the morning, wrapped in a warm shawl. And in Pierre's arms.

Horrified, she desperately tried to remember what had happened after their company left. The dull ache in her head was a clear sign pastis had been involved.

She lay still for a few moments, listening to Pierre's steady breath. Slowly she slipped out from under his arm. He stirred, mumbling something indistinct, and Nora sat on the edge of the couch, waiting to see if he would wake up.

Nora studied his handsome face. His brow was smooth, missing its usual tension. She resisted the urge to gently kiss it. If only he looked at her like this. She stood quietly and covered him with the shawl.

Atticus followed her up to the bedroom and once she was in bed, he climbed up and plastered his back to hers.

Nora's emotions were in a tangle—relief that the dogs were fine; confusion about what had transpired with Pierre.

Will he be upset with me? Should I be upset? Did we kiss? Had there been more? Did I pass out like a silly girl? Or...?

Chapter Thirty

NORA AWOKE TO THE SOUND OF ATTICUS SNORING AND the enticing smell of fresh coffee. She became aware of a dull ache in her head and remembered how her evening had ended. Well, partly remembered. *No, I don't remember how it ended. I only remember how I woke up during the night in Pierre's arms. What I need to know is how I got there.*

That was the thought hanging in her head as she stood in the shower. Would he still be in the kitchen when she went downstairs? She wondered how she was going to face him ... but just for a moment.

Common sense kicked in and she reprimanded herself for such immature thoughts. *So what if we kissed? Why should I mind? I'm attracted to him, but I'm not looking for anything. I should accept whatever happened and enjoy it. He needs to stop being uptight with me and I need to stop worrying about it. We need to be adults ... and friends.*

Pierre stood at the counter, looking out the open kitchen window. Birdsong filtered in, mixed with the *tuk-tuk-tuk* of the chickens foraging in the garden.

"Bonjour," Nora said, hoping her voice came out as casual and cheery.

"Bonjour!" His voice sounded light as he looked at her with a smile she couldn't quite read. "Would you like a café au lait?"

Nora shook her head, relieved that Pierre seemed relaxed and maybe even more friendly than before. "Thank you, but I think I need a strong espresso this morning."

Pierre chuckled. "Aha, yes. Pastis can do that to us."

"So I learned," Nora said with a sheepish grin. "But it does so in a pleasurable way."

While Pierre made them both an espresso, Nora excused herself for checking her messages on her phone. "This is rude, but I've been waiting for something from Canada."

"Hey, it's what we do these days, isn't it?" Pierre replied.

Nora said her message had not arrived and put her phone down. "Guilty as charged."

Pierre's face betrayed no emotion as he handed her a steaming espresso and sat across the table from her. "Alors, all is good with the world again; the dogs are safe and home."

He raised his cup in a toast and Nora did the same. "Grâce à Dieu."

He passed the basket of pastries to Nora, and she asked if he had already gone into the village. "Of course," he said, with a smile. "It's also what we do."

She thanked him and put a pain aux raisins on her plate. They chatted about the stress of the previous day.

"Honestly, it felt like I lost my child," Nora said. "I might have overreacted."

"Not at all. It's how something so stressful affects us. The good news is it all ended well."

"Yes. Thank you for staying behind."

"Of course. It was the least I could do. Now we should talk about how to get you and Atticus back to Paris. I can put you on the train... Or if you can stand a longer trip, I will be happy to drive you back."

"Please, I want to do whatever is the least burdensome for you."

"The drive is about seven hours. If we leave soon, we can be there in time for apéros."

Nora laughed. "Hmm, I might skip that today. But I'm fine with going by car, and I'm happy to help with the driving. We can take shifts if you like."

"That's kind of you," Pierre replied. "I frequently drive long distances and don't mind driving to Paris. Pas de problème. I will stay overnight with Olivier and Chloe and then carry on to Normandy tomorrow."

They tidied up the house and loaded the van, and Pierre suggested they have one last peek at the kids and nannies before they left.

Nora wondered if this new side of Pierre's personality would last. *Seven hours in the van together will put it to the test.*

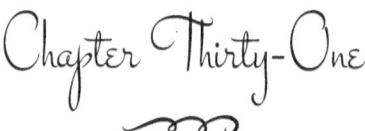

Chapter Thirty-One

SHORTLY AFTER THEY BEGAN THE DRIVE, PIERRE ASKED if Nora minded listening to music and if she cared whether it was French or English.

"Anything but rap," she said.

He frowned and said, "Non! That's my favorite."

For a split second, Nora thought her hope for them getting along might have already been dashed. He paused a moment for effect and then said with a smirk, "Not."

She laughed and told him, "The first thing I do when I get in my car is turn on my music."

He looked at her and smiled as he nodded. "Moi aussi."

They discovered they had similar musical likes and dislikes. He said he was impressed at Nora's knowledge of French singers and suggested they take turns choosing playlists.

Leonard Cohen was a shared favorite, though they debated which era of his music was the best. Their laughter grew when they discovered they were both fans of the soundtrack from *Saturday Night Fever*. Pierre arched an eyebrow in mock surprise when Nora admitted that The Weekend's "Blinding Lights" was often the go-to anthem to jump-start writing her rom-coms.

Seven hours in a van with a once-crabby-turned-moderately-cheery (and devastatingly handsome) Frenchman might turn out to be a test, but she felt it was off to a comfortable start.

Nora was glad her sense of humor was intact. She did enjoy road trips, and how could driving through France be anything but pleasing?

Atticus was definitely an icebreaker, although not in the best way in the beginning. The first two times he threw up, he quickly dispelled Nora's discomfort and embarrassment. He shared his affection with both of them and looked distraught when he was sick. Pierre seemed to respond to her sympathetic reaction to Atticus, and also displayed plenty of patience.

Fortunately, Pierre was a tidy person and had a box in his van with paper towels, cloths, and cleaning solutions. He insisted on cleaning up the mess each time while Nora took Atticus out for some air.

After the third incident, which seemed to indicate this happened every hundred kilometres, they discovered Atticus was just fine if he slept on Nora's lap. So, that was what he—all eighty-eight pounds of him—did. After a few hours, Nora wondered if she would be able to walk by the end of the trip.

When Atticus was awake, Pierre often had a chat with him. The dog looked intensely at Pierre, as if taking in every word he said. Nora told Pierre she thought they had developed a bromance. The term then required an explanation, which made Pierre laugh.

To her surprise, their conversation remained relaxed. Pierre seemed to enjoy sharing historical facts and local information as they passed through various départements.

He asked her what she liked about her life in Canada, and Nora asked him about growing up on the farm and how it compared to his life on the Côte d'Azur. He didn't venture to say anything about his marital history or divorce, nor did she mention being widowed. They stuck to light chatting about happy topics, and good background music filled in comfortable silences.

The look of disdain she had seen so often, or perhaps imagined, since they had met never showed itself. Now he radiated quiet, genuine interest.

Shortly after noon, he suggested they stop for lunch and turned off onto a country road. He told her about a tiny hamlet with an excellent kitchen in the local café. The road wound through gentle hills, occasionally passing a stone farmhouse, tucked behind a stone wall. Sometimes Nora could make out windows shuttered against the winter cold.

They arrived at a small square. Ancient stone houses huddled together, and smoke rose lazily from the chimneys. A weathered, hand-painted sign reading *Auberge du Coin*, framed by fairy lights and pine boughs, hung above the doorway of a public house.

A waiter greeted Pierre like an old friend. Pierre introduced Nora and Atticus to the affable owner, who seated them near the stone fireplace, which was filled with glowing embers. He spoke with them in French for a few minutes, and Nora felt pleased she understood the gist of what he said. *Maybe all my French Immersion lessons are kicking in.*

Their waitress moved a blackboard displaying the day's menu closer to their table. Before she took their order, she chatted with Atticus and asked them if she had permission to bring him a treat along with some water.

Pierre said the dog had not been well earlier in the trip and perhaps food wasn't a good idea. The waitress held up her hand and said she had just the thing in the kitchen to help him.

"This will be good for him, trust me," she said. "A little rice with ginger and a few small pieces of chicken."

Pierre looked at Nora, who nodded her approval.

"People treat their dogs so well in this country—I trust your advice completely." She smiled warmly at the waitress.

The plat du jour was confit du canard avec pommes de terres salardaises—duck confit with garlic parsley potatoes. When Nora said it was one of her favorite dishes, Pierre placed two orders. A simple green salad was served first.

The golden-brown skin of the duck was crisped to perfection, creating a savory burst of flavor right before tasting the tender, juicy meat. The potatoes were sautéed in duck fat, finished with garlic and parsley, and accompanied by a rich gravy.

Pierre gave Nora a satisfied look as they murmured their pleasure with each bite, but he frowned when she offered him the accompanying mushrooms. She had hesitated doing it but couldn't bear to see them go uneaten.

"I can't eat them," she explained. "I've some sort of allergy to them. I'd have to join Atticus in the vomitorium if I even taste one. Please, enjoy them."

A muscle twitched on Pierre's face, as if he couldn't decide whether to laugh or find her remark tasteless. But then he chuckled and shook a finger at Nora.

"You need to know that mushrooms are like a religion in France. You are missing out, but I'm the lucky recipient," Pierre said. He made the sign of the cross with his fork and accepted the food from her plate. "Mille mercis."

They toasted with their local red wine, which they declared delicious.

Food was the main topic of their lunch break, and Nora discovered Pierre had a fine palate and loved to cook. *What doesn't he do?*

Pierre also mentioned his parents had told him about their conversation with her about the war years. "They were touched by your interest."

"And I was touched by the stories of your grandparents' experiences. Do you know I've been meeting with Giselle's Tante Marie-Louise?"

He nodded. "Yes, Olivier told me."

"I hope to write her memoir, and the chat with your parents was most helpful in deepening my understanding of the time period. Of course, I've read about the war years in history classes and historical fiction novels, but hearing firsthand experiences is irreplaceable."

Pierre's face became solemn, the lines on his brow deepening.

His eyes flickered with emotion. His voice was quiet, edged in pride and pain as he said, "Our family was fortunate to survive... But surviving isn't forgetting. Some wounds never closed for those who lived through those years. My grandparents seldom spoke of those things to me. But I'm thankful they told the stories to my parents, who passed them on."

The waitress, who lingered at a discreet distance seemingly aware the conversation was serious, now appeared to take their plates and announce their dessert special.

"Crêpe Suzette," she told them.

Nora began to refuse, but Pierre reached over and took her hand. "Impossible! You have never tasted the way they make them here. You must have them."

Nora experienced a moment of surprise at the gentleness of Pierre's touch, which had been so completely unexpected.

The delicate crêpes were coated with a rich, orange-flavored butter and Grand Marnier sauce. Then the waitress ignited a ladle of cognac, with great theatrics, and poured the liquid over the crêpes to flambé.

They applauded, and the waitress gave a small bow as she proudly served them.

Nora was aware of Pierre's attention. She lifted a forkful of delicate dessert to her lips. The thin crêpe glistened with sauce—an irresistible combination of sweet and tangy with a faint crackle of caramelized sugar. Her eyebrows lifted and her eyes widened in sheer delight.

"You were right," Nora breathed with pleasure. "I needed these."

Pierre smiled with quiet satisfaction as he seemed to savor his dessert as much as Nora.

They relaxed with an espresso after the plates had been cleared, and Nora excused herself to find the ladies room. She discreetly asked the waitress for the bill, only to find Pierre had given her his card when they'd come in.

When she got back to the table, Nora graciously thanked

Pierre but also chided him, saying she had wanted to treat him as thanks for all his help and for driving.

He simply shook his head, saying, "Pas de problème."

The waitress wished them a bon voyage and gave Atticus a pat on the head as they left.

Nora thanked Pierre for the entire experience. "Out in the middle of nowhere! Amazing."

"C'est la France," he replied.

Nora thought to herself, *Or as Chloe would say, the French Effect.*

They chuckled about the garlic aromas they would have to live with in the van for the rest of the journey. Their comments now had an air of intimacy about them, and Nora felt even more of a cautious sense of friendship.

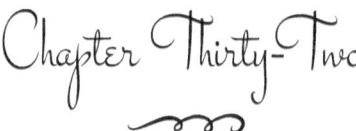

Chapter Thirty-Two

As Pierre had predicted, they drove onto Rue Lepic just in time for apéros at six p.m. When he turned off the ignition in front of her apartment building, Nora reached over and put her hand on his arm. "I can't thank you enough for everything. My visit to your family home was unforgettable."

He replied with the warmest smile Nora had seen from him. "It was a pleasure to spend time with you and so nice to know you as part of our family now."

"And I know Atticus is sorry about the vomiting," she added. Pierre gave her a rather puzzled look, and Nora wondered if she'd made another faux pas.

The dog's ears perked at the mention of his name, and he sat up on her lap where he had been sleeping.

Pierre gave Atticus a head scratch. "Pas de problème. I have grown to like this dog very much. There is a special aspect of sensitivity to his personality."

Nora, startled by his comment, said, "I guess I should apologize for being so hysterical when I thought he was lost."

Pierre shook his head. "Non! That was a time to be worried. As I was also."

"Your patience and help with finding Atticus are something I will remember always. Mille mille mille mercis."

Pierre opened the car door. "Je t'en prie. I'm thankful it all worked out. I will see you when I return from Normandy to load up the artwork. Chloe has been trying to convince me to stay in Paris for a skating party on the thirty-first."

Chloe and Olivier had been waiting in the apartment foyer and ran outside as the van pulled up. Nora had texted them along the way and given them a heads-up when they were about to arrive.

They joyfully greeted Atticus first, relieved he had been found. Then Chloe took charge of him as Olivier helped with the bags.

Pierre had a light overnight bag, as he planned to leave first thing in the morning for Normandy. Olivier gave an exaggerated show of staggering as he lifted Nora's bag. "How many santons did you buy?" he joked.

In the elevator, they chatted about the drive. Chloe stood behind Pierre and gave Nora questioning looks.

Arriving first at Nora's apartment, they were startled to see a dazzling floral arrangement in front of her door. Overflowing with breathtaking white amaryllis blooms, creamy peonies, icy blue hydrangea, and white roses, the effect was magical. It was highlighted by wintery details of frosted pinecones and long sprigs of juniper with blue berries and cedar boughs arcing outward. Wisps of curly willow rose above the florals and gave the whole thing a sense of windblown abandon.

"Oh my God," Chloe squealed. "How unbelievably beautiful! How did we not see this get delivered? It wasn't here when we went downstairs."

Oli reminded her they'd taken a box down to their cave, the underground stone storage space, before they waited in the foyer. "It must have come then."

Nora stood open-mouthed and a little embarrassed at the arrangement's extravagance.

"Mom! Open the card! Who on earth sent this?"

Nora put her key in the lock and pushed the door open. "Someone who knew when I was returning to Paris, for sure. I'll look once I'm inside."

She reached to pick up the arrangement, but Olivier insisted. "It's big. Let me get it."

Pierre left them and moved quickly toward Chloe's door down the hall. Chloe called out to him, "It's open!"

After Olivier dropped Nora's bags inside, Chloe suggested he join his dad and said she would be along in a moment.

As soon as he left, Chloe turned to her mom. "So? Are you two friends? Or more? Is there a spark there now? Seven hours on the road can be a challenge."

Nora's brow furrowed. "Oh Chloe, you still can't give that a rest? You really must!"

"I don't want to!" Chloe said, her pout returning. "I'm not giving up."

"I have to say, the trip was just fine. Pierre couldn't have been kinder or better company. We had good conversations, listened to music we both liked ... or at least pretended to. And he helped take care of poor Atticus."

With a look of concern, Chloe went over to the dog's bed by the window. He had gone straight to it and settled right in. She gave him a rub and murmured in a comforting voice, "Yes, poor baby. What a scare you gave us at the farm."

Atticus lay still. His ears drooped, and his eyes were without their customary brightness. His tail gave a few feeble wags. "He's certainly not himself," Chloe said.

"He's getting better now, thank goodness. Pierre thinks they ate scraps from the neighbor's lamb roast that didn't go down well. He checked with Denise, who is looking after the farm while everyone's gone, and Fantôme was sick today too."

Chloe grimaced.

Nora continued. "We had the most amazing lunch in a small café in the middle of nowhere. The waitress gave Atticus her special remedy for sick pups. It was very sweet of her, and I think it helped. And the meal! I'll never forget it. So, to answer your question... Yes, I believe we are friends."

"And he wasn't mean or grumpy?"

"Not at all. When we arrived here, he said he was happy to welcome me into the family. Which isn't mean at all, but it doesn't exactly sound like a love affair to me either."

"But look how jealous he seemed just now. He sure took off like a bullet when he saw these spectacular flowers!" Chloe said. "Ooo, open the card please."

Nora opened the envelope, which read:

Bienvenue chez toi et Bonne année! Vendredi, 3 Janvier, pour tango? Je t'embrasse chaleureusement. — Luc

Chloe read over her shoulder. "Oh, that man! How divine! 'Chaleureusement' is quite a romantic term! And tango again next Friday. Will you go?"

Nora's face flushed, which Chloe noticed. "You kind of like him, don't you? Can't say I blame you ... even if you are robbing the cradle. Maybe if it isn't Pierre, it'll be Luc who sweeps you off your feet." She giggled and pinched Nora's cheek.

Nora shook her head and threw her hands up in the air. She was not going to let Chloe's obsession with her love life irritate her anymore.

"My dear daughter, Luc is simply a good friend. Of course I will go on Friday. He's turning my stay in Paris into something I never imagined. And yes, he is younger than I am, but he doesn't seem to notice ... and so neither do I. He's looking after me as Giselle asked, and besides, I only have two more Fridays before she returns and I leave."

She decided not to mention she was meeting Luc for a tour of Notre Dame on the following Tuesday.

Chloe let out a soft laugh and threw her arms around her mother. "Who says you have to leave just because Giselle is back? Maybe you can rent the van Gogh apartment—that's what I call it. It's been vacant forever. Let's look into it! I can't imagine anything better!"

The suggestion stunned Nora. Staying longer in France had never occurred to her. But Chloe was right. There was no reason she had to leave in two weeks. And living in that apartment would definitely be cool. She still had a seed of a story she'd begun about the young artist, who resembled Vincent, and the waitress in Montmartre. She had just started it when she met Marie-Louise and got sidetracked. Maybe there were more stories to plan while living in that special apartment.

But she reminded herself she was not impulsive. She'd have to think about it.

Or maybe not. Maybe the French Effect was taking hold of her.

Chapter Thirty-Three

LONG WALKS WITH ATTICUS ON SATURDAY PROVIDED Nora with perfect writing breaks, since she was having trouble concentrating. Several times she stopped to rest. Bundled up and sitting on a park bench, she listened to the rest of her recordings with Marie-Louise.

Every session with her, and then going over their conversation later, provided an emotional challenge. Nora was transported back and forth from the Paris she loved to the terrible years of the Occupation. Without fail, the shift was jarring.

When she sat down to write in the studio, Atticus got up several times and leaned against her leg while she worked, as if he felt her sadness. She grew closer to him with each passing day. It was going to be hard to say goodbye.

She was almost caught up with transcribing her notes, and felt certain their next chat would edge close to being the last. Marie-Louise had reached the days when Paris hummed with barely-contained excitement—whispers of the approaching Allies had become louder. People hoped perhaps the war really would end soon.

Moving between the radiant Paris Nora adored and the bleak, suffocating years of the Occupation left her unsteady, as if her heart couldn't fully settle in either time. The joy of liberation was always shadowed by what had come before—the fear, the silence, the betrayal.

Reliving those moments was like crossing a fragile bridge between hope and despair, and the weight of both lingered long after she returned to the present. It was, in many ways, not unlike the intense grief she had experienced in the early months after losing Jeremy.

She was reminded of the calm support her dog Maggie had brought her. Now she experienced a similar relief from hugging and stroking Atticus. Eventually it brought her to a calmer state. If she was indulging in a Paris love affair, it was most definitely with him.

There was no question, she told herself, dog-sitting in Paris had evolved into something far more profound than she ever could have imagined.

It had transformed into a unique emotional journey through Marie-Louise's past, as Nora was drawn into the words steeped in heartbreak, resilience, and the haunting echoes of war.

But Nora felt other changes in herself as well. She'd fallen in love with Paris, Provence, the tango, and having a dog in her life again. She enjoyed life with Luc, as well as with Chloe and Oli. She was happy writing again and wasn't homesick for her little ski town, although she often thought fondly of her life there.

She considered all of that while she made herself a smoothie from the bag of fresh fruit she had cut up and put in the freezer. She felt overcome with gratitude at being so content, Going home after Giselle returned and her time with Attiticus was up, would send her off with a renewed attitude about living life.

Snuggled into the Moroccan cushions by the window, she gazed over the city. Atticus tucked himself beside her and Nora absentmindedly stroked his velvety ears. Her fingers moved in gentle circles and she stared off in the distance, lost in her thoughts.

She studied the sky and visions unfurled in her mind, delicate and slow-moving like the passing clouds. She loved her life at home, but these weeks in France had given her so much more than she'd anticipated.

She contemplated how France was rearranging her expectations of her trip —and perhaps, if she let it, her sense of self too. She wondered if she had settled too easily into life on her own in her small town back home. Maybe this trip had given her the nudge she needed to move forward and start a new chapter.

Maybe Chloe is right about me needing a change. She smiled at the thought that she might be feeling the French Effect, as Chloe put it. She thought about Luc's explanation of seduction and pleasure and realized she was beginning to understand it.

In the afternoon, Nora sat back down at her computer. If she stayed focused, she could get in another two hours of transcribing before the next walk.

She wrote far longer on the draft as the story took over. She loved how this happened when she wrote, as facts became more than mere details and led her fingers to words she hadn't anticipated. Even with the difficult subject matter, Marie-Louise's characters came alive and knew where the story should go.

Once in a while her mind wandered to Pierre's departure so early that morning. Chloe said he had left even before she and Oli awoke.

The next thing she knew, Atticus nudged her foot. Time for a walk.

While they walked, Nora's phone rang. It was Cynthia.

"Guess what? I'm in Paris," Cynthia squealed. "It was a last-minute thing. I'm only here for two days, as we have to be home for New Year's. Do you have room on your couch?"

"Omigawd! Cyn! Of course I do. What a nice surprise. What—"

"I'll tell you all about it when we're together. If you give me your address, I'll call an Uber and see you soon."

"Wait, have you had dinner?"

Cynthia replied she had not, so Nora said she would make a reservation while she waited for her to arrive. "What a fabulous surprise! Get over here!"

Nora was beside herself with excitement. *Trust Cynthia to just land here out of the blue. So typical of her.*

Within an hour, Cynthia had arrived by taxi. She dropped off her backpack, met Atticus, and raved about the apartment and the view. They popped in to see Chloe and Olivier, and now Nora sat across from her friend at a cozy bistro down the street. Atticus sat at Nora's feet, and Cynthia was telling her how the Italians were as crazy as the French about dogs.

"You are such a welcome sight!" Nora said, her eyes sparkling. "I've been having an amazing time, but it's even more fun to have you here. How did it happen?"

"First, let's take a selfie to send the Girls." Unable to stop grinning, they took a few, and the waiter stepped in to help out. They couldn't resist taking one shot that included him.

After a long sip of wine, Cynthia explained she had been in Lyon with three girlfriends. "They're in an English class I teach, and we've become good friends. Bella and Maria are Italian and from the area where I live. Salima is from Libya, and what a story she has. She arrived after a grueling, terrifying voyage on one of those overloaded, harrowing, migrant boats."

"I can't even begin to imagine how terrible that was," Nora said, her voice somber.

Cynthia nodded and told Nora some of the details of Salima's life: the risks, dangers, fears and courage. "We are all so glad we met each other and that we can help her settle into life in Italy."

"We have no excuse to complain about anything," Nora murmured.

They said nothing for a moment, lost in their own thoughts,

until Nora said, "But you still haven't explained how the four of you ended up here."

"We thought it would be fun to go somewhere for a few days after Christmas, since we were all on our own with the week off. We found a cheap flight from Pisa to Lyon. Maria has family there, and we rented an apartment that one of Maria's cousins owns."

Nora said, "Lyon is known as the Gastronomic Capital of the World, as I'm sure you're aware. I've never been but would love to go sometime."

"You should! I loved the city. It has great vibes. So, to continue…" Cynthia stopped talking and laughed.

"Bella argued that Paris should have the title of gastronomic capital, and when we realized it was only a four-and-a-half-hour drive from Lyon, without hesitation, we rented a car and were on our way to decide for ourselves."

"I can see you've found friends in Italy as adventuresome as you've always been." Nora chuckled as she raised her glass to meet the one Cynthia held up.

"Definitely! You will love them! They insisted that I connect with you tonight, and they checked into a hotel in the Latin Quarter. I was so excited I forgot to text you until we were already here. I wasn't thinking straight until we hit the suburbs. So, as you can see, it was spur of the moment… You know me!"

"I love that! Stay as long as you like. Chloe has a blow-up mattress we can use. You must see the fantastic Christmas decorations everywhere!"

"No, no." Cynthia put her hands up in refusal of the offer. "I love sleeping on couches, and with that view from yours, there's exactly where I want to wake up."

They both ordered moules et frites with curry sauce and talked nonstop. Nora plied her friend with questions about her life in Italy. Cynthia had originally gone to Italy to visit the seaside area from which her grandparents had immigrated to Canada. She had fallen in love with the coastal town of Cinquale and moved there a year later.

"Like I told you, moving there was the best decision I ever made. I love the village, the people, and the culture, and there are festivals every month! I do a bit of freelance online contract work. Between jobs, I live a peaceful existence, teaching English, fixing up my sweet little 250-year-old hovel by picking up treasures at markets. I love my new friends in Cinquale, but of course miss all of you at home. Thank goodness for video calls."

They smiled as the waitress quietly removed their bowls overflowing with mussel shells and brought empty ones that would soon be filled. Nora thanked her and asked her to tell the chef she thought he made the most delicious mussels in Paris.

"But enough about me. Tell me all about what's happening with you," Cynthia said.

The first thing Nora did was thank her.

"You know, it was that conversation I had with you in November, where you told me to take a chance and not miss spending six weeks with Chloe. It really put me over the edge. I grabbed my suitcase and packed."

Cynthia laughed and pumped her fist. "Brava, my friend! Isn't it fun to be impulsive? Which you never are... But from your photos, it looks like you're having a fantastic time. And Christmas in Provence? Bonus! Is Olivier's family nice?"

"His grandparents are a sweet couple and very welcoming. I would love to go back. Olivier's father is nice enough but still dealing with a five-year-old acrimonious divorce and has his moments. However, he was extremely kind when Atticus was lost and, really, he was the one who figured out where the dogs were. Man, talk about a stressful situation. I was a basket case!"

"It sounds like quite a trip."

"Seriously, all the holiday traditions were so touching, and it's a stunning part of France. Apart from the fact I ate nonstop for three days, it was perfect. Provence is magic in so many ways. And ... there were baby goats at the farm."

Cynthia's eyes lit up. "Squee! So cool!"

"Unforgettable! And really, I've been here for four weeks now and there hasn't been a day I didn't feel content. Well, except when the dogs were missing, as I said. And to top it off, I speak French most of the time! Such as it is."

"Formidable! I always loved that word in French. I'm doing the same with Italian. Total immersion is the only way. Although it can make for some interesting misunderstandings."

"You've got that right."

They shared some of their more impressive bloopers.

They had dressed for the cool weather, so they walked down to the small marché de Noël for a chocolat chaud after dinner. Cynthia described the holiday traditions she had discovered in Italy.

"Would you ever expect Italians to be playing bagpipes at Christmas?'

"Whaaa?"

"True fact! It's a beloved tradition. The Zampognari dress like shepherds in sheepskins and woolen cloaks, and they wear peaked hats. They play carols on what look like rustic bagpipe-type instruments. Everyone loves them!"

"I'll have to look them up," Nora said, but Cynthia pulled some photos up on her phone. "Take a look at the videos."

Nora watched a few short ones. "I'm enchanted! That's so sweet, in an unusual way... And loud!"

Cynthia agreed. "Always very loud. So Italian! To be honest, at first I thought it was a joke, but everyone adores them!"

She continued, adding, "The nine days before Christmas are called La Novena, and each day is marked by street performances and concerts. Children go from house to house, reciting poetry or singing carols, and collecting money for charity. On the first day, each family sets up its presepio, a manger scene. It's a pretty religious time, and everyone goes to church a lot."

They continued comparing experiences for a while longer until Cynthia began to apologize for stifling yawns.

"Oh my God, I'm sorry to keep you talking! You must be exhausted after the day you've had!" Nora said.

Back at the apartment, Cynthia stood in front of the floral arrangement with her arms spread wide. "This is magnificent! What's the story?"

Nora looked sheepish. "It's a bit over the top, isn't it? But also beautiful, and I convinced myself to simply enjoy it. I've never had anyone send me such gorgeous flowers."

"So ... tell me more," Cynthia pressed her.

"The arrangement was sent by Giselle's friend, Luc, who has taken me under his wing. He's in Mexico right now, visiting Giselle with his daughter. He's just a friend…"

"Hmm, that's not exactly a 'friendly' arrangement. Looks serious to me. If I wasn't so pooped, I'd beg for more details. Tomorrow, you have to promise to tell me more. Whoever he is, he has exquisite taste."

Nora nodded, happy to change the subject.

"But before we go to sleep," she said, "let me tell you something, in case I forget in the morning." She told Cynthia about the history of the van Gogh brothers living in the apartment next door.

"That's so cool! And it's the kind of thing that can only happen in Europe. Those kinds of stories just can't possibly be part of the history of a country as young as Canada."

Nora described having visions of Vincent—lurking in the hallway, drifting down the stairwell, and wandering all around the neighborhood. They grinned at the absurdity of it, but there was something oddly touching in the way Nora described it. "It almost feels like he is a lost spirit, and it inspires me to write."

"There's so much just in this apartment to set your imagination on fire. That beamed ceiling gives the place such atmosphere, and the view is to die for! Imagine Vincent being your neighbor. I love everything about this."

In spite of being tired, they talked well into the night, their conversation dotted with long yawns and lots of laughter. It wasn't only about catching up but also reflecting on the options available to them at this stage in their lives.

"It hadn't occurred to me that I might be a bit stuck in my life at home. I love living in our little ski town," Nora told her, "even though Chloe keeps suggesting I might need a change."

Cynthia's knowing glance indicated no need for words.

Nora continued, "Even on days when I don't do anything in particular here, I feel more alive and happier. Much of it has to do with this guy." She reached down and gave Atticus a scratch around his ears. He climbed onto the sofa and snuggled beside her.

"It's obvious you two have bonded." Cynthia chuckled and gave him a rub too.

"I adore him. Really, do we need much more company than a loving pet? I've been reminded of that here. I might even get a dog again when I get back home. A rescue, already trained. I don't think I could survive the puppy stage now."

Their chat moved to pets and memories for a few minutes, interspersed with even longer yawns and drooping eyelids.

"We better get to sleep," Nora mumbled.

Cynthia stretched and yawned again in agreement. "But it's so much fun to share these new experiences we're having. We need to video chat more often."

"Absolutely. I'll just end by saying that much of my happiness here has to do with people I've met who have passed on to me their passion for living in France. It's deeply contagious."

Cynthia was in complete agreement, saying she had the same experience in Italy. "We both know the kinds of choices we're making aren't open to everyone at our age, but they might be in later years. Change is good, that's the lesson I've learned. You don't have to move to Europe to do it."

"Although it doesn't hurt."

Chapter Thirty-Four

WAKING TO THE RINGING OF CHURCH BELLS ON SUNDAY morning, Cynthia and Nora agreed the sound was a favorite part of living in Europe.

They began the day by having crêpes for breakfast with Chloe and Olivier at the Moulin. After that, Nora gave Cynthia a tour around Montmartre as though she was a local.

"Wow! You know this neighborhood inside out and backward."

"That's because I've stayed here three times for a month visiting Chloe and Olivier. Walking is the best thing to do in Paris. The city really lends itself to exploring on foot."

When they stopped for a coffee, Cynthia said she needed to order a croissant too. "Italy has fabulous pastries, but I confess they don't make croissants as delicious as the French do."

"I couldn't agree more. I'll join you."

They took their time eating, savoring each bite. Cynthia gushed over the buttery goodness. The conversation returned to their late-night talk about living in Europe.

"I'm not saying I'll stay in my little Italian village forever. But for now, it's definitely where I want to be. If the graphic design company I worked for hadn't offered me a package after Covid eased up, I couldn't have made the move. Being able to freelance remotely changed the game for me."

Nora was quiet for a moment, processing those words. "I could do my work from here too. The real estate market at home is so hot that renting my house wouldn't be a problem. I've always enjoyed my visits to Chloe but never thought about staying for an extended time."

"Getting divorced and turning fifty-five also did it for me, if I'm honest," Cynthia admitted, her voice softening. "I'd spent so many years focused on other people—raising kids, keeping a marriage afloat, juggling work—and suddenly, there I was, standing in the middle of my life wondering where it had all gone. It was like time was passing me by, like I was watching it from the sidelines instead of living it. The realization hit me hard."

They sat in silence for a moment, before Nora spoke. "I hear you. I was feeling kind of invisible ... as we know journalists write about women our age. But, Cyn, you were always so positive. Of all our group, you were the one who kept us laughing."

Cynthia closed her eyes and rubbed her hands over her face, letting out a slow breath. "Right. I'm not saying I was depressed. I just knew something had to give ... big time. A real shift. You know how it is when the kids get going on their own lives, and you're left wondering what happened to yours."

Nora nodded slowly. "That was an issue for me too. I kept living in the past, talking about everything with Jeremy's ghost. These few weeks here have really helped me to get a grip on that. Of course, I still miss him terribly, but I'm beginning to realize this life—what's left of it anyway—is mine to live now."

Cynthia grinned. "Chloe whispered to me I should ask you about a certain someone named Luc."

"Ha! That girl is on a mission in spite of what I say to her. Chloe's waiting for me to be swept away by what she calls 'the French Effect'. She says I will know it, when it happens." With surprising ease, she told Cynthia about Giselle and Luc and all that had transpired since she'd arrived.

"Luc is the reason for that floral extravaganza."

"Oh wow, the man has taste! What an adventure! Dancing the tango—of all the sultry, romantic things—with a handsome younger man? No wonder you're falling in love with life here!"

"Chloe really hopes something will click between her hottie father-in-law and me. She's disappointed it isn't happening. I don't seem to be his type, and although he can be charming, he's got a grumpy side that isn't attractive."

They clinked their coffee cups together. "Here's to so many choices right now, and the courage to actually go after a few," said Cynthia.

"To be honest, this whole experience has been something of a reawakening," Nora said, her voice thoughtful. "I'd gotten comfortable—maybe too comfortable—at home. Change just didn't seem necessary anymore. But the kindness and attention I've felt here... It's stirred something in me. I've started to realize I need to be more intentional about my life and not just live out love stories by writing my rom-coms."

Cynthia reached over and took Nora's hand. "Brava! I told you, didn't I? Being in our fifties doesn't mean the end of romance. And romance doesn't necessarily mean a love affair with someone else. It could be with a new country! Perché no? Why not?"

They looked at each other and laughed.

"It's all about a new chapter, Nor," Cynthia added. "Stay open to it, bella—these moments are yours to claim. I mean, I love reading your rom-coms. But you need to write the story of your life now."

They met each other's gaze, and a quiet understanding passed between them as they exchanged a firm, encouraging nod.

Cynthia was also fascinated to hear about the writing Nora was working on with Marie-Louise.

"That's incredible. What a special opportunity to be drawn

into the history of those years by someone who lived it. Being exposed to the unfiltered truth about those World War II years... It's got to be both powerful and deeply sobering."

They sat in silence for a moment. Then in a quiet voice, Nora said, "Experiencing those years as a child is ugly, unbelievable, and deeply heartbreaking. It's devastating no matter who tells the story—but from a child's point of view, it feels even more raw. More immediate. Maybe because children aren't meant to carry memories like that. That's what strikes me most. Even though Marie-Louise speaks now as an adult, she's reaching back to her childhood emotions—and they still burn."

Their conversation remained serious as Nora opened up about the emotional strain of moving between the two timelines. She described how the past had come vividly alive when she went back to Marie-Louise's old neighborhood.

"I understand. We walk in the steps of history everywhere we go over here. When you hear true stories of events that occurred where you're standing, how can you not feel troubled? But this is part of the importance of telling these stories. I envy you, Nor. You are truly blessed to have this extraordinary experience."

Cynthia continued, saying, "You should come to visit me. The Germans were in Italy too, of course, but not for nearly as long as here. I see so many Italians who look like they are well over a hundred. There must be some unbelievable stories there too."

After lunch, Cynthia left to meet her friends at the Louvre and Nora made plans to rendezvous with them in the Latin Quarter for dinner. They hugged before they parted and agreed how they both did miss the Canadian hug in their new surroundings.

"After dinner, we'll go the Magie de Noël," Nora said. "So save room for an amazing selection of festive treats."

Nora worked on her transcriptions all afternoon, reorganizing and doing rough edits so Marie-Louise could see how her words and thoughts were being interpreted. Nora hoped Marie-Louise would help guide any changes she felt might be necessary.

It looked like the final draft would come in at around 25,000 words, which surprised Nora. She hadn't anticipated writing an entire novella but felt it had been necessary to justify the stories that Marie-Louise had shared.

Nora planned to show the work to Marie-Louise this week, and it felt like Nora's time in Paris was running out. Chloe's words to her about possibly staying longer and renting the van Gogh brothers' apartment regularly resurfaced in her thoughts.

Luc called to say he was back in the city. Nora thought it curious that his replies were quite short to her questions about his and his daughter's visit to Giselle.

"I will tell you everything when we see each other. Of course we have a date on Friday, but are we still fine for a tour of Notre Dame on Tuesday? It's our pride and joy, as you know, and the restoration is remarkable. Do you have other plans?"

"I have no other plans during the day and would be thrilled to do the tour. Chloe and Olivier have apparently made some plans for New Year's Eve, but I don't know the details yet. Otherwise, I am quite flexible."

"Magnifique! I will collect you at ten o'clock, and we can have lunch after, if that works for you."

"I'm already excited about it," Nora said. "See you then." He didn't mention anything about Tuesday also being New Year's Eve. But she was happy at the prospect of seeing Notre Dame … and even more so about seeing Luc.

Darkness had fallen when Cynthia texted they were heading to the Tuileries.

> Cynthia: We voted to skip dinner and want to eat our way through the market.

Nora called an Uber. She planned to meet them at the igloo-shaped Champagne bar.

> Nora: It's an easy place to find; it's sponsored by the famous Pommery Champagne House. We will take a coupe of champagne and get on the nearby Ferris wheel just before the top of the hour. That way, we can toast the show when the lights on Eiffel Tower sparkle.
>
> Cynthia: 🥂🥂🥂 Sounds like a plan!

The plan worked out, and they were all seated on la grande roue, plastic champagne cups in hand, as the Eiffel Tower twinkled in all its glory. Cheering and toasting, it was the first event of the fun-filled evening for the five women who were swept up in the festive charm of the season.

Cynthia's friends were good company and each one a very interesting woman. Nora wasn't surprised, as Cynthia always had a warmth that drew people to her. Her confidence, easy laughter, and genuine interest in others made people want to live more fully. Nora had always admired that quality in her.

"A girls' night out in any language is such a good time!" said Cynthia. It became the mantra for the night. The five women strolled through the market, laughing and savoring the magic of Noël. They sampled many of the different foods: escargots, roasted chestnuts, waffles, crêpes, sausages, cheese, and vin chaud, the best beverage on a chilly night.

Nora enjoyed the pleasure of the company only girlfriends could provide. It had been missing these past weeks, and she decided it would be nice to have from time to time. She vowed to make it a priority if she stayed longer in Paris. She knew there would be writing groups to join and made a mental note to look into that.

It was close to midnight when they finally bade Cynthia's friends goodnight, and at the apartment, it didn't take long for Cynthia and Nora to collapse.

Chloe had taken Atticus for his evening walk.

"We'll worry about tomorrow in the morning," Nora said. "Bonne nuit, ma belle amie."

"Dormi bene, dolce amica."

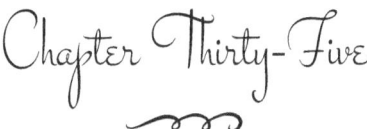

Chapter Thirty-Five

Two weeks left staying with Atticus

On Monday morning, Nora and Chloe met the other women at Angelina's in Galeries Lafayette for breakfast. The café's reputation since 1903 for chocolat chaud was not to be denied, Nora assured them.

The ladies' murmurs of delight confirmed Nora's proclamation. "We know chocolate in Italy, trust me, but this is hard to beat," Bella declared.

"And three cheers for the magnificent croissant," Maria said. "We don't make them this good in Italy."

"Here's a fact you may not have known," Nora said. "Breakfast really wasn't a thing in Paris until after the second World War. But even when it did start to be more accepted it was simple and carbohydrate based."

"I didn't know that," said Cynthia.

Nora added, "Really, it's only quite recently that English and North American bacon-and-egg breakfasts showed up here. Too bad I don't have time to take you to the Breakfast in America diner in the Latin Quarter for the best blueberry pancakes. Sooo not French but fun!"

Bella said to Nora, "In Italy in the morning, it's all about the espresso, biscotti, and cornetto."

"Which is?" Nora asked.

"The yummiest pastry," Bella said. "Kind of like a croissant but softer and filled with jam or custard. Or—"

"Nutella!" Cynthia interrupted and squealed softly as the others laughed and nodded. "I've become a Nutella addict!"

"Welcome to the club," Nora congratulated her.

Salima described her favorite Libyan breakfast. "Shakshuka! It's a dish of tomatoes, onions, pepper, spices, and eggs. A great way to start the day. But I might be persuaded differently by this French food."

They spent the rest of the morning picking up souvenirs and checking out the department store windows. The women separated for an hour of serious retail therapy before meeting back up and wandering over to the Marché de Noël at Place de la Concorde around noon.

In the afternoon, the visitors planned to take their time strolling the Champs Elysees and then grab the Hop On, Hop Off bus. They would end up in Montmartre so Nora could show them around.

"Cynthia fell in love with your neighborhood and insists we see it too," Salima said.

"With pleasure," Nora told them. "Let's meet at my apartment at five for apéros."

After a light lunch, Nora and Atticus arrived at Marie-Louise's door with gifts from Provence in her panier.

"Bonjour, Madam Bennett," Yvette greeted her. "Welcome back! Did you enjoy your fête de Noël in Provence?"

"Bonjour, Yvette. Thank you, yes. We had a wonderful family celebration, and—" Her response was interrupted by Marie-Louise calling them.

Yvette hurried into the salon with Nora right behind her. To their relief, Marie-Louise was fine. She apologized for calling out and beckoned Nora over for an extended bise, saying, "I simply did not want you to have to repeat yourself. We both want to hear all about your experience."

Yvette tut-tutted her. "Madam! You gave us a scare. I must attend to something, but I will be only a minute." She gave Nora a subtle eyeroll on her way out.

Marie-Louise patted the chair beside her. "Dis-moi, s'il te plaît. Tell me everything, please. I love Provence so much! Yvette, please stay with us."

When Yvette returned, Nora handed out her gifts of santons, sachets, and soaps, all of which had been beautifully wrapped in the shops or stalls, a French custom she admired.

She described how she loved all the festivities and traditions she had experienced.

When Nora rhapsodized about the meals, Marie-Louise burst into laughter and insisted on hearing everything in detail.

"Alors, what memories," she murmured many times, her voice filled with melancholy. "It makes me sad to think I may never go back there."

"Canadians like to say, 'never say never.' You may well go back again if you really wish to." Nora patted her hand.

"We say the same," Marie-Louise told her. "Ne dis jamais 'jamais.' How many times have I said that to myself or to others. But I feel now I must accept things I refused to before. Being ninety brings its own truths along with it."

Yvette quietly excused herself after thanking Nora for her gifts. As she left the room, she smiled warmly at Marie-Louise and said, "Now I want to go to Provence soon again too. Madame, perhaps we will go together."

"I am at an age where I must be realistic, ma belle," Marie-Louise called out after her. She turned to Nora and continued her train of thought. "There comes a time when we need to be happy with our memories and accept they are enough. This is where I find myself now ... and I'm content, although I have a few regrets. My advice to you is, try to live your life with no regrets. Keep making memories."

Nora reached over and gently patted her hand. "We have spent so much time talking about the worst time in your life. Today, why don't you tell me about some of the best? We can go back to the other memories tomorrow."

"Bonne idée! Let us linger on happy reminiscences today."

Yvette's timing was impeccable, and she brought in a tray with a pot of tea and still-warm scones, jam, and clotted cream. She suggested they move to a small table and chairs by the window. Once she had assisted Marie-Louise, she filled their elegant teacups.

Marie-Louise let out a quiet laugh. "Bless Yvette. I gave her a hint that I would like to share with you some of my history in England after the war, and look at this. She is so very thoughtful."

Nora knew Marie-Louise had been in England after the war, and this afternoon she would get to hear the details. As the older woman disclosed more information, Nora asked if she could record. Marie-Louise agreed.

"I am not going to speak of the last year of the war or the following months now. We can get back to that tomorrow. I want to tell you how and why I went to England." She rang a little bell hanging from her chair, and Yvette appeared right away.

After a few words of instruction, Yvette left and returned with a small wooden box, which she placed in front of Marie-Louise.

"In the summer of 1945, I turned thirteen. Life was still hard in Paris. Food was scarce, people were tired—of everything. There had been a lot of suspicion and revenge. I won't speak of that now. But around my birthday, a happy stage in my life began." She opened the box and took out a tattered envelope, from which she carefully withdrew a letter, yellowed with age.

"This letter was hand-delivered to my mother. We still did not know if my father was alive, and she was taking care of everything. The envelope was sealed. See? There is a little of the wax. It was very official and frightened us." She handed it to Nora.

Nora's hand trembled as she realized it was dated eighty years prior and it was from the French Government.

She handed it back, asking Marie-Louise to read it in French. She did, and then proudly translated it into English for Nora without looking at the paper:

In recognition of extraordinary service in the defense of France during the occupation, Mademoiselle Marie-Louise Tremblay is hereby invited to attend Kingsmoor School in Glossop, Derbyshire, as part of a program to restore the education of young patriots.

"Can you imagine how many times I have read that? I will never forget the first time ... and the second ... and the third. I did not really understand it. My mother had mixed feelings about my leaving. She was excited about the wonderful academic opportunity but so afraid of us being apart. When I discovered two of my friends had also been invited, I became all for it.

"Maman explained we would take a train to Calais and then a ferry to England. I had never been on a boat, and that part was a bit scary. I already knew what it was like to feel true fear, and this was not even close. Being parted from Maman was most scary of all."

Nora sat quietly for a moment, considering what a momentous journey the opportunity would have been for those children. But she also tried to put herself in their place. They had faced fear and bravery—and everything in between—for almost five years in the most extreme ways. She wondered how they could even feel anything after that.

She felt a lump in her throat that was hard to swallow.

As if reading her thoughts, Marie-Louise said, "Eh bien. There is much for us to talk about regarding this time, and we will save it for tomorrow. I just wanted to show you how I first got to England. Let us continue with happy memories now."

She carefully refolded the paper, put it in the tattered envelope, and returned it to the box.

"Before I knew it, Maman and I were on the train to Calais with five other children from Paris. There were no other parents, and I learned later I was the only one who still had a mother. A few had fathers, but they still could not travel and were protected. The only people I knew were my friend Nicole and her sister, whom I had met in school before the war. I did not know they were couriers too. Then there were four boys I had never seen before. My mother only went as far as Calais. A man in a soldier's uniform helped us board the boat and then remained on board with us."

"How did you feel about leaving your mother?" Nora asked, feeling a deep sense of sadness.

"I have often thought about it through the years. I have reached the conclusion that we were all accustomed to not showing emotion during the war. How sad is that? We children were more excited about getting ice cream on the boat."

"And your mother? Was she emotional?"

"She whispered she loved me and would be waiting for me to come home. We had held our emotions in check for almost five years. It was not easy to show them then."

"I can understand that ... but it is difficult." Nora put her arm on the table and her chin in her hand. It almost hurt to try to understand.

"We will talk about it more tomorrow. Now for the happy times. I am just going to tell you how the change began for me, and then we will be finished for today."

Nora sat up straight again and encouraged her friend. "Certainly, you should only share what you wish."

Marie-Louise sipped her tea. When she spoke again, her voice was quiet and solemn.

"What I want you to write about is the Occupation and the way some French children were affected. It does not compare in any way to the unforgivable treatment of the Jewish people. But it is important to share, and I thank you for helping me find my voice. My happy times do not have a place in this story."

Nora nodded and picked up her tea. She and Marie-Louise looked at each other with understanding.

The air between them held the weight of memories—unspoken ones—that didn't need describing anymore.

Their teacups clinked softly on the saucers as the ladies set them down.

Nora shifted her gaze to the window. Outside, a breeze moved through the garden, rattling the late roses against the windowpane and rustling the dried ivy that clung to the stone walls.

Closing her eyes, as if taking herself back to the school set in the rural countryside of Derbyshire, Marie-Louise drew on her memory to describe the location. "It was a half-day's train ride northwest of London and not far from Manchester. I remember seeing much devastation in Manchester as we took a bus to the school. I worried about where we were going."

Nora nodded, her mind going along with the story. "How could anyone, let alone a child, fathom how one area could be devastated beyond belief while others nearby remained almost untouched? Such starkly contrasting faces of war."

Marie-Louise met Nora's gaze, and for a fleeting moment, Nora saw in her eyes confusion, hurt, and fear that mirrored the woman's younger soul. The glimpse vanished quickly but startled Nora. It had taken her back over eighty years in an instant.

Marie-Louise suddenly sat up straighter. "The further we traveled from the city, the scenery was magical. Somehow it was as if there had never been a war. It was so green, and there were beautiful rolling hillsides, open meadows, and ancient forests. It all seemed so untouched, and when we reached our destination, the main manor house looked like a king's castle."

"It must have been surreal to find yourself in such a safe and welcoming environment."

"I recall being unable to say anything. I followed along willingly but can still feel the uncertainty I experienced. I remember being wary of everything for some time. But I had the dearest roommate who helped me more than anything. We remained the best of friends until she passed away a few years ago."

Marie-Louise spoke of her school days and learning English, and how her mother visited twice during the school year. The first summer she went home to Paris, but after that she remained in England with her roommate's family and three years later went on to university. The French students were often invited to ceremonies marking important dates of the war.

Her eyes sparkled as she described the British army major with whom she fell in love. "He was much older than I, but after my experience during the Occupation, I had a maturity beyond my years."

She paused for a moment, and her voice took on a soft and wistful tone. "I can tell you we had a most passionate love affair for two years before we could even imagine someone marrying us. Although we were discreet, of course some people figured it out."

Nora felt Marie-Louise's gaze penetrating into her soul as she said, "So now you know how happiness came back into my life. Those were my reckless years in England, my dear, filled with a very different kind of courage and daring compared to those terrible years in Paris. I highly recommend embracing the spirit I discovered. It's never too late to take a chance on love."

Nora smiled and felt a bit like a schoolgirl as Marie-Louise continued. "You are in the perfect city for a love affair, my dear. Trust me. It's part of what makes France the country it is—deeply rooted in seduction."

Nora tried to sort out how to respond to these lessons on love from a ninety-three-year-old woman. All she knew was that it was all quite moving, undeniably wonderful.

"I was married to my *amant*, or paramour, as he was called back in the day, for fifty-seven years." The sweetest smile spread across her face.

"We remained in England for ten years, and I worked as a translator for the government, helping with war documents.

Then we moved to Paris and were happy to be back and be part of its rebirth."

Yvette brought a fresh pot of tea to them and some cookies that made Nora chuckle when she recognized them. They also turned the conversation to something less intimate. "Aha! McVitie's Digestives! I have a friend at home who always serves those with her tea," Nora said.

"Bien sûr!" Marie-Louise said. "I learned to call them Hobnobs in England, and they are the quintessential British tea biscuit. Do you know they were first created in 1892 by two British doctors?"

They laughed together, amused at the history such simple biscuits carried with them.

"Who knew?" Nora said.

"Indeed. Add in a fine pot of tea as a delicious accompaniment, and now you know how happiness came back into my life after the most horrifying years of war."

Nora remained for a while longer. They chatted about the new year arriving in two days and how they would celebrate.

"I know very well I will be sound asleep before the midnight bells ring," Marie-Louise assured Nora. "But I trust you will celebrate for me."

"You never know," Nora replied. "There have been many New Year's Eves where I, too, have been asleep long before midnight. However, this time, Chloe has a busy night planned, beginning with skating at Le Grands Palais."

"Ah yes, I have heard of the new use of the beautiful Palais. Do you know it was built for the 1900 World's Fair? I read about the skating rink being the largest in the world. What fun!"

"I'm looking forward to it, although Olivier's father will be with us and we never know whether his grumpy personality or his cheery one will show up. I seem to set off the crabby side. Time will tell."

"Ah Nora, you do make me laugh. I hope to hear about the

evening. To confirm, we will meet January first in the afternoon, oui? A good start to another year."

"Definitely!" Nora agreed. "We're quickly running out of days. It will soon be time for Giselle to return, and I will go back to Canada. Gosh, I'll miss all of this."

"Well," said Marie-Louise, "we never know what might happen. Plans often change in an instant."

The rather cryptic reply startled Nora, but before she could question her friend's words, Marie-Louise rose and Yvette appeared, as if by magic, at her side to help her say goodbye. Atticus was on his feet as well.

Nora touched her cheek subconsciously and wondered what the quick goodbye had been about as she and Atticus walked down the street.

Chapter Thirty-Six

LATE IN THE EVENING, NORA TOOK ATTICUS FOR HIS bedtime walk. She was bundled up with a toque—a wool scarf wrapped around her neck—and her hands were tucked into warm mittens. Snow drifted gently over Montmartre, coating the crooked rooftops in a thin, shimmering veil.

The usual buzz of cafés was subdued. Inside, people huddled over glasses of vin chaud, their breath fogging the windows. Outside, life seemed to pause, wrapped in white.

The lamps along Rue Lepic glowed amber through the flurries, flickering like candlelight. Once again, Nora had an image of Vincent shuffling along ahead of her. She shook her head to clear it and hurried Atticus along, carefully watching her step on the slick cobblestones. It was time for bed.

Not only was she emotionally drained, but in a good way this time, from her afternoon with Marie-Louise, but the evening had taken its toll too. She'd given Cynthia and her friends the quickie tour of Montmartre. They'd ended up in the cozy atmosphere of Nora's favorite wood-fired pizza place, known for its fresh ingredients. There was no lingering, as they had decided to drive back to Lyon that night rather than pay for another night in a hotel.

After endless hugs with Atticus, they left in a flurry of grazies, arrivedercis, and bisous, exclaiming they were in love with Paris and vowing to return. They invited Nora to visit them in Italy, and she promised she would. Cynthia assured them she would make certain Nora kept her promise.

Luc had called late in the afternoon to confirm he would collect her in the morning for a special tour of the newly reopened Notre Dame Cathedral. Nora was excited to see the amazing restoration, which had been completed on schedule—a miraculous feat in itself. But she had to admit she was even happier at the thought of spending time with Luc once again.

She fell into bed and chuckled as she listened to Atticus snoring lightly before her eyes were closed.

The words of Marie-Louise filtered into her mind. Nora always had so much to reflect upon after their visits. Usually she thought about the horror the war had inflicted on that little girl as well as the entire country. She had so much more to process than she'd anticipated. Of course, everyone in her generation was aware of the history of that time, but Marie-Louise had been taking her back to it in almost real time. It was a lot.

And then, on a completely different topic, which always made Nora smile inside, she recalled Marie-Louise's words of encouragement to let love into her life again. That was something completely unexpected, but not easy to ignore, coming from this wise woman.

And those cryptic words when they had parted, about plans changing. Did she know something Nora didn't?

By morning, Nora hadn't stopped thinking about Marie-Louise's last words, but now she set them aside. She looked forward to being surrounded by peace and beauty at Notre Dame, and she felt blessed to live in a time where those options were available to her. More than ever, it was not lost to her.

Punctual as always, Luc texted to say he was just minutes

away. Nora replied she would meet him outside so he wouldn't have to park. The snowy weather had left cars in disarray as people parked more chaotically than usual. She chuckled thinking of the heavy snowstorms she was used to and how one of those would have spelled disaster in Montmartre.

Luc had left the engine idling and stood at the door of her building when she reached it. His lightly tanned face lit up when he saw her. His stunning hazel eyes held hers.

Nora's smile unfolded slowly and with a sensation she felt down to her toes as he approached. Her breath caught at the intimate way he looked at her. She leaned into his tender, lingering bise. The kiss to her cheeks, as well as his sensuous, citrusy scent, still warmed her skin after he stepped back.

Even though it had only been ten days since she'd last seen him, Nora was instantly pulled into his orbit. He did make her happy.

They chatted nonstop, trading stories of their experiences over the holidays, as Luc guided the car through the slushy streets. His descriptions of the property and villa where Giselle was staying created sumptuous visuals of lush gardens with birdsong and trickling fountains, terra-cotta-colored adobe walls, and mosaic tiles hand-painted with jewel-tone glazes.

He asked about Nora's fête de Noël in the heart of Provence, and she kept him laughing with tales of the food and the goats and chickens, and of her efforts to speak French every day.

She dramatized the story of the dogs' disappearance, which shocked him greatly until she reached the happy ending.

"Honestly, Luc, I can't recall ever being so frightened. I was so worried Atticus was lost for good. Knowing there were hunters and wild boar out and about had really gotten into my head."

He reached over and lightly squeezed her hand. "I can well imagine what a fright it was. Grâce à Dieu, everything worked out. What good luck that Pierre thought to call his friend."

They reached the cathedral in what seemed like minutes. A private guide greeted them at the front façade and pointed out the immaculate Gothic carvings and statues of saints, as well as the restored rose windows. As soon as she entered, Nora gasped. The change between the time she had visited Notre Dame with Jeremy on their honeymoon and now was so dramatic.

Instead of the old dark, muted interior, everything had been cleaned to a soft limestone glow. The whole space felt lighter, brighter, and more open. After years of careful restoration by the caring hands of specialists, the sculptures had emerged from centuries of grime with more clarity.

The guide's words carried such meaning as he said, "These once-darkened saints, angels, and prophets are not just preserved, but reawakened. The Cathedral of Notre Dame has been revived, and our hearts beat with pride."

Two hours after they'd entered, Luc took Nora's hand as they stood outside taking a last look.

A long sigh escaped Nora's lips. "That was so emotional. Thank you for arranging the tour. It has been unforgettable. But, am I wrong to tell you I missed the dark, mystical atmosphere of the old gloomy interior? I appreciate all of the restoration that has been done but ..." Her voice trailed off.

Luc grinned. "Pas du tout. You are not alone with those feelings. The new interior takes some adjusting and I'm happy you shared that thought with me. I've attended mass a few times here since the cathedral reopened, and each time I go inside I feel the same emotional absence of the old play of shadows and stained glass light. It will take time to warm to the new brightness for some of us."

It was still snowing lightly, which made the experience of the morning that much more meaningful for Nora, as all snowfalls did.

Luc slipped Nora's arm though his. "Fais attention. It's slippery."

Nora was glad to have his help and enjoyed the intimacy of walking arm in arm. While Luc led her across the street to a charming bistro, he pointed out the nearby Quai de la Tournelle.

"In the summer, this is a good place to come dancing. You would love it. There are special swing dance events as well as salsa and tango nights. Dancing there under the stars is incredible. You must come back then, Nora."

It was an invitation Nora found most enticing.

As they finished their meals, Nora sensed a change in Luc's voice, as if he was holding something back. He gently placed his hand over Nora's, stilling her fingers as they fidgeted on the table.

"Nora," he began, his voice low and tender, but strained. "There is something I need to tell you."

She looked up and her eyes searched his face. After his recent personal disclosures, she wondered what he might want to tell her.

"I'm sorry to say it, but Giselle asked me to be the messenger. She didn't go to Mexico to visit friends but rather to have treatment at a clinic for ovarian cancer."

The words landed like cold water. For a moment, Nora couldn't move.

It was such unexpected news. Her fingers gripped Luc's.

"Oh no! How is she? Is she very ill? I'm so, so sad to hear this. We've FaceTimed often since she left, and she always looked fine."

"Yes, she manages to hide her illness very well. She has been battling this for some time, and treatments here in Paris did not seem to be helping. Last summer she went to a clinic in Mexico and after two months under the care of their physicians, her condition improved dramatically. She came home with new medications and felt so much better."

Nora struggled to regain her composure and asked, "Why did she go back there? Did her condition deteriorate?" Faint worry lines had appeared on Luc's forehead.

"Yes. She had scans here in November which indicated the situation was worsening. That was why she needed you to come so quickly after her usual dog-sitter became ill."

A lone tear trickled down Nora's cheek, and Luc reached over to wipe it away. "It's so crazy," Nora whispered. "We only had those three days together, and yet I feel so close to her. Living in her space, caring for Atticus... And she made a massive impression on me. In those few days, she shared such passion for everything... Life, Paris, Atticus, her painting... She awakened feelings I had forgotten."

"That has always been Giselle's gift." Luc's voice caught as he spoke. "In any case, the doctors are hopeful their advanced treatment will give her more time. The clinic has the highest reputation, and I've been most impressed with the care when I went to meetings with her. So, we all need to stay positive."

They sat without saying anything for a few moments. *Words seem so futile,* Nora thought.

Luc began to speak again, their fingers still entwined. "Giselle is going to call you this afternoon around four, but she wanted me to explain the situation first, to make the conversation easier. Will that time be convenient?"

"Definitely. I won't go anywhere this afternoon until I hear from her. Chloe has plans for us later in the day. I keep forgetting it's New Year's Eve tonight. Apparently, we are going skating at Le Grand Palais. She even had me send my skates over before I left Canada."

"Ah! Bravo! Every year for quite some time now, Le Grand Palais is transformed from an international exhibition hall into a Palais des Glaces for December and part of January. I hear it's a great time. What a good idea!"

Luc became somber again. "I only flew home for a meeting yesterday and to see you today and then my wife and daughter tonight. I should have told you I always spend New Year's Eve with Mathilde. I apologize for not thinking to tell you before."

Nora shook her head and raised a hand in quiet acknowledgment, her expression marked by deep respect for Luc's relationship with his family.

"Dominique and I always dress formally and take Mathilde a gorgeous new dressing gown with an orchid corsage. The home organizes a lovely short concert of chamber music, and everyone gathers in their elegant salon. The kitchen prepares a fine dinner, and we have champagne, of course. Even Mathilde has a sip. We always hope for some sign of awareness, but sadly there is none."

After they ate, Luc took Nora home and accompanied her in the elevator up to her apartment.

"You must come in and see the magnificent flowers you sent," she said. "It still looks like it was just delivered."

Nora smiled as she gestured to the arrangement on the table. Luc gave an admiring nod. "Dominique helped plan it and the florist did an excellent job of following directions. Wow!"

"I've been enjoying it tremendously. And thank you for the tour today," Nora said. "It was so very special."

"I wanted to be the one to take you to see the restoration and was getting worried you would run out of time."

"Je vous souhaite, et aussie Dominique et Mathilde, meilleurs vœux pour la nouvelle année," Nora said. "Did I get it right and wish you all a Happy New Year?"

Luc laughed. "Très bien fait! You are speaking like you belong here!"

"Luc, I want to say how much I respect your life with Mathilde and Dominique. You are a fine man."

Their eyes met, and the emotion they both felt was obvious. But it was emotion that perhaps would never be acted upon.

As they parted, Nora said, "Luc, the news about Giselle is so difficult to accept. I will not be able to do anything until she calls, and I will let you know after we have talked."

Luc nodded solemnly and they touched their foreheads together before he turned and left.

Chapter Thirty-Seven

JUST AFTER FOUR O'CLOCK THAT AFTERNOON, GISELLE called Nora for a video chat. She sat in a garden surrounded by the most vivid purple bougainvillea and looked like someone in the best of health. Her eyes sparkled and her vibrant red hair tumbled in soft waves to her shoulders.

"Bonjour chérie!" she sang, her voice as lively as always.

"Giselle! I'm so happy to see you."

"And I know also ... so unhappy to hear my news." She followed her words with tinkling laughter and a wave of her hands.

Nora nodded, surprised by Giselle's light-hearted manner, but didn't have time to reply, as her friend continued. "As you Canadians say, it is a bummer! I learned that word from Chloe. And really, my dear, we do not need to talk about it. It is what it is, and I'm certain darling Luc gave you the details."

"He did, Giselle. Yes, this news is truly a bummer. My heart is with you." Nora felt awkward speaking in such a casual way about such a serious situation.

They chatted for several minutes, and Giselle basically repeated what Luc had said. But then her mood changed to become more somber.

"I need to be here for another month. Is there any chance you can stay longer with our sweet boy Atticus?"

This was so unexpected. Nora's natural resistance to being impulsive began to rise within her. But one look at Giselle's pleading expression changed her mind. More than anything, Nora wanted to help.

"It's not a problem. I'm happy to help in any way possible. Chloe will be devastated to know why, but—"

Giselle interrupted. "Let me tell you some good news. Staying here an extra month gives me more time to continue the treatment, and honnêtement, it is working ... just like last time. Amazingly, I still have not lost my hair ... now that would be a disaster!"

"That is such good news!" Nora agreed, trying to sound light-hearted, when she really was feeling shattered.

"Yes, it seems I can keep going for some time by coming here for two months every year. At least that is how it looks at the moment. As we know, nothing is certain with these nasty diseases. I feel good, and hopeful, and I need to get back to Atticus and my beloved Paris and my painting."

Nora asked if she was painting there, and Giselle walked her through the magnificent garden to a spot where an easel held a work in progress. "En plein air, ma belle! Isn't this gorgeous?"

"Stunning! It's so you! Luc told me he and Dominique had a wonderful Christmas with you."

Giselle's face lit up as she spoke lovingly about their visit and all the special memories they had made. "Dominique is such a force, a wonderful young woman. And her dad adores her. We had such fun!"

She asked question after question about Nora's visit to Oli's family home in Provence and laughed uproariously when she heard about the kids and nannies. "Oh, that is the best! Please send me the videos you took."

Nora decided it wouldn't do any good to mention Atticus getting lost and the worrying situation it had caused. *All's well that ends well*, she thought.

Nora promised she would send the videos, and then Giselle said she had been speaking with Marie-Louise over the holidays. "Nora, you have been a gift to my dear aunt. I cannot express how happy she is to be sharing her story with you. She said it is such a load off her mind, even though she had not been aware of it."

"Yes, she kept those memories buried for a very long time."

They talked for quite a while about the difficult challenges Nora experienced as she worked on the story. Nora described how conflicted and deeply sad she felt at times. "It truly is a journey for me. But I'm so happy to help her, and I know your entire family will hold her memoir deep in your hearts. She's such a wise woman and an example of how one can overcome the most drastic of experiences. I'm learning so much from her."

"She is a treasure," Giselle agreed. "She has always been the guiding light in our family, and after our many efforts to convince her to tell her story, it's like a miracle you came to Paris when you did."

Nora replied with modesty and said it seemed more like Marie-Louise was a miracle in her life. *Something I never could have imagined.*

They ended the conversation after Giselle had a little chat with Atticus. He sat very still and stared intently at the screen while his stubby tale thumped madly. "He sees you! I know he misses you too and will be happy to have you home again." It was all the effort Nora could make to keep her tone cheery. Her heart ached.

"Bonne année, ma chère amie!" Giselle said, blowing kisses, which Nora returned in kind. She hoped the tears she'd fought to hold back hadn't been apparent.

Chapter Thirty-Eight

THE STREETS OF PARIS WERE ALREADY BUSY WITH NEW Year's revelers when a taxi delivered Nora, Chloe, and Olivier to Le Grand Palais just before nine o'clock that evening.

They could spot the stunning glass and steel dome of the iconic structure long before they pulled up to the ornate classical façade, which featured stone columns and sculptures.

"This building is so beautiful just to see from the outside, even if one never gets to go in," Nora said as they stopped at the entrance.

"Trust me, Mom. Living here doesn't ever take away from any of the beauty for me. None of this ever becomes ordinary."

Chloe and Olivier waved to a cluster of people of mixed ages, just past the ticket takers. The group, which included Pierre, were gathered to welcome in the new year at a grand skating party, complete with champagne. Reservations required changing their skates for shoes in time for a midnight Réveillon menu of fine dining in the Belle Époque atmosphere of Le Grand Café, located within the premises.

Pierre had arrived back from Normandy earlier in the day and appeared to be in good humor, engaging in lively conversation with everyone. It was the first time Nora had seen him so relaxed and laughing so much.

The Palais was transformed into a glacial wonderland. Olivier described it as an extraordinary blend of Belle Époque elegance and modern festivity. Beneath twinkling fairy lights, couples waltzed. Kids did spins and raced each other under the watchful eyes of rink attendants.

A DJ kept the skaters in constant motion by spinning an eclectic mix of electro, disco, pop, and French house favorites. In the center of the rink, an LED-lit ice sculpture glowed like a frozen jewel. There was a continual line to take selfies and group shots.

Food stalls tucked under the colonnades offered steaming cups of vin chaud, buttery crêpes, and other enticements. Olivier kept reminding everyone to save their appetites for the midnight meal.

Nora had met several of Chloe and Olivier's friends, and they all went out of their way to include her by switching skating partners and taking breaks with her in the relaxation spaces.

To her surprise, at one point, Pierre offered his arm and invited her to skate with him. They chatted easily about his trip to Normandy and his plans to leave the following week to drive the art to Nice.

Nora still wondered from time to time exactly what had transpired between them in Provence after her overindulgence with pastis. She had more or less decided it was in the past and just left it at that.

As the group prepared to leave the rink, a sudden commotion shattered the festive buzz. A heavyset skater, arms flailing wildly and obviously out of control, barreled at high speed across the ice, straight at Nora. She was gliding leisurely toward the edge of the rink after snapping a few photos, when she became aware of the impending collision.

Before she knew what had happened, Pierre lunged in front of her and absorbed the full force of the impact.

The crash echoed across the rink—the sound of bodies colliding, followed by the sharp scrape of skates on ice and a collective gasp from nearby skaters. Pierre hit the ice hard and got the wind knocked out of him, while the out-of-control skater tumbled beside him in a jumble of limbs.

Nora spun around, stunned. "Pierre!" she cried, dropping to her knees beside him. His face was contorted in pain, but he was conscious and already trying to sit up.

"I'm okay," he managed, wincing. "You?"

"I didn't even see him," she said in a shaky voice as other skaters rushed over to help. For a moment, she hoped Pierre wouldn't blame her for his fall, given her previous track record.

Olivier and a rink attendant arrived at the same time and asked onlookers to stand back.

The other skater, dazed but unharmed, mumbled an apology as another attendant helped him off the rink. Security was waiting to check if he was inebriated.

Pierre gave a shaky laugh and insisted he was fine as Olivier brushed ice off his father's clothes. It appeared his legs were fine, but he said he had a lot of pain in his left shoulder and chest, although he was trying to put on a brave front.

Nora still clutched his right arm. Her shock had worn off and was replaced by something tender. "You could have been seriously hurt. Thank you."

"Better me than you," Pierre murmured.

Nora was certain she saw pain register in his face.

"I'd do it again," he said quietly, his eyes meeting hers. Nora blinked, taken aback. She hoped her surprise at his kind words wasn't obvious.

Nora ended up sitting beside Pierre at dinner, with Olivier on her other side and Chloe across from her.

Waiters opened and served bottles of champagne. After a

countdown to midnight, fireworks seen through the glass domes accompanied cheers and cries of "Bonne Année et Bonne Santé! Meilleurs voeux!" Bises were exchanged with everyone. Even Pierre.

When the main course was served, it became apparent Pierre had an injury that needed attention. He couldn't lift his arm to cut the meat on his plate. Despite his protestations, Nora took charge and did it for him.

He agreed that no one should miss out on the delicious meal and muttered that what had been injured most was his pride.

When dinner was over, Olivier insisted he and Pierre go to the hospital for an X-ray. They left with everyone's good wishes when the Uber arrived.

Chloe and Nora went home and waited for the result. Olivier texted a short while later:

> Olivier: He has a broken collarbone that will take six to twelve weeks to heal.

"Poor Pierre," Chloe said. "He'll be so upset. He has so many plans for January, not least of which is driving our art to his gallery in Nice."

"And of course, it had to happen because of me. Seriously, if he didn't like me before, he's really not going to want to be around me now."

"I heard him tell you it wasn't your fault," Chloe argued. "In fact, I thought I heard him speak very sweetly to you after he fell."

"Well, he must not have been thinking straight. Just wait until he comes back with a sling and directions to take it easy for twelve weeks." She stopped talking for a moment, horror-stricken. "What about your art? Who will drive it to the coast now? Oh merde!"

Chloe sat quietly and then said, "Well, Mom, you know how you always tell me everything will work out, even though you worry about everything more than I do... Let's wait and see how it all works out. Maybe Olivier and I will have to do the drive, even though we can't afford to take the time off."

Olivier and Pierre arrived home just before five in the morning. "The emergency department was packed on New Year's Eve, as you can imagine," Olivier told them, describing some of the chaos.

Pierre was calm and quiet. "The pain pills have kicked in, and all I want to do is go to sleep."

Nora thanked him again. "I'm so sorry this has ended up a painful beginning to the new year. Thank you again for being so chivalrous."

Pierre said, "Pas de problème. Je suis content que tu ne sois pas blessée."

Nora again noted what seemed to be genuine appreciation that she hadn't been injured. She said goodnight, giving a hug to Chloe, a bise to Oli, and an awkward wave to Pierre. "I hope you are able to sleep," she told him.

Chapter Thirty-Nine

Before the chaos of New Year's Eve, Nora had promised herself the first day of the new year should begin with a sleep-in.

However, Pierre's accident had put an end to her plan, and she was awakened at eight o'clock by a text.

> Chloe: P didn't sleep well. Going to see about stronger pain pills. Calling our doctor.
>
> Nora: Should I come over and offer sympathy?
>
> Chloe: Nope, but thanks. He's dozed off. Will tell him when he wakes up. I'm sure he'll be happy to see you then.

Nora was still a little concerned Pierre might not be as happy to see her as Chloe predicted. It was because of her, after all, that he was in pain now.

She felt terrible.

Across the city church bells heralded the new year anyway. Guilt got the better of her and she soon got up, making espresso.

She was still tired, even with the shot of caffeine. Thanks to the busy trip to Provence and then the surprise visit from Cynthia and her friends, she'd had no down time, and she needed more rest. She made a promise to go to bed early.

After a long shower and another good jolt of caffeine, it was time to get the day underway. Nora bundled up against the blustery wind and Atticus wore a sporty red-and-black plaid fleece, his Christmas gift from Chloe and Olivier. Although he had previously refused to wear a coat, he seemed to love the feel of the fleece. Nora was certain he had a jauntier spring in his step with it on.

They set off on a longer walk, and Nora hoped the brisk, fresh air would snap her out of her fog and spark some energy. Atticus often enjoyed socializing with other dogs they came across in the little park in Square Nadar at the foot of Sacré-Coeur. The friendly way dogs got along with each other always made Nora smile. Conflict was a rare occurrence.

Her writer's mind focused on Marie-Louise's memoir. She was anxious to get through the next few days, anticipating all the haunting stories yet to come. She felt they would be the most daunting of their time together ... both for her and the sweet lady. Marie-Louise had indicated as much at their last meeting.

Taking on writing this memoir was so much more than she had anticipated, and she wanted desperately to get it right. Better than right.

Never had she been the witness of such intimate, important memories and she thought now about the narrative arc. She knew it needed to transform the narrator from the person they were at the beginning of the story to the person they had become by the end. All the information had to support and reveal the transformation.

She remembered her English professor stressing that a memoir must have constraints and not be about a whole life, but rather a time in life. Never would Nora have imagined she would one day write about this particular time and this particular young girl.

She felt honored ... and challenged.

She realized that with all the commotion at the skating party, she still hadn't told Chloe and Olivier she was remaining in Paris for another month. Or why. The news about Giselle would be difficult for them to hear.

Stopping in at her favorite Boulangerie Alexine, located just down the road from their apartment building, she picked up baguettes and two quiches; one for herself and one for the 'youngsters'. She also bought four tartes aux citron meringue, mainly because they were her favorite. She berated herself for being paranoid Pierre might not like her choice. *I've got to get that out of my head.*

She texted Chloe to make sure it was a good time to drop by, and when she got a positive reply, she went to their apartment.

Chloe squealed with delight when she saw Atticus wearing his fancy coat they had given him. She gave him hugs and told him how handsome he looked. They all laughed as his ears perked right up.

Pierre was up and reading on the sofa. He began to slowly rise when Nora came in the room, but she gestured for him to stay seated.

"I can see from your eyes that moving isn't fun. I'm so sorry."

He smiled ruefully. "C'est vrai. Too true! It's going to hurt for a while."

Chloe and Olivier greeted Nora with the usual bises, and they sat down to chat.

"Thank you so much for the quiches," Chloe said, and added with a big grin, "Now I don't have to cook. Oli can make a salad, and we'll be all set for dinner."

Both men agreed that after the delicious feast at the Palais, a small meal was exactly what they wanted.

"Thank you again for helping me out with my dinner last night, Nora. I was not going to miss eating the exquisite filet mignon, no matter how much my shoulder hurt."

"I offer my services as your découpeur de viande any time," Nora said, and they all laughed. "Is that even a thing?"

In the midst of the merriment, she awkwardly decided she could not delay telling them the unhappy news about Giselle's health. "I did not want to tell you this before our New Year's fête, but I need to share it with you now."

Nora took a deep breath and looked at the suddenly concerned faces waiting for her to speak.

"Luc shared this with me first and then Giselle called me yesterday. The reason she's in Mexico is because she has been suffering from ovarian cancer and goes to a clinic there for treatment. This is her second visit, and they have been quite successful at keeping her condition from progressing."

Pierre said he hadn't seen her in quite a while and was sad to hear she was ill. "Every time I have encountered her through the years, she has radiated warmth and vitality. She instantly brightens a day."

Chloe and Olivier were shocked. They expressed loving feelings about Giselle, since she was like family to them. Chloe murmured, "She always seems to be the picture of health and so full of energy. I have never heard her complain ... about anything..."

Nora agreed. "In the few days I spent with her, she made such an impression on me and, honestly, she gave me such a gift of joy – pure unabashed passion for everything in life. Seriously!"

"When will she come home?" asked Chloe.

"She isn't coming home for another month."

Chloe looked at Nora in anticipation. "And?"

"And she asked if I would stay on with Atticus."

"And?"

"Well, you know I don't make impulsive decisions."

"Maman! Tell us! Did you say you would stay longer?"

"Yes ... I said I would."

A look of relief lit up Chloe's face.

"Well, that at least is some good news. I was already getting sad about you leaving and talked to Olivier this morning, if you can believe it, about you renting the van Gogh apartment. Right, Oli?"

Olivier nodded. "I am so upset about Giselle. Who knew? I'm glad you have offered this help, Nora. Also, it will be a pleasure to have you here longer."

Chloe got up from the couch, wiped away tears, and threw her arms around Nora. "We have to think positively about Giselle and hope she'll go into remission. In the meantime, I'm glad you're able to help her by staying, and I'm selfishly glad I have my maman here for another month."

Olivier got up and hugged Nora as well. He looked at his father and said, with a smirk, "You see, Chloe has made me a hugger too. It's nice!"

Pierre had been watching all the interactions and said, "It is refreshing to see how close you all are. This is how a family should be."

An awkward silence followed, and then Nora said, "I must have a rest before I visit Marie-Louise. If I don't, I'm afraid I might not be able to keep my eyes open, no matter how important her words are."

"Mom, why don't you stay for lunch and then go?"

"As I said, my dear—I've got to have a little nap. I'm not joking."

Chapter Forty

ANOTHER FIVE WEEKS WITH ATTICUS

Even though Nora didn't usually make impulsive decisions, she was glad she had agreed to Giselle's request to stay longer in Paris. The news of her friend's illness was distressing, and she felt watching Atticus and the apartment was one small way she could help.

Nora was tired from all of the New Year's Eve excitement, but she'd promised to visit Marie-Louise that afternoon.

In her typical amusing manner, Marie-Louise texted Nora.

> Marie-Louise: Bonne Année! Everyone is recovering from overdoing everything last night … but not when you are ninety-three.

Just after two o'clock, Nora and the sartorially elegant Atticus arrived for their visit. The dog's eye-catching red-and-black plaid flannel coat had garnered many compliments on the walk over.

"Bonne Année, vous deux! Ah, Monsieur Atticus!" Marie-Louise exclaimed, after a warm bise with Nora. "Comme tu es beau! How elegant!"

"I'm certain he feels quite proud of himself," Nora said with a chuckle. She handed Yvette a bag of apple beignets she had bought at the bakery, knowing they were favorites of both women.

Yvette thanked her and rushed to get her phone. "Don't take his coat off yet, please! We need photos!"

Marie-Louise was full of questions for Nora about the skating party and was horrified when she heard about Pierre's accident. "People just don't understand how to act in public anymore. It makes me very sad."

Nora had decided not to say anything about Giselle unless Marie-Louise brought up the subject. It was possible she didn't know of her niece's illness, and Nora made a mental note to check with Luc about the matter.

Soon, Yvette appeared with her tea tray. Today's baked treat was mini-macarons and slices of lemon-poppyseed loaf. After exchanging a 'bonne année' bise with Nora and slipping Atticus a biscuit, she retired to the kitchen.

Marie-Louise asked Nora for even more patience today. "The last time I told you about my happy time in England after the war. I was not ready to tell you what I am going to share today.

"Yes, we did talk about your postwar life."

"Now I am going to tell you something I have never shared with anyone. Not even my beloved mother. The memory has been buried deep within me, but lately it has returned to haunt me. It is part of the reason I decided to tell my story to you."

She described the summer of 1943, in shocking detail, as a time when conditions had become unbearable. People behaved desperately, sometimes betraying a neighbor for their own benefit. Food supplies were scarce and rationed, electricity worked inconsistently, rats and dirt were everywhere. Medicine wasn't available but Monsieur Chartrand, the local pharmacist, risked his life to acquire supplies on the black market in order to help those who needed it most. Fear hung in the air everywhere.

"The Resistance fighters were becoming bolder. They were our heroes. We children pretended to be them. Is it hard to understand that sometimes we played games in the midst of all the horror? Can you imagine the confusion in our heads?"

The women looked at each other wordlessly. Moments of silence were sometimes as powerful as words, their eyes said.

Marie-Louise continued in a low voice. "Most days, Paris felt dark and quiet. The usual sounds of traffic and people going to work had all but disappeared. People stayed home. We peeked from behind curtains. But even so some days the sun shone, and birds even sang, and I couldn't understand how the day could feel so beautiful and yet know it was not. My mother told me we needed to remember to keep going. She was always so strong.

"Some days, different scents came to us on the breeze. It was confusing because there were smells we loved from the boulangeries—bread continued to be baked—and in the spring, the sweetness of chestnut blossoms was there. But it was mixed with sewer smells and..."

She began to cough, and Nora passed her a tissue, asking if she was all right. Marie-Louise nodded, and after clearing her throat, continued to speak.

"Did you know fear has a smell?" Marie-Louise's voice was quiet but unwavering. "I have never forgotten it. I couldn't describe it if I tried, but I would know it anywhere. It gets into everything."

Her words lingered in the air, heavy and inescapable. Nora felt them settle over her like a weight. How sad to understand what Marie-Louise had experienced.

"I took my job as a courier seriously. Some teenagers helped adults in the Resistance. They knew what I did and let me in on a scheme they had, although I knew no details until much later. All I knew was that I was to pretend to trip and fall in front of a drunken soldier—a heavy drinker who had been targeted by the Resistance. Then I was to go home, taking an indirect route, and tell no one what I did. I was scared but bold."

She said it wasn't until the war ended that her friend and neighbor, Emil Gagnon, told her the entire story.

Marie-Louise stopped talking. Nora asked if she was in distress, and the older woman said she needed a moment to collect herself and asked for a glass of water. Yvette appeared with one immediately. After a few little sips, Marie-Louise continued. Her voice was clear and strong.

"The neighborhood boys had been asked by the Resistance to steal a German uniform. German soldiers liked to eat at certain restaurants. The boys targeted one on a very dark street. A waitress kept flirting and refilling the wine glass of a soldier sitting by himself. I was pretending to be playing in the street and when he staggered out, I tripped right in front of him on purpose. When he stumbled over me, the boys hit him over the head with bricks. They dragged him into the hallway of a neighboring building and closed the door."

She paused again for another sip of water. "I saw none of that, as I was already zigging and zagging my way home through alleyways. I could only walk so I would not attract attention.

"Monsieur Chartrand had given them a bottle of ether and a cloth. It knocked out the soldier and then the Resistance fighter garroted him. The instructions said they didn't want any blood on the uniform. Garrote... I didn't learn that word until later."

Nora couldn't fathom how a little girl had the courage to act as she did. She was learning how fear and hatred could instill courage.

She sat frozen, unable to speak.

Marie-Louise continued without faltering.

"Emil said they stripped the German to his underwear and shoved him into the basement where they rolled his body into an old, unused well. The man from the Resistance took the clothes in a sack and disappeared. It all happened in minutes."

She looked off into space for a moment, seeing something that was visible only to her. Nora felt ill.

"The next morning, the Germans yelled for everyone to come out on the street. They said someone killed a soldier, so they were going to shoot one of us in return. We were all terrified. But Emil

Gagnon, I can still see him clearly, told the soldiers he saw a drunk soldier go down a cramped passageway with a hooker. The soldiers took off in that direction and for whatever reason never came back. We were lucky. Others might have shot us."

Nora took both of Marie-Louise's hands in hers. Their four hands were strong together. She looked deeply into the old woman's eyes with respect and admiration. "You helped. You were brave. You did something important. That is what you need to remember. It was more than most people could do."

"I know. I'm not sorry. I never allowed myself to think of the German soldier's humanity. Whether he was a father or not. He was certainly a son. But he was doing evil. He represented evil. I was a child, yet I helped kill him. I needed to say it out loud before I die, and I have. Now I do not carry it alone."

"No," Nora said. "Never alone again."

Marie-Louise wasn't finished with her recollections. "One more thing colored the remainder of my life, after the war ended, and after I had been in England for a few months. I could not stop thinking how one word felt burned into my soul. The word was hate. I had grown to hate so many things. The Germans, whether they were soldiers or not. The starvation. The fear. The suspicion. The hate. I hated the hate."

She looked at Nora, pursed her lips, and shook her head. "That hate—resentment for collaborators, accusations, revenge, ideological differences—kind of exploded in Paris in the days after the war ended. The joy of the liberation and the arrival of the Allies was not really the end for the French. Not yet."

Marie-Louise dabbed her eyes with a tissue. Her face creased with pain.

"Next came l'épuration sauvage, the wild purge. A need for revenge. The government had an official épuration, but the citizens had their own. It was horrid and, in some ways, as terrifying as the Occupation."

"Thousands of people accused of collaborating with the Germans were publicly executed without proper trial. Women suspected of treason had their heads publicly shaved and were paraded through the streets to be spat upon and have garbage and other unmentionable things thrown at them. It was so scary because it was French killing French. Neighbors accusing neighbors. It was mob justice, and I remember hiding in my mother's arms from the shouting and screams."

Nora could only shake her head. She felt so inadequate in offering consolation, but knew Marie-Louise wasn't looking to be affirmed or reassured.

"So all that hate affected the remainder of my life. I banished the word from my vocabulary, and I worked with organizations to help create peace in the world, at least in the small part of the world I could reach. We took our messages into schools and supported others hoping to achieve similar goals."

There was silence. Nora sensed Marie-Louise was searching for words, then she said in almost a whisper, "I wish I did not have to say this. Today I see the word *hate* coming back into society, and it is heartbreaking. How can the world not have learned?"

Fatigue began to show on her friend's face. It had been an emotionally draining afternoon, and Nora felt relief at reaching an end to their discussion.

"I know you are returning to Canada soon, dear Nora. I shall miss your company. But I am so grateful to you for drawing these memories from me. I want my family to know what I and so many other children experienced in our early years and why we grew up to be the people we are."

Nora didn't mention she would be staying longer. She would tell Marie-Louise in due course.

The sun blazed in a cloudless sky as Nora and Atticus walked home. The temperature had risen dramatically, and the streets were full of pedestrians enjoying a promising start to the new year.

Nora felt cold and empty inside. Her thoughts remained stuck in the visuals of the stories she'd just heard. Children woke each day to fear and horror. She couldn't stop thinking that it was happening again in so many places in the world right now. The details were different, but the results the same: death, starvation, hatred, fear. She usually avoided watching much of the world news so she wouldn't see too much of it. It always made her wonder why, as Marie-Louise had asked, lessons hadn't been learned.

Eventually, being drawn into Marie-Louise's stories from the past brought her sharply back to the present. It was difficult not to feel hopeless about humanity, but she had to rise above her personal reactions now and do her best at bringing Marie-Louise's words to life. Even if it was only for the sake of the woman's family, while Marie-Louise still had time.

Instead of taking the direct route to her building, Nora and Atticus stayed out for more than an hour. Breathing the crisp air and feeling the warmth of the sun on her face slowly brought Nora around to the beauty of the day and how good it was to be alive. Not just alive, but alive in Paris. She felt grateful for the charm—and safety—of her surroundings.

By the time they arrived home, the sun had dropped to the horizon. She was often amazed, particularly when she was outside, at how quickly it happened this time of year.

She texted Chloe, who had invited her for dinner.

> Nora: Thanks, dear, I'm having an early dinner and working on a new copyedit job, then I'll be off to bed. It's been a most emotional afternoon. How is P?

She was quite certain she knew the answer to that question. Pierre would still be sore, not just around his shoulder and his chest, but all over, after that huge man landed on top of him. And he wouldn't be happy about his lack of privacy.

Her phone dinged with a reply.

> Chloe: Understood. Hope the writing goes well. Pierre still in a lot of discomfort. Sleeping a lot now as meds kick in. Still insisting he can drive the art to Nice. Says he needs a week to adjust. He's checking with a few friends. Don't see how he can do it. Time will tell.

Luc had left a voicemail earlier in the afternoon sending New Year's wishes and asking if Nora was still fine for tango on Friday. She returned his call.

Luc asked about the skating party and Nora said she'd save the story for when they were together on Friday. He said he was intrigued when she told him it wasn't quite the midnight celebration they'd all anticipated. But Nora insisted he had to wait and wonder until they got together.

They chatted only briefly, as he said he was preparing to go to Switzerland with Dominique.

"She has a new apartment, so I'm going to see it and spend a couple of days with her. I'll be back Friday afternoon and pick you up around nine o'clock. Sound good?"

"That sounds better than good, Luc. I'll be more than ready for some tango therapy. See you then."

The conversation lifted Nora's spirits even more. She spent the evening working on a copyedit a client had sent over the holidays. Now that she had extra time in France, she felt less pressure to stay working on Marie-Louise's memoir. She would take tonight off and devote herself to it for the rest of the week.

She felt happy to welcome positive thoughts and poured herself a glass of white wine before she settled at her computer.

Chapter Forty-One

As Nora and Atticus returned from their early-morning walk the next day, Pierre was strolling down the street toward them.

"Bonjour!" Nora said. "It's nice to see you up and around. How are you feeling? Chloe said she thought the medications are giving you some relief from the pain."

Pierre nodded—still no bise, Nora noted—and attempted a smile. "Lots of discomfort, but the pain is dulled most of the time. At least until the pills wear off, and then there will be more to take. Hopefully it will just be a few days like this. I've got a thing about taking pills, so I want to be off them soon."

Nora was sympathetic. "Don't rush it. If the pills take away the pain, let them."

They looked at each other awkwardly, and then Pierre said, "Would you like to join me for a coffee or crêpe, or both, at Le Moulin?" He patted Atticus on the head and asked him, "What do you say, mon ami?"

Nora tried to disguise her amazement. "Well ... um ... yes! Great idea."

She experienced a mental tizzy of disbelief. *Pierre just invited me to join him at breakfast. Could I be any more surprised? OMG.*

She turned around and they walked to Le Moulin at the end of the street. Pierre kept up a casual chatter about the skating party and the excellence of their midnight meal. Nora wondered what kind of meds he was on, because she was seeing a totally relaxed Pierre she had only caught glimpses of before. He was even more friendly than when they had driven back to Paris.

Nora ordered her crêpe with Nutella, and Pierre teased her. "Ah yes, this is the flavor that brought you and Chloe to song the last time we were here together."

Nora chuckled. "You remembered. How embarrassing."

"Not at all," Pierre said. "I have noticed how close you and Chloe are … and how close you are with Olivier too, for that matter. I like that very much."

He looked at her, his gaze sincere, and repeated, "Yes, I like seeing that very much. Watching the three of you together these past weeks has reminded me of what I have been missing."

Nora was taken aback at his candor. She hesitated to collect herself before replying, "I love Chloe and Olivier very much. I'm so happy they found each other, and it is an absolute pleasure to spend time with them."

"This is what I mean," Pierre said softly. "You express your love of family so easily, while I have struggled with it for a long time."

Nora sensed he had more to say. She looked at him with what she hoped was encouragement, and he continued. "With Annalise, my first wife and Olivier's mother, the three of us shared the love I see you enjoying with Chloe. We were a happy small family. After she died, I tried my best to be both father and mother. I know you experienced much the same situation."

Nora nodded, and her eyes filled with sympathy. Before she could say anything, Pierre spoke again.

"My second marriage, sadly, was a mistake. I saw too late Angelique was not cut out for a family situation, although before we were wed, she pretended to be. Her desire to party caused us a lot of arguments and quarrels. I could see it affecting Olivier and felt guilty about it."

"I'm so sorry, Pierre. Sometimes things don't work out the way we hope they will."

Pierre nodded. "Yes. I do not need to go on about it. It's just that since our divorce, I have mostly avoided close family situations and have not been the kind of parent I would like to be to Olivier ... and to Chloe too. I've always been hard to get along with. Grumpy. I know it's because I felt so angry and bitter about Angelique's behavior. I didn't handle it well. For reasons that are not their fault. "

Nora said, "We often can't control what happens in life and have to deal with it and move on. I need to have peace and happiness in my life, and I steer clear of conflict whenever I can. My writing helps me with this."

"I have begun to paint again," Pierre said. "For the first time in a long time. And I have never felt happier with the kids than I did this Christmas, and also now. They are being so kind and thoughtful ... and fun. I want to thank you for that."

Taking a long sip of coffee, Nora collected her thoughts. She had sat in shock listening to his unexpected confession. *But he seems very sincere and almost relieved to be saying his thoughts out loud.*

"We share a lovely family with those two, Pierre. I'm glad you're feeling differently about being around them now. To have a happy family is the most important thing to me. My video chats with them help me feel better about being so far away from them."

Pierre looked away and then back into her eyes with an intense gaze. "Thank you, Nora. That's what I've been trying to say. Thank you for making me feel part of my family again."

Nora smiled warmly and tried to hide her disbelief at this intimate disclosure. "I've enjoyed our family time together too and look forward to more."

The waiter appeared with the bill and a treat for Atticus.

They walked straight back home, and Nora and Pierre parted at her door. To add to her shock, Pierre leaned in to quickly bise her as he said goodbye.

"See you later," he said. "Chloe said something about you joining us for dinner tonight."

After she closed the door, Nora stood looking out the window into the distance, stunned by the entire episode with Pierre. His revelations had been intense. And then a bise! That elusive bise! She felt he had happily accepted her as family.

She couldn't wait to speak with Chloe about it and see if Pierre had said anything to her about their talk. Or maybe Chloe would notice a change in his attitude toward her and Olivier. Whatever had happened, it could only be positive. It was satisfying to think she and Pierre could be friends and share the best interests of their children.

Or it could've just been the meds talking.

Her thoughts were interrupted by the phone ringing. "Luc! What a lovely surprise! How is everything in Lucerne?"

"Everything is magnifique," he replied. "This is such a charming town in a spectacular setting. We actually went skiing this morning. Engelberg is just a half-hour away by train, and it was a glorious sunny day on the slopes. After four hours, we were ready to come home."

"How convenient! I'm happy for you."

"Thanks. I'm happy for us too. It's been a while since I skied with Dominique. She blew me away! What have you been doing?"

"Have you seen the weather here? I've been staying in and working on Marie-Louise's memoir. Atticus is annoyed because his walks are so short. I actually just picked up my umbrella and promised him we would stay out longer this time."

"Off you go then. I just called to say hello. I am looking

forward to our evening together. You can tell me all about the progress on the memoir then."

"I'm looking forward to seeing you tomorrow too."

"Je t'embrasse, Nora."

"Moi aussi."

Nora felt a flicker of awkwardness and didn't know if her response had been the right thing to say. There was something so tender about 'je t'embrasse'—just 'I kiss you' in French. But it sounded much more intimate.

The call from Luc, so unexpected, brightened her day. He was an interesting conundrum.

There was no question Nora found him attractive in every way. He was gorgeous—a hottie, as the Girls had agreed when she sent them a photo. And his personality made him the perfect subject for the love interest in one of her novels. He was charming, intelligent, fun, suave, compassionate, empathic, with solid values and a strong sense of humanity. He was someone it might be easy to fall in love with. *Readers would love him.*

Knowing he was married and the tragic circumstances of his relationship with his wife only made Nora care more for him. She loved him as the best kind of friend and she'd never had that kind of male friend in her life, except Jeremy. Luc had taught her so much… And not just tango. But tango was definitely part of the pleasure she was learning to appreciate from him…

Meeting him—and spending time together—during her short time in Paris had been serendipitous. Rather than trying to make sense of their friendship, she decided to simply continue to enjoy it.

A knock on her door startled her out of her daydreaming, and Chloe burst in.

"Mom! I can't believe you didn't text me about Pierre inviting you for breakfast. That must have been quite a surprise."

"That's putting it mildly," Nora replied with a chuckle.

"So tell me all about it!" Chloe hopped up and down with excitement.

Nora couldn't stop laughing. "Chloe, get a grip, dear child of mine. I think his meds are affecting him. Have you noticed any change in his behavior?"

"As a matter of fact, yes. Big time. He's turned into the nicest guy and can't seem to do enough for us. In fact, that's why I'm here. He made a big pot of French onion soup and told us to invite you to join us for dinner. Want to come?"

"Well, I'm never one to turn down a good bowl of French onion soup," Nora said.

"Olivier claims it's the best. Pierre used to make it all the time when Oli was small but hasn't done so in years. Apparently, he shopped for all the ingredients this afternoon, picked up fresh baguette, and voilà, dinner is made. And we'll have a simple green salad with vinaigrette followed by some fine cheeses."

"So," Nora persisted, "do you agree with me that it's probably the pain medication that's created a change in him? He actually gave me a bise when we came home after breakfast!"

"Whaaaa? Unbelievable!" Chloe was wide-eyed and her jaw dropped open. "Finally!"

"Well, when should I come over?" Nora asked.

"Now! He suggested you come now for apéros. He's making limoncello spritzes. I just came over to tell you about his change in behavior."

They both giggled as they went into the hall.

"I want some of what he's taking," Nora whispered.

"Aw, Mom!" Chloe whispered back. "You don't need anything like that. You're always chill. But we are enjoying this new Pierre."

Pierre's soup was outstanding, and he happily shared the recipe with Nora. "The secret is to cook the onions with loving care, and add a touch of sugar and good sherry."

"Dad, I remember you making this all the time many years ago," Olivier said.

"C'est vrai. You're right, son. I've been doing some thinking about those early years and I miss them. I owe you an apology… And you too, Chloe. I have a lot to make up for."

Olivier got up to get another bottle of wine and put his hand on his father's shoulder. Chloe smiled at the intimate moment.

When Olivier refilled everyone's wine glasses, he raised his and the others did the same and echoed his toast: "To the future."

The evening was relaxed and filled with good conversation. Much of it was about the coming art exhibit at Pierre's gallery in Nice and how the art was going to get there now that he was injured.

"I'm telling you I will be able to drive it down. I just need another week to heal a bit more. No problem."

Chapter Forty-Two

Rain was in the forecast, and on Friday it rolled in with a vengeance. At times a heavy downpour and other times a drizzle, but steady. Dog walks were brief—they went straight to Atticus's favorite potty place and back home. He seemed as happy as Nora to get out of the showers.

It meant more play time inside. Tug-of-war was their best indoor game, and it gave him a decent workout. Today it reminded Nora she was missing having more physical outdoor activity than dog-walking. Listening to Luc talk about skiing caused her a twinge of homesickness. Thoughts about days on the slopes with the Girls made her smile. One more month in Paris would still get her home for the rest of ski season, and that timing might be perfect.

She wondered if she had let herself get too caught up with living in Paris. Maybe she did need to go home. But ... maybe Paris had uncovered a version of her she hadn't known existed. She had been happy at home. But she was also happy in France ... a different kind of happy that embellished what she had before.

She looked over the view that filled her with joy every day and hugged Atticus, who had snuggled beside her on the sofa. *I still have a lot to think about, a lot of decisions to make... Time will tell...*

The inclement weather also meant she had much more time to work on her transcripts, notes, and recordings. The memoir's page count grew. Marie-Louise had gifted her with an incredible story. In some ways she felt disappointed it wouldn't be shared widely, but she was learning so much as she wrote it—from an emotional perspective as well as craft.

What a coincidence that coming to help Giselle had led to the opportunity not simply to meet Marie-Louise, but then to be invited to write her memoir. When Nora stopped to think about it, which she did often these days, if she hadn't been impulsive and responded to the last-minute request to dog-sit, none of this would have happened.

As she found her thoughts drifting off, Nora decided to take a break as it was close to lunch time anyway. She heated up a slice of leek, chèvre, and salmon quiche from a previous lunch and sat at the counter to eat. *Cynthia is right about taking chances in life,* she thought. *Particularly at our age, when our family responsibilities have changed so much. Our kids are busy building their lives, and we need to keep building ours. I'm so glad she came for a surprise visit, and we got to talk about that so much more.*

On a whim, she picked up the phone and hit the video button on WhatsApp to call Cynthia.

"Buon giorno, bella!" Cynthia's gleaming smile filled the screen, and she held up a forkful of pasta. "Linguini alla vongole! What are you having for lunch?"

Nora laughed and showed her plate, which contained what was left of the quiche. "A delicious quiche—leek, chèvre, and salmon. Your lunch looks delish too!"

"And I'm enjoying some prosecco with it. How about you?"

"Nothing so good! Plain old Perrier, I'm afraid. If I had prosecco now, I wouldn't get anything done for the rest of the day."

"Well, that's kind of my plan," Cynthia replied. "I worked my buns off all New Year's Day on an emergency request, so today I'm actually celebrating the new year two days after the fact. Slightly belated, but chissenfrega! I just learned that word. It means who cares, and is fun to say. At least I think so! Chissenfrega! So Italian!"

"I knew you'd have me laughing in no time."

"How do you say who cares in French?"

Nora thought for a minute. "Hmm. I would say on s'en fout. I think that's actually who the fuck cares. I'll have to check. Haven't said it for a while but maybe I'll start again."

Cynthia gave her a wide-eyed stare. "Really? What's going on?"

"Well, I'm up to my eyeballs right now working on the memoir I told you about. It's so intense, powerful. It's got me thinking about a lot of things, and for the first time I had a moment of homesickness. And then I remembered what you said about taking chances at our age. So I picked up the phone to see your smiling face, and I'm glad I did!"

"Me too! I love it when video calls come in out of the blue. I have absolutely nothing to report since I saw you ... just last week!" She squealed. "What fun to be able to say that!"

Nora nodded. "So fun! And I may get to visit you for a few days soon, because I'm staying in Paris for another month."

"Woo-hoo! Great news. How did that happen?"

Nora explained the situation and Cynthia expressed her concern for Giselle. "I'm so sorry for your new friend, Nor. Ovarian cancer is scary, but there's been a lot of progress in developing new treatments, from what I've read. I know how much you like her and hope everything goes well with her care."

"Yes, we have to hope for the best. So, I wanted to tell you I'm into taking chances now. But today I'm feeling conflicted. One moment I'm homesick and the next I'm thinking of renting the apartment next to Giselle's after she gets back. You know, the one I told you Vincent lived in for a short while with his brother."

"Awesome! Go for it!"

"The idea just kind of rolled into my head last night as I was falling asleep. We will see. I'll keep you posted on whether I'm coming or going. I'm having a crazy day!"

They chatted a bit more and exchanged stories about how they spent New Year's Eve. Cynthia's jaw dropped as she listened to Nora's experience.

Cynthia said, "Capodanno! That's what Italians call New Year's Eve. I'm happy to report no one sustained any personal injuries, but it was quite the party. For some reason, we all had to wear red underwear and there was a lot of flashing after midnight. So crazy! We set up the longest banquet table I've ever seen on the beach, and everyone came for a feast. All ages ... so much fun! And then fabulous fireworks at the end of the night. I'm not certain what time I got home. I know I saw the sunrise."

"Sounds like a party, all right," Nora agreed. "I'm really excited about coming to visit. Once I get my writing organized, we can talk about it. Is there any time that won't work in the next couple of months? In case I do stay here?"

Cynthia said she had no plans. "I need to stay close to home and make some money. But that's no hardship since this place is so wonderful. You let me know whenever it works for you."

Then she added, "Nor, feeling homesick is something we all experience when we make a decision to move away. I always feel it is a lovely reminder of the happy memories which are part of you. Don't let it stop you from making a decision to stay longer. It's all part of the process. Don't doubt yourself."

Nora nodded. "I hear you. It's bound to happen from time to time. I'm feeling better already, just talking to you. I think I'll organize a video chat with the Girls."

"Excellent! Include me too! Can't wait!"

Chapter Forty-Three

Nora ended the call and wondered what on earth had gotten into her. She hadn't seriously considered renting the van Gogh apartment until the minute she'd mentioned it to Cynthia. But now that she'd said it out loud, it didn't sound like a bad idea.

Never mind, she told herself. *I will simply carry on writing the memoir and other projects and see how I feel mid-February when Giselle comes back. I may very well feel it is time to go home.*

She worked on more of her recordings until noon, figuring out where they fit into the notes she had already taken and concentrating on getting all the dates and the timeline right. She knew when she felt herself being drawn into the pain and darkness of those days again, it was absolutely necessary. It had to be done to tell the story the right way.

When she was pleased with her progress, she put the work away for the day. With any luck, she might even get started on the final draft before the end of January. She'd already decided at that point she'd contact her editor in Canada to see if she would take a look at it. Nora was determined to give Marie-Louise a memoir she could be proud of.

She left Atticus at home after lunch and hopped on the Metro and then the RER to visit the Musée d'Orsay. Nora had read about a photography exhibit of Celine Laguarde—a retrospective showcasing her early twentieth century work—and noticed it was only on for a short while longer.

She'd first learned of Laguarde's work in an art course during her university program, many years ago. The article on the museum's website looked interesting, and Nora thought it would be a good break from all the writing she'd been doing.

Strolling the spacious exhibit halls of this former train station, relatively empty of tourists this time of year, Nora let her thoughts entertain the possibility of staying longer in Paris and enjoying more experiences like this one.

She stopped mid-afternoon for a coffee in the Café Campana. The setting was dramatic thanks to the massive ornate clock, preserved from the original Gare d'Orsay.

Before she left to go back downstairs, Nora went out to the terrace and took a few photos. She had plenty of sunny shots of this panoramic view of the Right Bank, but perhaps inspired by Laguarde's stunning black and white photography, she wanted to try to capture the special allure of Paris in the rain.

As she returned on the Metro, she thought more about renting the van Gogh apartment and remaining in Paris for a few more months. If she did, would she overstay her welcome? Perhaps when Giselle returned, it would be time to give Chloe and Oli some space. *They've made me feel so welcome, but maybe I should go home and come back next year like I usually do. I still have five weeks to think about it.*

When she checked her phone on the way home, Luc had texted.

> Luc: May I collect you early to go for sushi before we go dancing? There's a special place I would love to show you. 7:30?
>
> Nora: I would never say no to sushi. Bonne idée!

Chapter Forty-Four

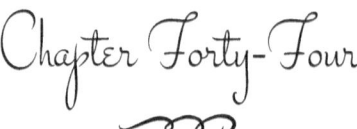

Luc was punctual as usual when he knocked on Nora's door. He presented a small basket to her containing two splits of chilled Vintage Brut champagne, a jar of fine foie gras, and a paquet of crostini.

"What do you think? Should we have a belated New Year's toast before we go out?"

Nora smiled at his suggestion. "Dear Luc, you are the perfect one-man party, complete with all the best ingredients."

He uncorked one split, and they toasted each other with warm wishes for the New Year. Nora asked about his special night with Dominique and Mathilde. His voice dropped as he described the lovely evening they had shared. Nora held his hand and said, "It sounds divine. I have so much respect for the time you spend with your family."

Luc nodded and kissed her cheek. "Thank you. It is so important to the three of us."

A quiet moment passed between them as they sipped their champagne. Then Luc said, "You hinted at some excitement during your festivities that night. What happened?"

Nora gave him the details of the skating party, embellishing the scenario and reminding herself it really had been an enjoyable outing, with the exception of Pierre's unfortunate accident.

"I feel badly because he was protecting me. I'm sorry he has such an inconvenient injury, especially regarding his plans to drive back to the coast with Chloe and Olivier's art."

Luc was sympathetic to Pierre's bad luck. "We never know when something like that is going to happen. As the saying goes, le malheur n'arrive jamais seul. I think you English say, trouble comes knocking when we least expect it. I hope it all works out for him."

Now Nora had a sudden flash of bumping into Pierre unexpectedly while with Luc. It would be just her luck. If it did happen, she hoped he wouldn't react as he had that first time.

The sushi restaurant was the most refined Nora had ever seen, an artful fusion of Japanese tradition and Parisian elegance. The minimalist interior consisted of pale, untreated wood walls, which provided a quiet background for tables of hand-finished wood or stone, and chairs of leather or wood. Each dish was a work of art and a gustatorial experience.

"I'm almost afraid to speak in here," Nora said, drawing a soft chuckle from Luc.

"It is rather like a religious experience, you are right," Luc said. "But isn't the fish outstanding? Next time I will take you to my other favorite sushi place. It is more like a Tokyo backstreet bar —loud and colorful and also delicious. We can make all the noise we want there."

They talked more about some of their favorite restaurants, feeling grateful to have so many options.

Their friends at the dance club welcomed Nora and Luc back after their holiday break, and Nora was happy to return to the congenial, relaxed atmosphere. The music carried her away, and she quickly lost her nervousness as Luc swept her into his embrace.

Tonight, employees of the club offered some instruction from time to time, helping the patrons weave some of the more complicated steps into the dances. The subtle footwork, elegant turns, and timing cues were fun to try and sometimes ended in entertaining chaos for everyone and the applause of friends appreciating each other's effort.

By the end of the evening Nora was exhausted, not just from dancing but from concentrating so intently. She smiled to herself as she considered how tango had become such an enjoyable part of her life. As they drove home, she told Luc she had never seen anyone dance tango at home, and he was quite incredulous.

"I pose this as a challenge to you, ma belle, when you return to Canada. You must find people to dance tango with you and tell me about it. But that will not be for a while, now you are helping Giselle by staying longer. So we can continue to refine your increasing grace and confidence on the dance floor."

Nora laughed, blushed, and accused him of giving her delusions of tango grandeur. This led to a conversation as to when she might return to her home and then, more importantly, when she would next come to Paris.

Luc then mentioned he was leaving on Sunday to spend some time with Giselle in Mexico. "We will call you and give you an update on how she is doing," he said.

"Oh, please do. We text often, and she says things are going well. But, of course, it's easy to say that in a text. I worry about her."

She opened her door and Atticus bounded up to greet them. Luc knelt and gave him a good rub. "I miss having a dog, but my travels spoil that idea. I can see what good company Atticus is and why you and Giselle adore him."

When they parted, Luc looked deeply into Nora's eyes. "Thank you for all you give to me. You are such a special part of my life, and I don't want to think about when you are not here anymore. I'll be back in a week or so and hopefully we will carry on ... as we do."

He leaned in and left a warm bise on each of Nora's cheeks.

"I look forward to your return. Be safe," Nora said. She placed her hand lightly on his cheek, thankful for such an open and honest friendship without feeling the pressure or uncertainty of there being any other expectations.

Chapter Forty-Five

The rain finally eased up on the weekend, although the temperatures were still cold enough to be an invitation to sleep in and spend time reading in front of the electric fireplace.

Chloe, Olivier, and Pierre were all under the weather with the flu, and blamed the week's rainy, cool weather. Nora made a big pot of leek and potato soup for them and texted Chloe when she left it at their door. Chloe had warned her not to consider entering into 'Germ Central.'"

When she and Atticus were preparing to go for walks these days, he pointedly looked at his fleecy coat. He seemed to have decided he liked it … a lot. She had sent Giselle a photo of them—he wore the red-and-black plaid fleece and she had on a matching scarf she had found at a local market. She'd captioned it: *Do you think I'm getting too involved with this boy?*

On Monday, Nora called Marie-Louise to set a time to visit her. She was missing being together with her and had questions to confirm some details from her notes.

"Bonjour, Yvette. My family are all battling the flu. I made a large batch of soup and thought you and Marie-Louise might like to have it as well."

"Merci beaucoup. We have been so fortunate to stay healthy this winter. I'm certain we will enjoy it."

Marie-Louise greeted Nora in the parlor with a welcoming smile. "I've missed you so much, chérie. It has seemed strange not to take my mind back to the dark days. And to be honest, I am struggling a bit with that. I need spring to arrive and brighten my heart again."

Nora took Marie-Louise's hand and held it lightly. "We went on a journey together, and it will take us both some time to recover. I'm sad you are struggling. I hope you can move away from that soon. I'm afraid we have some time to wait before spring arrives. But I've brought you a beautiful photobook of the seasons in Paris. Maybe it will lift your spirits."

Marie-Louise was delighted with the stunning photography. They had a conversation about some of their favorite books and authors, and then Nora showed her some of the draft pages she'd been working on.

Tears filled the old woman's eyes as she read what Nora had written. She nodded her head slowly, taking her time with each page.

"Oh chérie, thank you for showing me these. You have already made me feel better about the stories I told you. You are bringing them to life in the best way, sad as they are."

"I'm so pleased you're content with these. There is still a long way to go, but it makes a difference to feel I am on the right track with your purpose for this memoir. I'll be here for a few more weeks and will continue to show you more pages. You must not hesitate if there's anything you want me to change."

"I'm so happy to hear you are staying longer. Giselle called me to say she was staying longer in Mexico. She does love it there."

This confirmed for Nora that Marie-Louise was unaware of Giselle's illness. Her heart ached for the aunt, but she knew she would have made the same decision in Giselle's place.

Marie-Louise continued. "I don't know how to thank you

adequately but will continue to try. And thank you, too, for the soup. Yvette and I will have it for dinner with great pleasure."

When she sat back down at her computer later, Nora felt a quiet surge of inspiration and gratitude about Marie-Louise's reaction to her writing. She'd been teetering on the edge of imposter syndrome the more she worked on the memoir, and worried that her transcribing of Marie-Louise's words did them the justice they deserved. The woman's warmth and encouragement buoyed Nora's spirits and her faith in the way the story was unfolding.

Chapter Forty-Six

FOUR MORE WEEKS WITH ATTICUS

By Wednesday, the flu symptoms had been vanquished at Germ Central and Chloe and Olivier were back at work.

Chloe called Nora that afternoon. "Whew! Problems solved here. Pierre's good friend Felix, from Normandy, is here to spend today and tomorrow helping some other friends of ours wrap all the art and load it into the van. It will be parked in a secure space with proper thermostat control. Then he will come back in two weeks and drive to Nice with Pierre."

"Oh, thank goodness! I know Pierre was anxious about the situation."

Chloe continued, saying, "It's unbelievable the lengths they have to go to with some of the pieces—building wooden support frames and stuff like that. It's a much bigger job than I expected. Now they're installing racks in the van to hold everything in place during the drive."

"Would you like to stop by my place for a celebratory drink after work?"

"Actually," Chloe replied, "we just decided we're going to work here until half past seven and then take Felix out for dinner. Come and meet us at La Boite aux Lettres at eight. Sound good?"

"Excellent, I adore that place. I'll see you there! Is Pierre with you?"

"Yes. We are all here and going a little crazy. You can calm us down."

Dinner ended up being a lively, raucous affair. Several of Olivier's young friends who were helping pack and load the art came along, and the mood was light and irreverent. There was much laughter and clinking of glasses as everyone relaxed after a stressful day. There was more work to be done the next day, but it was obvious tonight was going to be a party.

Nora sat across from Pierre and Felix. It was interesting to listen to them talk about their exploits as young artists in the 90s, struggling to make names for themselves in such a competitive business.

Pierre had gone from art college in Marseille to the prestigious Beaux Arts in Paris. There he met Felix, who had come from Deauville, where he'd grown up.

Nora enjoyed the stories of Pierre being such an accomplished painter. He was modest about giving up his brushes to focus on opening a gallery and searching out new talent to champion.

Felix continued to paint and specialized in seascapes and coastal landscapes. He seemed to assume that Pierre and Nora were an item until at one point Pierre corrected him.

"Ah non, we are family."

Nora was amused and not insulted.

When Pierre had introduced Nora, he told Felix she was a writer and explained about the memoir she was working on.

"Oh Nora, you need to come to Normandy," said Felix. "You will find stories there that will intrigue and inspire you. The people of Normandy have never forgotten what went on during the Occupation and the arrival of the Allies. In that part of

France, the stories have lived on vividly through the generations. You must come. And besides, it is a beautiful place."

Pierre agreed and suggested perhaps he and Nora could take Olivier's car and drive up for a day.

His suggestion took Nora by surprise, but she liked the idea. She insisted she would be the driver.

Pierre slammed his fist lightly on the table. "I keep forgetting about this stupid injury. But whenever I make a sudden move, I'm reminded."

Nora and Pierre walked back to the apartment together, leaving Felix and the rest of the crew to continue their revelry.

"I'm not up to partying yet," Pierre said. "But I have to say, my pain level is much lower and I am not taking pills anymore."

"I'm glad to hear it," Nora said. "It was lovely to meet Felix. You two have quite a history! And by the way, I meant what I said. I would be happy to be the driver and do a day trip up to Normandy, if you were serious about it."

"I was," Pierre replied. "But I'm sorry I just blurted the idea out without asking you first. I can be like that."

"Let's talk about it next week, once you're feeling even better. Hopefully, the new brace the doctor ordered for you will help."

"Goodnight, Nora. Thank you for your friendship." He leaned in and gave her a light bise. It made Nora smile, but she managed to hide her surprise.

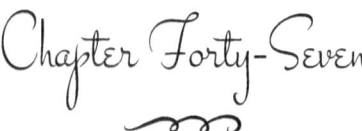

Chapter Forty-Seven

It had been a week since Pierre's terrible mishap at the skating party.

Early Tuesday morning, Chloe texted Nora.

> Chloe: Mom! Emergency! Olivier was going to drive P to the hospital for his appointment. Now we both have a very important out-of-town meeting this morning. Could you drive him in our car? We will drive with a colleague to our meeting."
>
> Nora: Of course. What time?
>
> Chloe: Can you come to our place right now, for a minute?
>
> Nora: Be right there.

Still in her jeans from her morning walk with Atticus, she went next door to Chloe's and found her standing quietly at the kitchen island while Olivier and his dad were engaged in a heated discussion at the table.

Pierre insisted he was fine to drive himself to the hospital, while Olivier argued it was too soon.

"You were told to do no driving for at least three weeks," said Olivier.

They stopped when they noticed Nora. "Hey, can I help?" she asked. "I'm happy to drive. No problem."

Pierre was still in his Mr. Nice Guy persona and calmly replied, "It's okay. I'm sure I can do it on my own."

"Well, why don't you try it out, and I'll just come along for moral support."

"I don't want to inconvenience you, Nora," Pierre replied, looking slightly irritated but accepting.

She assured him it would be no trouble at all. The argument came to an abrupt end. It was settled.

Two hours later, they were on their way to the hospital and Nora was driving. Pierre had winced as he struggled getting himself seated in the car and made the sensible decision before he even put his seatbelt on. "I guess it is a bit too soon."

In the busy Paris traffic, Pierre gave good directions, and they reached the hospital parking lot in just over half an hour. She said she would wait there for him.

"But you never know how long this will take. You know how doctors can get behind schedule. There's a very nice cafeteria that might be more comfortable."

Nora hadn't wanted Pierre to feel she was being overly protective by going into the hospital with him, but it did make sense. He seemed to feel at ease with her walking in with him.

It had been a good call. Two hours later Pierre appeared in the café, looking extremely irritated. He was apologetic for her having to wait so long.

"Hey, no worries," she told him. "I'm reading a great novel, and this gave me more time than I would have taken at home to relax and enjoy it. Good coffee here too!"

"You are too agreeable," Pierre said. "If it were me, I would be steaming. No, I was steaming! But so was every person in the waiting room."

"But exactly what did that accomplish?" Nora asked. "The

doctor probably got held up in surgery or had some other emergency. Honestly, Pierre, it's such a waste of time and energy to get upset about things like this. About anything that isn't immoral or life-threatening."

He blinked, looking at her as though she was crazy, and repeated, "Immoral or life-threatening? What do those things have to do with waiting for a doctor?"

Nora laughed. "I learned this lesson from a parenting guru when Chloe was small, when I kept getting my knickers in a twist about her behavior."

"Your knickers in a twist? Immoral and life-threatening? I'm not really sure what you are trying to tell me," Pierre said, looking confused.

She explained everything on the way out to the car and by the time they reached it, they were both laughing.

"Do you like Thai food? I know a great little hole-in-the-wall restaurant just around the corner," Pierre said.

While they ate, he told Nora what the doctor had said about his injury.

"They have ordered a new brace and will put it on me when it arrives. He thinks I will be able to move much more freely then, and maybe even drive … but not for long distances. Bah! I'm sure by then I will be fine."

"Don't push it, Pierre. You don't want to make the problem worse by rushing."

"Yes, but I do need to get back to Nice with the art. I have so much to do to prepare for the exhibit. Deliveries will be coming in a few weeks, and I have to be there. This could not have happened at a worse time."

Nora was understanding. "It's bad timing, for sure."

Pierre shrugged. "Felix said he can do it in two or three weeks, but that's too long to wait. I'm asking around and so is Olivier. Between us, we should find someone. It's not that bad of a drive. It can be done in one long day if we took the autoroutes, although

I would prefer to use backroads with all that art. And, in truth, I avoid the autoroutes whenever I can."

He described a few possible routes, and all of them sounded appealing. She asked questions about some of the places on his proposed routes.

"I haven't traveled much in France," she confessed. "I usually spend all my time in Paris. Chloe and Oli took me to the Loire Valley for a few days once, which was wonderful. And, of course, visiting your family home in Provence was an unforgettable experience. I need to plan to see more of the country in future visits."

"You will never run out of new travel plans in this country. Every département offers very different experiences in beauty, culture, history, cuisine, and wine. I have read my country described as a layered masterpiece and could not agree more," Pierre said proudly.

"Even staying in one town for several days can give you many incredible road trips. I never get tired of exploring. And trust me, I have done a lot."

Their conversation lasted far longer than their meal. The owners had started subtly cleaning up and making noises about closing until the dinner hour when Pierre said they should leave.

Nora realized with a start that Atticus would be anxiously awaiting her return. "He will have his legs crossed," she said and Pierre gave her a strange look. Nora thought how she seemed to have a knack for putting her foot in her mouth when she was with him.

Chapter Forty-Eight

THE REMAINDER OF THE WEEK PASSED UNEVENTFULLY. Nora focused on her writing business. The new year had brought several requests for copyedits, which she was busy scheduling. Between those and the memoir, her work calendar was full.

She also made time to do some plotting for what she called her 'van Gogh romance' and looked forward to doing more research for it. She'd noticed the young artist was still around, frequenting some of the same cafés she did—although the waitress was nowhere to be seen. But Nora had enough of a concept for the story in her head. She still wanted to pursue the project once she finished the memoir.

And she hadn't stopped thinking about renting the next-door apartment. Her fascination with Vincent having lived there hadn't diminished, and she had not stopped escaping into fantasies about it. When she'd mentioned her idea to rent the apartment to Chloe recently, her daughter had smiled knowingly and said, "It's like I keep telling you, it's all part of the French Effect."

Nora was pleased when Pierre asked if she would consider driving him back to the hospital, this time in the van, to get the new brace put on. He expressed high hopes the change would help him to move around more easily.

Atticus went with them so Nora could take him for a walk instead of waiting in the hospital's cafeteria. She had noticed a large park nearby as they'd left the previous appointment and thought the two of them could go exploring.

The doctor wasn't behind with his appointments, and everything went smoothly. Although Pierre wore the new brace, he was still required to wear a sling for another few weeks.

He showed the brace to Nora. It fit snugly and looked like it offered great stability for his collarbone. The new sling was much sleeker and Pierre said it was more comfortable.

He asked Nora if she would mind if he drove home.

"If you feel you're ready, go for it. But please, don't push yourself. If driving causes pain, just stop."

He pulled himself up into the van without any apparent trouble or discomfort. When they reached the apartment, he climbed out quickly and went around to open Nora's door.

"Come on, let's celebrate and go down to Le Moulin for a glass of wine."

Atticus settled under the table with his treat from the waiter as they toasted to Pierre feeling better.

After a bit of small talk, he looked at Nora intently. "Nora, I have a proposition for you. Well, not a proposition, that's the wrong word... Sorry, I didn't mean that. I can't think of the right word. Er, proposal. Non! Okay, a suggestion. That works!"

Nora laughed as he fumbled for the word he wanted. She thought it endearing that a hint of embarrassment flickered across his face.

"Yes, a suggestion. You always seem interested when I talk about road trips, and you appeared to enjoy our drive back to Paris."

Nora's face registered her enthusiasm. "I've been a fan of road trips my entire life. When I was a child, our vacations were road trips, and they have continued to be a part of my life. We took a lot of trips when I was married, and Chloe and I have always loved to take them together."

Pierre raised his glass to her. "I am desperate to get back to Nice. I have an assistant keeping my gallery open, but as I mentioned earlier, I have a lot of work to do to prepare for the upcoming exhibit. Also, I have been here far longer than I would ever want to stay. I feel like I am now living with the kids."

Nora noticed him tap his fingers nervously on the table.

"I'm sure staying with them hasn't been easy in such a small space. But I know they have been happy to help you while you recover. And I've enjoyed your company. We've had a chance to get to know each other, and I…" She paused for a moment. "I feel our little family has grown stronger. I like knowing that when I'm so far away, they have you to rely on. It's so important to me."

"Yes, I am happy about that too. So, here is my suggestion. My idea." Now he began to speak quickly, hardly stopping to breathe, as if he needed to get the words out before he lost his nerve.

"I know I cannot do the drive home myself. How would you like to go with me and help? I will plan a trip on the back roads so you will see more wonderful areas. We can make some stops, and we can take Atticus with us. I even looked up how we can help him with his car sickness."

He stopped suddenly and didn't break eye contact as he took a long sip of wine.

Nora was stunned. Obviously, Pierre had given the plan a great deal of thought.

"Wow. That's quite an idea. It actually sounds wonderful. But are you certain you want to take so much time getting back to Nice?" She laughed and added, "With me?"

Pierre's eyes were serious and he smiled wryly. "I understand perhaps you are surprised. And maybe it doesn't appeal to you. But, yes to all of it. The fast drive to Nice is one long day on the autoroutes, which I always avoid. This way we could spend three

THE FRENCH EFFECT

or four days getting there, and you would see some places I know you will love."

He took a long sip of wine and signaled to the waiter for another round, asking Nora with his eyes if it was okay. She nodded.

Then he added, "Since you have never been to the south of France, I know when you get to the coast you will be thrilled with the beauty around you. I predict you will fall in love with the area. Everyone does!"

"Well it's a persuasive enticement. How could I refuse?" she teased. "But seriously, we'll have to agree on a few things. Our playlists are a must and we will definitely share the driving. You need to continue to take care of your injury. We'll share the costs of meals and I will pay all my own expenses."

"I may insist on buying you a glass of wine once in a while," he said. And then he added, "Or pastis," with a twinkle in his eye.

Nora thought back to the night at the mas and wondered if there was a hidden message in his words. But she quickly brushed off the thought as paranoia. Getting to know Pierre over the last few weeks, she didn't think that was his style.

"D'accord. And I may buy you a glass of wine ... or pastis... too," she said.

They both laughed and raised their wine glasses.

"Seriously," Pierre said as they walked back to the apartment. "Think about it for a day or two. If you agree, then we can leave as soon as you are ready."

When Nora got home, she texted Chloe asking her to call when she had a chance.

Chloe called immediately. "What's up? Although I think I might know."

"Are you kidding me?" Nora asked.

"Not at all," Chloe answered. "I assume Pierre's appointment went well and then he invited you on a road trip."

Nora laughed in surprise, floundering for words.

"Pierre talked to us about his idea yesterday. He wanted to

know if you'd think he was crazy or if you might feel awkward. And did you?"

Nora spoke slowly. "Wow. I'm impressed he talked to you kids about it. I like that."

"Yes. We were blown away by the fact he very much wanted our opinions. Honestly, Mom, the change in him since Christmas has been nothing short of unbelievable. And he's not on any meds now so we can't point to that. Olivier says this is the father he remembers having long ago. We're so happy about it all."

Nora carefully digested Chloe's words.

"To say I was surprised by his suggestion is the biggest understatement ever. But I feel good about it. I think it would be a wonderful trip with such interesting stops. He put a lot of thought into it."

"Pierre is very sincere about all of this. Like I told you before, he feels you are family. He's excited to show you where he lives too. You're going to go bonkers when you get to Nice. It's so beautiful in so many ways. I would live there if we could. Who knows, maybe further down the road..."

"Well, I more or less said I'd be happy to go. Pierre said to think about it, but I don't need to. I'll go pack! See? I'm being impulsive!"

Chloe laughed. "Brava! You're becoming surprisingly good at it."

Chapter Forty-Nine

THREE MORE WEEKS WITH ATTICUS

Two days later, Pierre and Olivier doublechecked the art to ensure it was still securely in place. A spot between the front seats was prepared for Atticus with his favorite blanket.

Pierre and Nora set off before dawn to avoid rush hour on their road trip to the south. They planned to share their Spotify playlists as before, since that worked so well on their previous trip. They'd brought plenty of water, and Chloe had prepared a basket of fruit, cheese, and cookies for them.

Chloe and Olivier waved them off, wishing them safe travels and asking for regular text updates and perhaps even a few photos.

Pierre had agreed Nora would drive out of Paris, since that part of the journey required the most abrupt stops and had the craziest drivers. Pierre's directions were clear, and he guided her out of the city and into the countryside with no problems. He'd printed out their itinerary and organized their driving schedule.

"Always subject to any changes we want," he assured Nora. "For the most part, it's going to be an easy trip. But of course we may run into road work or the like."

"Flexibility is the key to any successful road trip," Nora concurred.

Just an hour and a half after entering the pastoral countryside, they reached the town of Auxerre. They agreed they didn't want to stop but detoured through the town to drive past the sixteenth century Abbaye Saint-Germain and follow along the Yonne River.

"This town is known as the City of Speech and Sound," Pierre said.

"That's kind of odd," Nora commented. "Why?"

"It goes back to the early centuries of the Abbaye and its history of monastic chants." Pierre looked at a tour book he'd brought and told her what he had read. "The town has a deep-rooted emphasis on vocal and acoustic cultural expression. Apparently, many artists of all kinds come here to study spoken word, vocal performance, and sonic art."

"Who knew? You are the perfect tour guide," Nora said, sincerity in her compliment.

"Merci!" Pierre said with a chuckle. "And now onward to Dijon, where we will spend the night. I'll drive now, if that's okay. I know exactly where to stop for lunch."

Of course you do. Nora smiled in anticipation.

Lunch was delicious; Nora expected nothing less from Pierre's choice. They'd stopped in a tiny hamlet of stone buildings covered with trailing vines growing around weathered shutters. The local Bar du Place was unassuming, the air thick with the scents of garlic, wine, and roasting meats. They each chose a local specialty from the chalkboard menu, forgoing dessert so they wouldn't feel sluggish during the afternoon drive.

Chloe's cookies, an apple, and cheese might be the best dessert anyway, they agreed.

The day went by quickly as they drove through the countryside. The roads were not busy, and the countryside was unfailingly beautiful—a rolling tapestry of crops, livestock, and vineyards. All along the route they passed serious cyclists, often in groups.

Atticus probably hadn't ever enjoyed such picturesque pit stops. Nora chuckled to herself each time they took him for a short walk. At Pierre's suggestion, she'd gone to see Atticus's vet, who gave her some medication which settled his car sickness. He was a happy pup and enjoyed the drive as he sat contentedly between them when he wasn't snoozing.

They arrived in Dijon midafternoon and checked into a quaint hotel. For a few hours they followed little owl symbols embedded in the cobbled streets, which led them on a tour of the charming old town and even the cathedral.

Pierre had made reservations for dinner. Nora was amazed again at how he knew just where to stop, where to eat, and what to see. Their appetizer was a rustic terrine of the region, accompanied—not surprisingly—by a sizeable dollop of Dijon mustard.

Despite all the hours in the van, there was never a problem with conversation. It flowed freely and was always enjoyable. As she'd begun to see on their drive back to Paris after Christmas, she continued to discover Pierre was quick-witted and laughed easily. His humor was warm, and he could find the absurd in the ordinary. He showed a different personality than he had displayed when they'd first met. Including crooning French songs in a seductive tenor, making her both amused and quite unsettled, in a good but surprising way.

More than once he referred to their time at Christmas as being so important to him. He thanked Nora for helping him to acknowledge his flaws and show his love for his family rather than keeping it buried under years of bitterness.

They also talked about Nora's life in Canada and how she had dealt with her grief when Jeremy died. Pierre was interested in her writing, and they spoke a lot about art. She asked why he had given up painting. He told her the story and confessed he hadn't talked about it in such detail for many years. He said he appreciated her interest.

The next morning, they met at the front desk at eight for coffee and pastries and set off once again.

The morning drive toward Beaune went along the Route des Grand Crus, and Nora recognized one famous Burgundy winery after another. They stopped in at a couple and took turns doing light tastings on their way to their lunch destination. Experiencing the Burgundy wines in their actual vineyards thrilled Nora.

She discovered Pierre was a light drinker like her, and they saved their indulgences for a good meal in the evening. They happily declared themselves to be compatible traveling companions.

After lunch, they decided to carry on to Lyon and checked into their hotel just in time to head out for their dinner reservation. Pierre explained the city was known as the Gastronomic Capital of the World, and they had to decide whether to dine in a bouchon that served the old-style grandmothers' recipes of the region, or a Michelin-star restaurant. They opted for a bouchon, with its red and white curtains and simple décor that matched the authentic meals.

The next morning, they took an early bus tour around the city. Nora said she'd like to return to Lyon, and Pierre heartily agreed it was worth doing. "You could spend a week here, easily."

But they were happy to get back underway after lunch. They'd need to drive more kilometres today, but Pierre promised Nora a surprise for their dinner and overnight accommodations.

When they crossed into the Provence area in late afternoon, Nora recognized familiar road signs she'd seen on their visit for the holidays. Avignon was their destination.

However, just before they reached Avignon, Pierre turned onto a side road that looked vaguely familiar to Nora, until he turned into the driveway to his family farm. She looked at him in disbelief.

"Pierre, what a surprise! This is incredible!" she exclaimed. She was certain she felt tingling from her toes all the way to her heart.

He beamed with delight at her reaction, and wrinkles crinkled around his eyes. Nora was beginning to think of them as adorable.

He grinned. "I hope it is a good surprise."

"The best," Nora said through her smile. She ran her fingers through her hair and hoped she looked presentable after their days on the road.

They got out of the van, and Mami and Papi rushed outside with joyful greetings and affectionate bises. "Bienvenue! We are so happy to see you both," said Mami.

The evening was filled with warm conversation as they devoured Mami's deeply satisfying boeuf bourguignon, perfect for such a chilly winter evening. A roaring fire in the nearby hearth was the perfect touch to the comfortable ambiance. It felt like home should.

The four of them spent a relaxed breakfast together and, after a visit to the goats, who were now bigger and calmer, Nora got behind the wheel and they were back on the road. Pierre planned to drive when they reached the coast so Nora could fully enjoy the Mediterranean.

Chapter Fifty

Pierre knew the precise place to stop for a coffee and to switch drivers. Soon, the countryside changed to lighter brush, which he described as garrigue, and olive groves amongst vineyards. Dramatic Aleppo pine trees silhouetted some hilltops. After a short while back on the road, they crested a hill and Pierre pulled over to the shoulder. Nora gasped.

Before them in all of its glory was the sparkling Mediterranean Sea, kissed by the sun. Brilliant turquoise shades blended into deeper blues farther out. The French Riviera. La Côte d'Azur.

Pierre drove down to the shore and stopped at a sun-bleached restaurant with tables right on the sand. He explained to Nora that by the time they reached Nice the beaches would all consist of galets—pebbles.

As always, Atticus was greeted first by the restaurant staff. The owner came to say hello and looked at Pierre first with a wide grin and then a frown once he took in Pierre's splint. It was obvious they were friends, and he demanded an explanation of the injury, after he had been introduced to Nora and greeted her with a bise.

The owner guided them to a table on the beach in the shade

of a gnarly fig tree, and he and Pierre chatted in the fastest French Nora thought she had ever heard.

The smells of grilled fish, olive oil, and garlic were hard to ignore as Nora and Pierre made their menu selections. They dined on freshly caught dorade seasoned with lemon and fennel, accompanied by a simple green salad with vinaigrette and what Nora declared to be the best frites ever. When they finished, the owner pulled up a chair and brought them each a digestif.

Back in the car, Nora thanked Pierre for such a memorable introduction to the Riviera. He smiled and said, "Ce n'est que le début, ma belle."

Nora loved that he'd said it was just the beginning and even more loved that he had called her 'ma belle.' It was a first. And she liked it.

In two hours, they were less than an hour from Nice and Nora commented on the heavier traffic.

Pierre shrugged. "Unfortunately, every season is tourist season around here now. Although this is nothing compared to the summer."

They followed along the coast as the two-lane road wove past sun-drenched rocky shorelines and through seaside towns, not yet packed with tourists.

Pierre suggested they roll down the windows, and the van filled with the scents of salt, pine, and aromatic herbs growing alongside the road.

"In France la Mediterranée is often referred to as La Grande Bleue and you can see how the colors change as the waters stretch toward Africa. We love this sea. It offers a unique way of life, and a special Mediterranean culture and cuisine. Generations come here and create their own special history. It's hard to believe that until the late nineteenth century, people did not swim in the sea for recreation. Fishermen ruled the waves. Artists came for the unique light. And you know the history of the twentieth century —after the first World War is when the glamorous Riviera life really began. Artists, aristocrats and dreamers arrived, ushering in an era of glamor, jazz and sun-soaked decadence."

"I love your history lessons," Nora said. "Keep telling me more." And he did.

She couldn't stop commenting on the colors of the water. They changed from brilliant turquoise in the rocky coves near the shore to sapphire in calmer water, and then to a deep indigo in the distance. The waves glistened in the sun as windsurfers in wetsuits and small wooden fishing boats shared the water with gleaming mega-yachts.

Now, after having shared so many interesting stories along the trip, Pierre checked to make certain Nora was not getting tired of them. She said no, and he told her they were on the Bord de Mer, his favorite coastal road which connected Antibes to Nice.

The traffic was heavy. Cars and cyclists shared the road, which ran right alongside beaches for most of the thirty-minute drive.

"Antibes is the town I love best on the Riviera and I will bring you back soon, if you like. This is the newer part, but what you need to see and will love—I guarantee it—is the old town which goes back to Roman times and even before."

In just over a half hour, they were driving along the Promenade des Anglais, the storied street bordering the sea from one side of Nice to the other. The broad Promenade was busy with cyclists, runners, and people strolling or sitting in the iconic blue chairs, which offered rest and perfect spots to contemplate the sea.

As they drove slowly along, Pierre gave Nora a short history of the area, going back thousands of years. She kept sighing and murmuring about the beauty of all she saw. At one point, she reached over and took Pierre's hand.

"Thank you so much for bringing me on this trip. It was incredibly special in every way. Every minute of it was unforgettable."

Unable to lift his hand from the wheel, he maneuvered his hand in the splint to touch her arm. "I am glad. I love my country and am happy to show it to you."

Once they reached the heart of the old town, he drove into an underground parking facility and pulled into a spot under the market street of Cours Saleya. Pierre said to leave everything except Atticus in the van, and then they walked up a short flight of stairs and stepped outside.

When she commented on being in the middle of a street full of restaurants, Pierre explained the road served as the market street every morning, then transitioned to outdoor patios at lunchtime and became a bustling street pulsing with life at night.

Nora could not stop looking around and exclaiming about the colors of the buildings and the completely different vibe from Paris. Pierre was right. She could fall in love with this town.

"Un coup de foudre!" He told her. Love at first sight.

They walked through the labyrinth of narrow cobbled streets where pastel-colored three- and four-story buildings leaned in close. The scents of baking, butter, and garlic drifted around them. Pierre's gallery took over the ground floor of a corner building, and he was heartily welcomed back by two young men and a middle-aged woman. He introduced Nora and invited her to sit in one of the comfortable armchairs, but Nora was too intrigued by the old town.

"What if I go and explore and meet you back here in an hour?"

Pierre smiled. "Perfect! See you then!"

Nora set the GPS on her phone and disappeared with Atticus into the rabbits' warren of winding alleyways.

As promised, they returned in an hour, Nora wearing a wide grin. "I love it here already."

Pierre laughed and said, "This is just a little taste of what Nice has to offer. I'm so glad you feel this way. Let's go to my apartment and the guys will bring up our stuff. We're going to unload the art early tomorrow, so we can unwind from our trip or do whatever you wish. I can't wait to show you around."

A few minutes' walk from the gallery, they came to an unassuming apartment building. Pierre pressed a code into a callbox set in the stone wall next to double doors Nora guessed were at least two hundred years old. He pushed the door open, and they stood in a foyer with a wide marble staircase in front of them.

"Sorry, there is no elevator. The building is three hundred years old."

"C'est la France," Nora said. But her mind was boggled. Just like in Paris, she could never get over living in buildings that had existed for so long.

Climbing to the third floor, Nora commented she was glad not to have any bags with her. Although she noted that the wide marble stairs had been designed so it didn't feel like a hard climb. She discovered that in her building in Paris too. As long as the steps weren't narrow and steep, stairs in France seemed different. Easier.

Pierre said there was a very small freight elevator they could use to send up bags and groceries, so the situation wasn't as bad as it looked.

"I like the sound of that," Nora said.

She also liked what she found in the apartment, which took up the entire top floor of the building. Pierre showed her around. The space had three bedrooms, one of which was an office, and two bathrooms. Nora's smile lit up when she saw the bathtub.

She was wide-eyed with surprise at the walls that were covered with an eclectic display of artwork—vivid paintings, vintage posters and abstract sketches—an almost chaotic celebration of creativity. She had not expected this from what she knew so far of Pierre and was eager to discover more.

A terrace ran along one wall. It overlooked the market street and beyond, to a breathtaking view of the Mediterranean. She stood there speechless. This panorama, this apartment, would be in a future novel. Her head spun with ideas, and she had only just arrived.

"What would you like to do now?" Pierre asked.

"To be honest, I would love to soak in the tub and then sit on the terrace with a glass of rosé. That's what first comes to my mind. How does this sound to you?"

"Well, I won't join you in the bathtub, but the terrace plan sounds good to me."

They both laughed.

He continued, saying, "I will take care of some paperwork and put your bag in your room when the guys send them up. The rosé and I will be waiting on the terrace for you."

My life is truly charmed was all she could think as she prepared her bath in Pierre's beautiful tub. She'd never seen so many clawfoot bathtubs anywhere else she'd traveled as she had on this trip to France.

She texted Chloe after she sank into the soothing water.

> Nora: We have arrived! La Côte d'Azur is truly magnificent! Our road trip was a dream. Go figure. Pierre has been so kind and thoughtful. Surprise stop at his parents' last night. Imagine!

She sent her a photo of her toes at the end of the bathtub.

> Nora: Have you been to this apartment?

> Chloe: No. When we visited him, he put us up in a hotel because his previous place was so small. He just bought the new place last year. We've only seen a few photos.

> Nora: It is spectacular. I will send a video.

Chloe: Well, he did say before he left, we should come to visit when the exhibit is on and he had room for us to stay with him. It's the new and improved Pierre. I wonder if this would have happened if you hadn't come here and been with us at the mas at Christmas. I think not. Funny how some things work out.

Nora: Quite unbelievable. I'll let you know when Atticus and I are flying back to Paris. xoxo

Nora flipped through some photo books about Nice that were by the bathtub. Everything she read excited her more.

"I've decided this town is pure magic," she said to Pierre as they toasted with their first glass of rosé on the terrace.

Her bags from the car had arrived and she was comfortably dressed in lighter clothes than she'd worn around Paris. Although it was not so warm that they didn't need the heaters on the terrace to be comfortable.

"The weather feels more like Paris right now, that's for certain."

Pierre agreed, adding, "Throughout the winter, we have some cooler days and then other days we can eat outside, no heaters. So you never know. But do you notice the light? You will understand why painters have been coming here and do not want to leave. The winter light in particular is so special. The mistral wind blows down from the Alps and clears everything from the air."

Nora looked out to the Mediterranean and then at the lively scene below of people wining and dining. All she had seen in the short time they'd been there—the sparkling sea, colorful buildings, intriguing narrow passageways, stunning Belle Epoque architecture, busy terraces—gave an impression of a vibrant culture inviting everyone to join in.

It was still early for dinner, but people of all ages and cultures sat at outdoor tables enjoying apéros. Music filled the air. "It's all so joyful," she said.

"It gets crazy noisy here. Especially in the summer, but I don't mind. It reminds me people are happy and enjoying their good fortune at being in such beautiful surroundings."

"We're blessed with good fortune to be here," Nora agreed.

"And by the way," Pierre said with a grin, "we love to dance tango in Nice. I'll show you when my arm is better."

Nora smiled at him, with a hint of shyness, and wondered if he was referring to Luc. For a brief moment, her thoughts wandered to him and her heart was filled with gratitude for all she had learned from him. He would forever be a true friend.

As dusk began to fall, Pierre asked, "What would you like to do for dinner? As you can see, we simply walk outside and have our choice of fantastic food. Or I can order anything from a charcuterie board to a gourmet meal. You decide."

Nora didn't have to think long. "We've had so many fabulous meals this week, I would be happy to sit here, watch the sun set, and graze a charcuterie board."

"Magnifique! You read my mind," Pierre said.

Chapter Fifty-One

WHEN NORA AWOKE THE NEXT MORNING, PIERRE WAS gone. He had left a note that they were unloading the art into a storeroom and he would be home around noon. She wondered what he meant by "don't jump too high when you hear the cannon go off".

At the stroke of noon, a loud cannon blast caused her to shriek out loud. Then she laughed. At least he had warned her and she would get an explanation from him.

The following days caused Nora to feel she was living a dream.

Pierre removed his sling and stated he was fine, only feeling a little stiffness, which he could deal with. "I want to be the full-time chauffeur while you are here."

He drove to nearby breathtaking locations: Villefranche-sur-Mer, Eze, Antibes, Menton, Mougins, St. Paul de Vence and even Gourdon, perched high on a clifftop. They laughed and sang as they traveled along the winding coastal corniches and maneuvered breathtaking switchback curves high into the hills. Memories were made as they visited galleries, browsed markets, took photos of crumbling castles, explored vibrant neighborhoods, and hiked challenging trails to be rewarded with stunning views. All the while they were embraced by the glorious beauty and culture of the Côte d'Azur.

Meals were a celebration of the simple pleasure and wellness offered by the Mediterranean diet, presented with creativity. "Some of these plates are almost too artistic to eat," Nora said as she tried not to become someone who took photos of every serving.

> Chloe texted: Mom! You are making me crave seafood so badly.
>
> Nora : I've never eaten fish served in so many irresistible ways and always so fresh.

This part of the world lived up to all Nora had ever heard, and then some. Her writer's heart felt it was in some ways a state of mind, the romantic blended with the real. History and art were alive everywhere and enfolded her.

In places of immense beauty, even on the streets of Nice, Nora encountered remembrances for women and men like ones she had come to know in Marie-Louise's stories. No part of the country had been untouched by war. Memorials stood in town squares, names etched in stone, flowers carefully laid beneath plaques that told of sacrifice and sorrow. She felt a deep and growing respect for such enduring reverence.

All these experiences inspired Nora to write, and each night before she fell asleep, she filled pages in a journal, something she had never done before. Her mind brimmed with ideas.

Her mind was alive with possibilities as Nora considered endless options facing her. She thought back to what had come before Nice and what could come after. Life. With all its choices.

Before Nora realized it, a week had flown by. In between their explorations and excursions, she had worked on Marie-Louise's memoir while Pierre spent time at the gallery. She was pleased to feel she was refining a final draft and eager to sit with Marie-Louise again and present it to her for her thoughts. Nora wondered if she would ever be able to adequately express her gratitude for all the experience had personally given to her and how deeply she had been touched.

Every time she mentioned to Pierre she should return to Paris, he had another reason to ask her to stay a while longer. But always, it was her choice. She never felt pressured and was aware of how deeply she did not want to leave. At least not for good.

Pierre invited her to his gallery on days when he had business there and asked her opinion about displays and promotional materials for exhibits. He introduced her to artists and sometimes encouraged her to bring her laptop to work on her writing in his office. Occasionally she stayed behind, writing in the quiet of the apartment or looking over the turquoise sea or in the peaceful surroundings of a shady park. She was writing every day.

Being with Pierre became effortlessly comfortable. The initial excitement of the new surroundings began to soften into something warm and welcoming for Nora. Their time together felt like a blend of mutual respect and companionship, even intimacy ... but not sexual. When he tenderly took her in his arms to dance to a song, it was always accompanied by laughter. They were two good friends enjoying life together.

Except they were becoming more than good friends. When Nora met his deep blue gaze, she saw something unmistakable reflecting back—something like love, steady and true. The question was, which of them was brave enough to say it out loud?

She hadn't forgotten he had displayed some unpleasant behavior when they'd first met, and from time to time she wondered if it might resurface. They spoke about it and Pierre admitted again to the bitterness and anger he had let consume him after his painful divorce. He spoke about the relief he felt when Nora came into his life and how, without her knowing, she had given him the strength to take a look at himself and let go.

Days after they arrived in Nice, Luc had called. Giselle wasn't doing well, and he planned to stay longer with her in Mexico.

Nora spoke with him about her feelings for the south of France and about Pierre, and Luc shared wise words with her.

"Nora, live your life doing what makes you happy. I understand how people fall in love with the south of France. There are reasons why painters, writers, and lovers have been attracted there for centuries. It sounds to me like Pierre may be an important part of why you are so happy, and that makes me pleased for you. You deserve this and I will always treasure your friendship."

"Yes, Luc, always," Nora murmured.

Then Giselle came on the phone. Her voice was tinged with sadness as she told Nora her health was failing, but she remained hopeful it would improve in time. Then she surprised Nora with another request.

"My dear Nora, I am so grateful for all the help you have offered me. As you now know, I am not certain when I will be able to return to Paris. Luc tells me you and Atticus are very close. And I could feel that in our texts and video calls. I wonder if you would consider making him your own. I'm afraid when I return, if I do, I will not be able to care for him as he needs."

Nora's heart broke at this news, but she would do anything she could to help Giselle.. "Of course. I'll keep Atticus for as long as he needs to be with me. I love him very much and I know you do too. When you feel differently at any point, I will have him waiting for you. He'll always be your sweet boy."

She didn't stop to consider the logistics. What mattered now was offering kindness and support. As a last resort, Jezebel might have to learn to love Atticus.

During all the time Nora and Pierre spent together, they hadn't addressed what was quickly becoming the elephant in the room. Exactly what was the nature of their relationship? It was as if they both avoided the obvious.

Occasionally Pierre held her hand as they walked along the

cobblestone laneways, but when they said goodnight to each other in the hallway, it was still a bise. Although she had to admit these kisses had started to last longer. And she'd noticed a change in the way he looked at her. It was how she wanted to look at him but was wary to do so.

At the start of their third week together, they sat at the small patio table on Pierre's terrace in the evening, enjoying a glass of rosé.

"Pierre, I think I must go back to Paris. I love life in Nice, but what am I doing? You've been so incredibly thoughtful in showing me around and teaching me about this amazing part of the world, but I should go back to Giselle's apartment."

Reaching across the table, he traced his fingers along her cheek and then took her hands. "Is it wrong if I tell you I wish you would stay?"

Nora felt herself being drawn into his gaze, unsteady in the quiet intensity between them. "But why is that? I wonder why we are so happy together, and if that's enough of a reason to stay."

"Nora."

Pierre's voice was thick with emotion. His eyes, achingly sincere, did not leave hers. "Je t'aime avec tout mon coeur. Je veux passer le reste de ma vie avec toi. I'm in love with you, with all my heart. I know it. With absolute certainty I want to spend the rest of my life with you. I've been reluctant to say it in case it frightens you away."

Nora's reaction was instinctive. Her heart surged. She ached with that sweet, terrifying weight only love can carry. She didn't think now, but simply felt.

She reached for him, her voice soft and sure. "Oh Pierre, je t'adore aussi. Every day I'm falling more in love with you too." She paused, her voice catching, "And you said it. I'm scared—but only because this feels so real."

He stood up and went to her, still holding her hands as he gently pulled her up to stand with him. With their hands entwined, she felt the tender brush of his lips on hers. Her response, tentative at first, grew more certain—inviting, asking for more. As their kiss deepened, they moved in perfect harmony, matching each other in longing and desire, as though they'd each been waiting for this moment.

They kissed again and again, passionately and hungrily, as their arms slipped around each other, pulling closer with every breath. In that embrace, time seemed to vanish and the world fell away, leaving only the quiet truth between them: they had found their way home – to each other.

The morning sun blazed through the bedroom window, which had the shutters flung open. Opening her eyes, Nora realized she was caught in a jumble of arms and legs—a full-body embrace. She looked at Pierre to find his eyes on her.

"I love watching you sleep," he said, kissing her forehead.

"I love that you love that." Nora met his gaze, warm and full of feeling.

They lay together in the quiet afterglow, wrapped in the intimacy of all they had shared through the night.

"Are we still friends?" he whispered.

"The very best," she whispered back. "And always will be."

They spent the day drifting in and out of bed, in the bliss of being alone together. At one point, Nora made coffee, and Pierre pulled on clothes and dashed out to the boulangerie next door. Breakfast was in bed—pain aux raisins for Nora, of course. They ate leftovers from the charcuterie board in bed for lunch. They slept. They made love. They talked. And made love again. And talked some more—slow and unhurried. It felt like the beginning of forever.

They agreed they didn't know where this ... this ... whatever it was, it was ... was going. But wherever they were headed, they wanted to be there together.

They were not young lovers. They'd lived a lot of life. They had known their own loss, pain, and loneliness, and had moved forward in their own ways.

There were options.

Pierre suggested they could rent the van Gogh apartment and go back and forth to Paris to spend time with Chloe and Olivier. He would always have business in the north of the country.

Nora wanted to focus on completing Marie-Louise's memoir to her satisfaction and start working on something else. She could feel the once-familiar urge to write inspiring her again, filling her with energy and curiosity for the next story.

They could go to her home in Canada and stay for a while. They had the freedom to go where they wanted and still do the work they needed to do.

"Let's try it, Nora, mon amour. A new chapter for both of us."

The next few mornings, after nights filled with passionate lovemaking, Nora went for long walks with Atticus along the nearby paths on Mount Boron, which offered solitude. She had much to consider.

She replayed her conversations with Cynthia.

She had long phone calls with Chloe and heartfelt zoom chats with the Girls.

And she thought of Jeremy. She knew he would be happy for her. This would be what he wanted … for her to have her heart filled with love again. He was letting her go.

Really, what was there to lose? She loved her friends and life back home, but did that mean she couldn't make a change? Because she also loved what had been happening to her in France.

And she felt certain of her blossoming love for Pierre. Her friendship with Luc had opened her mind to accepting the possibility of a love of life with a man who was not Jeremy. He had taught her to trust an embrace ... and enjoy the pleasure and seduction of tango. She chuckled at that.

Pierre had opened her heart.

Very early one morning when she couldn't sleep, she kissed Pierre's cheek, left a note, and slipped out with Atticus to watch the sunrise.

The area was well lit where she had already discovered a bench on her favorite path overlooking the sea. As soon as she sat down, the first soft washes of blush and lavender painted the sky, delicate and fleeting. They quickly faded as golden rays of light spread across the horizon. Suddenly it was day. Quiet surrounded her.

She slipped her arm around Atticus, who sat faithfully beside her on the bench. He nuzzled her shoulder, warm and solid against her side. In the quiet of the morning, his presence grounded her—a comforting, constant, deeply-loved companion.

She was captivated with the newness and thrill of loving Pierre and being loved in return. But passion wasn't all that thrilled her. A decision this big couldn't rest on romance alone. It was love plus many other things filling her head and warming her heart. It was the undeniable sense of being fully alive. She was choosing her future on her own terms.

She hadn't come to France looking for love, but it had found her. She felt she'd learned even the most tangled of hearts could find something they hadn't known they were looking for.

Nora tried to put everything in perspective. But could she even do it? Sometimes good things happened in life. Sometimes bad. She knew this. Certainly, Marie-Louise had taken her on a journey of the harshest lessons life could offer. Discovering the personal tragedy in Luc's life had deeply touched her soul, while witnessing Giselle's passion for all things in life despite her health challenges, had inspired her profoundly. Each encounter became a reminder of resilience, of the power of healing, and of the strength that can emerge even in the midst of suffering.

She also had been blessed with wonderful occurrences since the day she arrived in Paris at the beginning of December. Perhaps it truly was her turn to embrace change—to take a chance.

As Chloe had predicted, perhaps Nora had found the French Effect. Now she was ready to see where it would take her.

She and Atticus hurried back to the apartment, almost breaking into a run. Just as they reached the entrance, Pierre appeared, his arms laden with bags of warm morning pastries. Atticus barked once, tail wagging furiously.

Nora laughed, dropped to give Atticus a quick pat, then sprang into Pierre's arms. She kissed his cheeks, his neck, his lips. Breathless, she whispered, "Yes, Pierre, yes! You're right. Let's do this together." Then she grinned and added, "But promise me—we will always hug. That part of me is forever Canadian."

Pierre held her close, returning her kisses before pausing to search her eyes. A slow smile spread across his face. "We'll definitely hug—a lot. And you've just proven this is true love."

Nora blinked, puzzled. "How's that?"

He lifted one of the crushed paper bags between them. "Because we're squashing the *pain aux raisins*, and you don't even care."

Their laughter mingled with Atticus's happy yips as they made their way up the stairs. The dog bounded ahead, nails clicking against the marble floor, while Nora and Pierre embraced and lingered on every landing—each step a quiet promise, carrying them toward the beginning of their new chapter together.

The End

Acknowledgments

In order to reach that exciting point where a manuscript is finally ready to publish, a tremendous amount of support and assistance is essential. None more so than that from my patient husband, whose unwavering support and understanding makes my writing process possible.

I feel fortunate to have a very special friend/reader who offers honest, helpful comments and reads all my first drafts and rewrites without losing her sense of humor. Thank you for giving so willingly of your time and opinions Gail Napier Johnston. You are a star!

Also in the star category are the wonderful ARC readers. Your enthusiasm and support are so appreciated. Annie Mondesir, your ideas and helpful assistance are a constant. My gratitude to all of you is infinite. I wish I could beam each one of you to France with me.

Merci mille fois to my extraordinary friend, Deborah Bine, who is always just a click away, no matter what the reason. The laughter we share is priceless.

Kerry Schafer (Kerry Anne King), you truly are an Author Genie and I would get nowhere without your priceless assistance in so many ways. I want to mention that Kerry is the creator of the cover reveal that I absolutely love and apparently so did many others.

I owe immense gratitude to Jessica Annand of Maeve + Co. Public Relations, who is giving so much of her time and expertise to help *The French Effect* soar.

Many thanks to my friend, superb author Camille Pagán, for her guidance and coaching skills, to Charlotte Dixon, a fine book coach who kept me on track with deadlines, and Two Bird Author Services who provided the essential editing and proofreading service.

Thank you to Lauren Faulkenberry for designing this gorgeous book cover. It was great fun working with you to get just the right effect. Thanks for your patience and insight.

I'm so grateful to the writing community of which I'm proud to be a part. The collegiality, friendship and support found within is truly remarkable. Writers helping writers is absolutely a mantra and it is an honour to connect with so many talented and generous men and women who go out of their way to encourage, share information and ideas and promote each other's writing.

Thank you to the many reviewers, bookstagrammers and bloggers who take the time to read our novels, review and write about them. I include in my thanks talented designers who create meaningful and beautiful graphics. You all are the lifeline to sharing news about our writing and helping expand our readership ~ an integral part of the literary village.

Big bouquets of thanks to my wonderful author sisters in Tall Poppy Writers and Blue Sky Book Chat. Your encouragement, wisdom, and camaraderie have been a constant source of support and inspiration on this journey. In particular, I am beyond grateful to novelist Ann Garvin, creator of Tall Poppy Writers, for the inspiration and joy of writing (and life in general!) you so generously share.

In this story, I reference *La Séduction* by Elaine Sciolino—a book I've returned to often when researching French culture. It has been an invaluable resource in shaping the cultural details across many of my stories.

Which leads to more gratitude to all the readers who buy our books. I love hearing from you and appreciate the time you take to share your thoughts with me and with others. If you write reviews and spread the word, even better. And if you do none of that, that's okay too. As long as you find pleasure in the books we write, that is our greatest reward.

Read for the love of it!

About the Author

Patricia Sands lives two hours north of Toronto, but her heart's other home is the South of France. An avid traveler, she spends part of each year on the Cote d'Azur and in the countryside of Provence. Her award-winning 2010 debut novel, *The Bridge Club,* is a book club favorite. *The Promise of Provence,* which launched her three-part Love in Provence series was a finalist for a 2013 USA Best Book Award and a 2014 National Indie Excellence Award, an Amazon Hot New Release in April 2013, and a 2015 nominee for a #RBRT Golden Rose award in the category of romance.

Drawing Lessons, Sands' fifth novel, also set in the south of France, was released by Lake Union Publishing in 2017 and was a Finalist in the Somerset Literary Book Award 2019. The *Villa des Violettes* 4-book miniseries released in 2019/23

The Secrets We Hide, published August, 2022, received the

2023 Book Excellence Award for Women's Fiction; Winner – Women's Literary Fiction—International Impact Book Awards, 20242; Finalist – Women's Fiction – American Fiction Awards, 2024.

In March, 2023, *Lost At Sea*, Book 8 in the nine-book *Sail Away* series was published.

On January 1, 2025, *A New Leash on Life*, Book 9, in the *Dragonfly Cove Dog Park* series was released.

In November, 2025, her 13th novel, *The French Effect*, will be published.

A lifelong photographer, follow her on Instagram @psands.stories .

Find out more at Patricia's Facebook Author Page, Amazon Author Page or her website where there are links to her books, social media, and monthly newsletter that has special giveaways and sneak peeks. She would love to hear from you!

facebook.com/AuthorPatriciaSands
instagram.com/psands.stories
goodreads.com/PatriciaSands
bookbub.com/authors/patricia-sands

The French Effect Playlist

I hope you enjoy the playlist I put together for The French Effect. I tried to follow the story line and include a mix of everything. The great thing about a playlist is how easy it is to move on to the next song if one comes on that doesn't grab you! LOL If you think of a song that should be included, let me know! Happy listening! ♪♫♪♫♪♫

www.ingramcontent.com/pod-product-compliance
Lightning Source LLC
Chambersburg PA
CBHW020353080526
44584CB00014B/1005